THE YEAR OF MY REBIRTH

BOOKS BY JESSE STUART

Man with a Bull-Tongue Plow
Head o' W-Hollow
Beyond Dark Hills
Trees of Heaven
Men of the Mountains
Taps for Private Tussie
Mongrel Mettle
Album of Destiny
Foretaste of Glory
Tales from the Plum Grove Hills
The Thread That Runs So True
Hie to the Hunters
Clearing in the Sky
Kentucky Is My Land
The Good Spirit of Laurel Ridge
The Year of My Rebirth

BOOKS FOR BOYS AND GIRLS
Penny's Worth of Character
The Beatinest Boy
Red Mule

Jesse Stuart

THE YEAR
OF MY
REBIRTH

ILLUSTRATIONS
by Barry Martin

McGraw-Hill Book Company, Inc.
NEW YORK   TORONTO   LONDON

THE YEAR OF MY REBIRTH

Library of Congress Catalog Card Number: 56-12275

Published by the McGraw-Hill Book Company, Inc.
Printed in the United States of America

For All Who Have the Will to Live

ACKNOWLEDGMENTS

Parts of this book, in a different form, have appeared in the following magazines: *Ladies' Home Journal, The Saturday Evening Post, Esquire, Country Gentleman, Better Farming, The American Magazine, The Saturday Review, The Southwest Review, The Georgia Review, Christian Herald, Frontiers, The National Educational Journal, Nature Magazine,* and *The American Forests.*

P R O L O G U E

One day in April of 1955, I found myself in pursuit of the first butterfly of spring. He was a large fellow, yellow with black trimmings on the wings, and flying against a stiff, cool morning wind. I didn't chase him, but I walked briskly to see where he was going. Why was I following a butterfly? I stopped in the front yard and started thinking.

When I was a small boy and played along the W-Hollow stream, I used to sit for hours, back a safe distance, where I could watch them drink the sun-warmed water from the sand bar. Wild honeybees often came to the same sand bar for a load of warm water. Loaded, they'd take off like a plane, get higher and higher, and then level off on their proper course. They went straight toward a wild-bee tree somewhere in the woods and I would course them until I found the tree. It was a lot of fun to sit for hours and watch the wild bees and the multicolored butterflies. I often scared the butterflies up from the sand into a brilliant cloud in the sunlight.

1

In those days I'd never seen a movie. Radio and television were unheard of then. I'd never read a novel, and we didn't take any magazines. My only recreation was observing the wildlife of bees, birds, and animals that lived around me. And I found more than bees and butterflies watering on sand bars along the streams. I found turtles' nests with white, tough-shelled eggs where the sun would heat the sand someday and hatch little turtles. I found terrapins' nests in the sand and water snakes sunning on logs and rocks above the stream. I watched silver minnows darting up and down the deep holes of blue water, waiting for some insect to drop from the air.

I read the landscapes, the streams, the air, and the skies. I took my time about doing it. I had plenty of time to live and to think. I had plenty of time to grow up in a world that I loved more and more as I grew older. I didn't know then how good a world it was to grow up in. I didn't know how fortunate I was until later, when I saw other American children in the big cities who had to play ball in a street and dodge automobiles. They always had to be on the lookout for something that might hurt them. I had never seen a car until I was seven years old.

I had so many good, carefree, lazy days as I was growing up. I never rushed at anything, unless we had a field to finish plowing before a rain came. And in "case of a pinch"—my father used to call it—I could do as much work as two or three my age. But normally I'd sit under the hickory trees and watch the gray squirrels eat, and never kill them. I liked to sit on a hilltop and listen to my hounds, Rags and Scout, chase a fox. I never got in a hurry up there unless I ran to a crossing to see the fox in the moonlight. When I possum-hunted, I never got in a hurry unless Sir Robert or Jerry-B-Boneyard, Don or Trusty-Red-Rusty caught something on the ground or was barking very fast at something in a small tree or in a shallow hole.

This was the kind of life I knew until I finished high school. Then I went to the steel mills. When the whistle blew in the morning, I had to be there. At noon, when it blew, I dropped whatever I was doing and ran to my boardinghouse, for I had only thirty minutes to eat and be back at work. When the whistle sounded at four, I could take my time walking to my boardinghouse, for the day was done. But at the steel mills I learned about whistles and what they meant. The sound of the whistle was a way of life. My way of life was changing.

I had tremendous strength and power. The strongest man I worked with in the blacksmith shop I once laid down in the dust. I got this strength by growing up slowly. I didn't have a balanced diet and all the vitamins. I had biscuits, fat pork, ham and red gravy, fried apples, and sometimes fried chicken for breakfast. And in season we often had squirrel for breakfast.

Now I was eating different food. I didn't get biscuits. I was eating toast. And lean hamburger instead of fat pork. But it wasn't the food that made the difference. It was the time that bothered me, and it bothered others. There was that eternal tension of keeping up with time. It was harder than the work. It geared one up until he lost his slow stride. I lost a part of the way I had lived on the farm. I watched people walking in cities. First it was very strange to watch everybody walking in a hurry, and I laughed. Even the city dogs, I thought, walked sidewise to keep from flying.

At a later date, in college, I didn't have any money, but had a will to work and a lot of confidence. So I started working my way through college. In one year I set a record at Lincoln Memorial University, for I never missed a meal in 365 days. I had to be there to wash the pots and pans. I thought the dining room couldn't open unless I was there. I was really getting into the swing of things. I went out for the cross-country, the two-mile, the quarter-mile, and low hurdles. I became editor of the college paper. When I went to read proofs of my paper, I walked from Harrogate, Tennessee, to Middlesboro, Kentucky, a distance of five miles, and through a long tunnel under Cumberland Gap. There were signs up saying, "Dangerous. Keep Out!" I disregarded the signs, for it saved time to walk through the hill and not over it. I was getting to be a keyed-up man. I had to make every minute count.

After graduating from college, I taught school and walked home seventeen miles—one way—on the weekends. I carried books to my pupils, not the state-prescribed list, but my list—good books I'd read. I saw the need of education, and I wasn't going to let anyone in a class of mine escape an education if I could help it. I'd teach

him and I'd get him books. I didn't have time now to watch butterflies, and I had forgotten how to course bees.

Life had changed for me. I didn't have time to fool with people
who were slow. I was kind to weakly people, but impatient with
them. When I carried 100-pound sacks to or from a truck on our
farm, I first carried one, then two, and I got up to three. Why lose
all that time carrying 100 pounds at a time? Besides, there was
something wrong with a man who couldn't carry twice his own
weight. Insects and small animals could. There were insects that
could lift forty times their own weight. I cut eighty-eight shocks
of corn, twelve hills square on a steep hillside, in one day when two
men my age, working on the opposite hill in corn the same size,
cut thirty-nine. When two men strained to lift a tile—and this on
my fortieth birthday—I told them to stand back. I lifted the 400-
pound concrete tile, reinforced with steel, up into the wheelbarrow.
Yet this wasn't twice my weight. That would have been 444 pounds.

I was really getting out of the rut now. The boys I knew and
liked were the huskies who wouldn't take no for an answer. I liked
these doers. I was one. Time would run out one of these days. Even
if I lived to be ninety, there was not time enough. My mother's
father, uncles, and aunts had averaged ninety-two years. Dad's
hadn't been so fortunate. Many of them had died younger because
they'd got tangled up with unfriendly mountain neighbors. But I
had the years ahead of me. And schools all over America needed
plenty done for them. In one year I made eighty-nine talks in thirty-
nine states. That year I had two books published, as well as a few
short stories and articles. I didn't have time to write poems any
more, except in airports and railway and bus stations.

No longer did I work a day on my farm and then walk slowly
five miles to the post office and back, stopping to sit along the way
by wild phlox or on the bank of a quiet stream and write poems. I'd
lost that good feel of earth, its beauty and sounds, I once had. I
didn't have time now. I'd made a road and owned a car, and I
couldn't waste time walking five miles. I'd once heard a friend of
mine say, "America is my lemon. Brother, how I love its juice." This
was the way I felt too. I was teaching, writing, buying more hill

acres and trying to farm them, and I was sought after as a lecturer. One night was long enough in any city where I lectured. I used every spare minute to see more of America. Drive, drive, like the drive wheels on a big Mallet engine. Once I liked the train rides across the Midwest, the fast trains that thundered across America. But these trains got too slow for me. I had to save time. I needed more time. I liked to take nonstop flights between Chicago and Dallas, and Chicago and New York, and Miami and Boston. I liked that world above the skies. I liked the company of hurrying people.

One night we landed in New Orleans and the limousine from the airport got behind some slowpoke. The fellow next to me started talking to the driver about our Louisiana hayride. I chimed in about the slow ride. We passed a wreck on the way, but so what! Wrecks were for other people. Not for a limousine on its way to distribute important folks like us to our hotels. This stranger and I made the driver mad, and we didn't tip him. He made us mad, too.

Another time, it took the limousine as long to get from the airport to downtown Chicago as it had taken me to fly from Huntington, West Virginia, to Chicago. I let the driver know I didn't like slow service. If he got me to Chicago in a hurry, he always got a good tip. I liked speed. I was a speedy American. I was getting into the swing of a life that had crept up on me so gradually I took it to be normal.

My wife, Naomi, was the first one to meddle with me. She said, "Why are you always in a hurry? You're even in a hurry to eat. You'd better slow down."

She's the only one who ever tried to halt me. I told her I was pushing on only three fronts now: writing, lecturing, and farming —tree farming, for I'd set 22,000 trees the last two years. I'd be too old to reap the benefit of those trees. But somebody would. I'd never been a selfish guy. Naomi shouldn't comment. I was forty-seven, but Mom's ancestors averaged ninety-two. I reminded Naomi of that. And she said, "Yes, but their world was different. It was a quiet country world, like you were born and grew up in."

I was glad it was different. I liked my day and time better. I wanted to live long enough to ride on a plane powered by cosmic rays. I'd been reading a lot in the papers about it. That would be the way to travel—fast!

But I had seen a few things I couldn't forget. Once I was in a hurry in Manhattan, so I rushed into a self-service place, where I would not have to starve while I waited on the slow waiters. As I was getting a piece of pie, I looked at a large heavy man with a small mustache, tired eyes, and a bow tie. He toppled over and almost took me with him. He fell like a sawed-down tree, but I jumped back and he missed me. There was a doctor inside and he made the people stand back. An ambulance was called, and the man was carried out, moaning and groaning, on the stretcher. I bought four or five papers that evening to see if he was important enough to be mentioned. He wasn't. He might have been just another small businessman. But I wanted to know what had happened to him. That was a strange thing to do, just fall over like that.

Another strange thing happened in Chicago. I was trying to pass a man, walking fast, on the sidewalk. I was already abreast of him, when he pitched forward. A cop saw him fall, and came running. Then he called an ambulance. But this man died while the cop and I stood there. Others gathered around to look. The ambulance and a doctor came, but it was too late. After they put him in the ambulance, someone said, "Well, we've all got to go. That's a nice way. He went in a hurry!"

That happened to this man all right. But each one gathered there was sure he wouldn't be next. Stress and strain. People always in a hurry. Death on the street. I knew this wasn't for me. I had almost a half century before me yet. This quick death was for others. But I did have worries. I didn't know exactly why. My debts were paid. I had money ahead. I had a home, a checking account, and a car. I had an agreeable wife, except she was always after me for hurrying. Sometimes she actually nagged at me about it. But I still held onto my male independence. Once she told me I might topple over if I didn't slow down. That was when I was telling her how to drive the car to beat the scoundrel that tried to hog the road. I told her to ram him. That was after the doctor gave me some little green pills to slow me down. His green pills didn't slow me down, because I slowed them down the drain.

Then, one day in September of 1954, I had some sort of pain in my chest. Nothing I took relieved me. I'd never had a pain like this one. I didn't think I could get my breath much longer. Finally, Naomi dragged me to the young doctor in my home town, and he laid me down on a table and put a pill under my tongue about the size of a No. 3 shot. Then I began to feel a little easier. The doctor told me to go to a heart specialist.

"Can't be my ticker, doc," I said. "For five generations on either side there has never been a heart attack."

"But you're living in a different age," he said.

Somebody had said that before.

I didn't want to go to the hospital, but they made me. I told the specialist exactly what had happened. Before I was through with him he called in a second specialist—a specialist's specialist, I guess—and I was in the hospital two nights and three days and had every test in the doctors' books thrown at me. But I was happy when they looked at this chest of mine and finally smiled and said, "Your trouble is muscular. Chest muscles, that's what's wrong."

No man ever left a hospital happier than I. America was my lemon again. In less than two weeks I was on a plane flying across Kentucky. Train was too slow. I had with me three books to read, four stories, and a dozen poems to revise. The following day I was to give two major talks, one in the morning to the teachers of Kentucky's First Educational District at Murray and one at Flora, Illinois, in the afternoon. A chartered plane would be at Murray to take me to Flora. This was nothing special. I had made three major talks in a day, shuttling from talk to talk by chartered plane. I'd done it once in Illinois, flying in a little chartered plane across a part of Chicago to the big airport. I loved it.

In the Murray State College auditorium I had a full house. The balcony was filled, and at the back they were standing. I was scheduled to speak an hour. I spoke over an hour for good

measure. When I finished, several were in the aisles to meet me.
I didn't have time to meet them. I had to hurry. The chartered
plane was waiting. I had to be on my way to carry the ball for
the schoolteachers of America. More than a hundred had come
from the auditorium, and they watched from the side lines when
the Opposition to Life broke through my imaginary defenses and
brought me down with a shoestring tackle prettier than any ever
made on a football field. My feet went higher than my head. *I
will not die, I will not die,* I said to myself as I went down. I
knew now what had happened to the man in the restaurant in
Manhattan and what had stopped the man on the street in Chicago.

I never knew when or how I got to the hospital. Later, I
learned I was blue and gasping for breath, that my crippled
heart was beating over 250 times a minute trying to pump blood
past the clot to save my life. Edith Meeker McDougall, who was
to become my day nurse, met the ambulance when it arrived. She
placed a resuscitator over my mouth and nose to give me extra
oxygen. This might have been the split-second action that saved
my life. I remember the kind face of this wonderful nurse when I
awoke to consciousness.

After my wife arrived in Murray and realized the seriousness
of my attack, she phoned our family physician, Dr. Charles E.
Vidt, of Ironton, Ohio, who, with Dr. Hugh Houston of Murray,
decided to call Dr. Woodford Troutman, a specialist from Louisville, to see me. I barely remember Dr. Troutman's visit. For, at
that time, it was a matter of life and death with me. A heart
attack wasn't anything like what I had a few times imagined one
would be. I have never suffered any kind of pain, and never will
again, comparable to the pain of a heart attack.

At this very minute two people are dying somewhere in America
of heart attacks. Out of every 160 people in the United States,
one person will die of a heart attack this year. And this victim
can as well be you as the other fellow. Approximately three heart-
attack victims out of every four survive, thanks to medical science
and our skilled heart specialists and our heart associations and
the great work they are doing. But of every five Americans who

will die this year, approximately three will die of heart trouble.

I was lying helpless when I awoke to consciousness on a narrow hospital bed under an oxygen tent. The cool wind I had taken to be that of home was the good cool oxygen blowing over me from the tank. And the sound of the winds and the hissing snakes I had heard in dreams was the sound of the oxygen blowing from the tanks that was making the difference between life and death for me. I knew what had happened to me. I couldn't think very clearly, but I could remember vaguely the pain and the falling. I was among strangers until my wife walked into the room.

"What's this all about?" I whispered. "Where am I? In what hospital? When did you get here?"

Then I learned from Naomi Deane and my day nurse, Mrs. McDougall, that I was brought by ambulance from Marvin Wrather's home in a hurry the previous Friday at noon. Naomi and our daughter, Jane, had left home as soon as Mr. Wrather phoned the news to Greenup, Kentucky. Since we didn't have a phone, the message was relayed to Naomi, by her parents. She and Jane, along with my brother-in-law, Herbert Liles, my sister Glennis, and my brother James, drove that afternoon and all night, 500 miles to Murray, and arrived at four Saturday morning.

Others had come and gone—my father and my oldest sister, Mrs. Henry Keeney; Mr. and Mrs. Orin Nelson; another sister and brother-in-law; and two nieces and their husbands. All I could remember was a red shirt someone had worn. No visitors were supposed to be allowed in my room, but after they had driven this far, they were allowed in. They looked at me under the oxygen tent and then went away. My father had pushed three automobile loads of people relentlessly across the length of the state to get to me. This was the farthest distance he had ever been away from home. I felt very deeply about their making this long trip, and Naomi said I spoke to them and called them by name. This I do not recollect, for I was busy in my dreams, working with my parents on the land we loved. Say what one will, I believe that when the end is close one will go back, in dreams at least, to his beginning.

I told Naomi where I had been and what I had been doing.

I was still tired. And somewhere close to my heart, my chest felt as if a hole had been torn in it. I could not lift my arms. I could not write, but I asked Naomi to take down a letter to Milton Eisenhower. I was sure I had seen Mrs. Milton Eisenhower. To this day I have never forgotten any detail of our meeting. Weeks after Naomi had sent the letter, it occurred to me that she had been dead for some time. Months before, I had read about her death in our local paper.

Then I dictated a second letter, to Glen Hilton, telling him to put lime on my ground to kill the broomsedge. My wife tried to stop me, but after the realistic dream I had of working with Glen Hilton, I insisted she send the letter. I wasn't thinking clearly when I did all this. But no one could have told me I wasn't. Dad was back home now trying to see that my orders for spreading lime, disking, and sowing were carried out as I had seen it done in my dream.

Living under this oxygen tent was a strange existence. I felt as if the sky had fallen in, that I was in my grave. I felt so powerless, so listless, I didn't want to move. Although my body was slow to come back, my mind came back more quickly. And when I was able to think, I was depressed to the extent that if there had been a weapon near and if I could have used my hands to reach it, I might have finished myself. This was not my way of thinking. Something had gone terribly wrong with me. Something had happened I couldn't help. Vaguely, I could remember harshly criticizing people for finishing their own lives when they were deeply afflicted by some incurable disease. Now I reasoned that they had been justified. Why come so near and not go all the way?

In these black days of depression, while I lay under the oxygen tent and saw only the faces of my wife, doctor, and nurses, I grew tired of each one. They were the dear people fighting the hardest to save my life. Yet the ones who did the most for me I cared for the least. I didn't have anything personal against them, but I couldn't warm up to them, couldn't feel thankful for their efforts. I reasoned very passively and calmly that they should let me

die, let me get out from under that tent where the sky had come
down and the grave had enclosed me.

They should let me die, let me have the second part of life, I
thought. I had thoroughly enjoyed the first, up until now. But
I was ready for the second half, the unknown. I was stirred by
curiosity about the long journey. Even in my drugged state of
body and mind, I could get a little excited about going. I would
close my eyes and pretend that I was going, and sleep.

*I entered a beautiful world long past, with sun I could not
hold in the sky, flowers I could not keep fresh on their stems,
and sumac leaves I could not keep from coloring and dying in
an autumn season and blowing away on the wind of 1916.*

*The sudden flight of a pheasant from the cluster of sawbriers
at my feet startled me. I stopped to watch the big bird rise up
on its whirring wings to go over and down beyond the brush fence
that enclosed our pasture field. I had scared this rooster pheasant
up, and often his mate with him, many times before. But I had
never found him in this part of the pasture where there was a
grove of pine seedlings. Sawbrier clusters, growing among these
young pines, made me careful where I stepped, since I was barefooted.*

*The sun was getting high in the blue sky, and I had not found
the cows yet. Gypsy was hiding. I had been down in the deep
Byrnes Hollow where the tall beeches grew. I always went there
first in the mornings to see the gray squirrels. They fed early and
went into their hollow dens in the giant beeches long before the
morning sun had dried the dew. But I was up early, too, and I
sat under the den trees and watched the young squirrels come
out of the holes and play on the big leafy branches.*

*I also knew where the wild birds' nests were—redbird, ground
sparrow, song sparrow, and thrush. I had found a whippoorwill's
nest once on a big leaf under an oak, and I had found a hummingbird's nest, too. I knew the crows had their nest in a tall pine
and the chicken hawks had theirs in the bushy top of a giant
whiteoak.*

I could find all these birds' nests, and I was usually able to
see snakes before they saw me. But Gypsy was hard to find in
this forty-acre pasture, and that's why I always came out before
my mother. There was a place where I drove Gypsy for her to
milk. That was under the big, bushy-topped whiteoak that didn't
shade anybody but Gypsy, my mother, and me.

"Jesse! Oh, Jesse!" Mom called. "What's keepin' you so?"

Mom's voice wasn't so pleasant. I'd know her voice anywhere
and any time. I had been a little slow this morning, watching
squirrels, listening to young hawks and crows as their parents fed
them. I liked to stand under the trees and just listen.

"Jesse, Jesse, do you hear me?" Mom's familiar voice was louder
and closer this time. "Answer me, Jesse! Have you found the cow?"

"No, Mom," I replied. "Gypsy's hidin' someplace."

"You've had time enough to have been over all the pasture
two or three times," she said. "I'll find the cow myself."

I put my feet down carefully between the clusters of sawbriers, for I was ever mindful of snakes. Often a dark stick on
the ground made me stop suddenly and jump back.

As I stepped between the sawbrier clusters, I touched the small
pines with my hands. There were dewdrops on the pine-tree
needles. These dewdrops weighted them like little lumps of polished silver until the sun lifted them skyward in white ribbons
of mist. There were dewdrops on the red-tinted sawbrier leaves,
the hard stems of the sawbriers, the milkweed and silkweed leaves,
which were shaped like stiff hog's ears, only they were green. And
the bright wind above me was filled with streamers of mist riding
from the wild flowers, leaves, buds, briers, and pines. This pasture
world was filled with the music of wild birds' singing and the soft
blowing of the June wind through the pine needles and sumac
leaves.

I knew my mother was hunting impatiently for Gypsy. But I
could not help but stand there, bareheaded and barefooted, and
breathe the fresh white mists into my lungs. In two springs and
summers of hunting Gypsy here, I had never seen the pasture
prettier. I hated to end it all by finding Gypsy and taking her
to the whiteoak to be milked.

If only I could command the sun to stop where it was in the sky and hold all the white mists where they were in the air. If I could keep the pasture daisies as white and the wild roses as pink as they were now. If I could keep the sawbriers in clusters with their red-tinted leaves. If I could make this pasture and time stand still, I'd do it! I'd keep this world just as it was.

My father was thirty-five years old, my mother thirty-three, and they were very old and very wise to me. I was nine in this year of 1916, and I loved everything about it.

I stepped from the grove of miniature pines into the narrow little path made by Gypsy's tracks. Where the path made a sharp U-turn around a sweet-apple tree, I almost walked into Gypsy. Here she stood munching on the blighted sweet apples that had fallen to the ground. She was a big bony cow with a pair of horns fox hunters had already spoken for at her death. My father had often said the reason she was bony was because her horns were so big it sapped her strength to carry them. I often wondered how she got through the brush and briers with such big horns. "Go on there, Gypsy," I scolded her loud enough for Mom to hear. "What are you doin' hidin' from me?"

Gypsy had moved under a patch of alders. She was a smart cow all right. There the biting flies would leave her alone. They couldn't stand alder leaves when the sun dried the dew and the leaves began to wilt.

"So, you've finally found her," Mom said. She had come up from the Byrnes Hollow and into the path behind me.

"She was back there in the alder bushes," I said, surprised to see my mother pleased and smiling. Mom was tall, just an inch under six feet, and her hair was black as the crows' wings. Mom's eyes were gray as the bark on the poplar tree, and her teeth between her smiling lips were as white as the daisy petals in the pasture.

"Come, Jesse," she said. "We must get the milking done."

Gypsy trotted on ahead of Mom and me, knowing there would be something special for her under the tree. Mom never missed bringing Gypsy something extra to eat while she milked her. Fresh-cut grass from the yard, apple peelings, sweet corn, corn shucks, or salt. This morning there was some salt under the tree.

When we reached the bushy-topped whiteoak where Mom milked, a gray squirrel ran out one of the long branches, jumped to the ground, and hopped over the hill toward the beech grove. My mother didn't even look up. She sat on a stool and milked with both hands. The streams of milk hitting the bottom of the big zinc bucket beat a rhythm all their own.

I stretched out upon the ground to look up into the whiteoak leaves. When the wind rustled the leaves I could see the blue sky. I half shut my eyes and looked through my eyelashes at the changing leaf pictures. I thought there might be another squirrel hidden among the trembling leaves.

I couldn't keep the pine seedlings from growing into saw-log timber. I couldn't stay the hunters' guns from pheasants, crows, hawks, and squirrels. I couldn't hold the wild rose and the blooming daisy beyond their seasons. I couldn't keep the young spring wind blowing over me. I suddenly wanted Mom to finish milking. I listened to hear her say, "Jesse, let's be goin'." For I was waking from this dream world I couldn't hold.

Instead of a warn June wind and green leaves above me, there was the hiss of oxygen in a cool tent. That wasn't my mother standing there. It was a nurse. My mother no longer milked Gypsy under the whiteoak. Mom rested at Plum Grove. And this wasn't 1916, it was 1954. But dream world or real, there was one thing I was certain of. I had been with an angel in that pasture.

Time came for me to move my arm, slowly, and I realized I was still wearing the trousers to the suit I had spoken in at the Murray College auditorium. I didn't know how many days had passed, but I couldn't figure out why I was still wearing part of my suit. Then came an embarrassing moment. Though no one had ever bathed me before, Mrs. McDougall and Naomi removed my trousers and bathed me now. They told me that before this time they had been afraid to move me to take them off.

Once, years ago, when I was in the hospital to have my scalp cleated after I had been blackjacked, the nurse, after washing my bloody head, wanted to wash my body, but I wouldn't let her. This nurse had gone to school to me. She'd been a pupil of mine when she was a small girl.

But this wasn't like having my scalp laid open with a blackjack until my skull showed. What had happened to me was much more serious. I lay powerless now, entirely in the hands of others. Mrs. McDougall was even brushing my teeth for me. The most I could do was to think hazily for a brief time, then I would fall asleep.

After Mrs. McDougall and Naomi had finished bathing me, they managed to get me on a bedpan, and rejoiced when I was successful. Again I was puzzled, I couldn't understand this. What was so astounding about performing successfully on a bedpan? Later I learned that the man in the room next door, who had also had a coronary occlusion, had just died an hour or so before in his tenth day at the hospital—on the bedpan. At this time I didn't know that I had had a coronary occlusion and double heart injury. In fact I didn't know exactly what this was.

There was one person I wanted to see from the moment I regained consciousness. I wanted to see Jane, our daughter. I wanted Jane to come in and stand close to my bed, to put her cold face down against mine while they changed the oxygen tanks. She had walked through the autumn winds and the frost, and I wanted to feel a touch of autumn and the outside world on Jane's face. I loved her more than I had ever loved her in my life. She was a child, and she wasn't trying to save me. She had come to Murray Saturday morning at four after a sleepless night of fast driving, and on Monday she found herself plunked down in a strange school. But she didn't utter a single word of complaint. I liked her pluck, I liked the stuff in her. And I liked the autumn in her cold face. I hesitated to hold her there, asking her to stay a minute longer, but she was my link with youth, with life.

A few days after I was taken from the oxygen tent, I was given a newspaper to read, to keep my mind off myself. But it worsened my frame of mind instead of helping. I'd had no idea that a heart attack could cause so many other defects in the human body. I was just beginning to learn that the heart is Mr. Life itself. When I looked at the big headlines in this paper, I couldn't read them. At forty-seven, I suppose, one shouldn't be surprised by deteriorating eyesight, but mine had always tested perfect up until now. I'd had 20-20 vision in both eyes. But now I couldn't read newspaper headlines, and this had happened to me overnight. The doctors told me that I would be wearing glasses probably for the rest of my life.

In the times when the sedatives hadn't put me to sleep, I asked Naomi to read the letters that were coming in to us. All of these I wanted to answer, by dictating replies to Naomi. I learned how much affectionate letters can mean. I had been knocked to the floor by Death, the referee was counting ten, but I could see my friends, hundreds of them, standing behind him urging me to get up. I was sorry now I'd never taken time to write letters to my friends in the hospital. But Dr. Hugh Houston found out and put a stop to my dictating replies. Then I asked Naomi to send to her mother to get certain books and manuscripts from our house. These I had her put, along with the letters, on the table near my bed. I wanted everything where I could see it.

I began to realize I wasn't through living. It became hard for me to believe I had ever thought about ending my life. I never wanted to tell anybody about this. I was ashamed of it. Though I could hardly move under that tent, I would look at the table by my side and tell myself I wasn't through. Not when I could see my books again. Often I pushed Naomi, when her hands must have been tired, to write friends, publishers, magazine editors. Write them, I told Naomi, that I'm not through, that I will be back someday, flooding the mails with book and story and poetry manuscripts.

I got to the point where I was actually glad to see Dr. Houston come in early each morning. He took my blood pressure, counted my pulse, and sat listening to my heart beat. He told me I looked better each day, and I enjoyed hearing him say it. I wanted to hold him longer than he could stay. Though I never took kindly to all that bloodletting, I could even be kind to Technician Beale, who came each morning just before breakfast to take blood from my arm. Mrs. McDougall seemed like an angel dressed in white. Now I was desperately in love with my wife again, she had worked so hard to save me.

Then, after eighteen days, they took the tent from over me one afternoon, and I felt that I was stepping out of my grave. A few days after that they took it away once and for all. But I still had nurses around the clock, and a hot-water bottle to my cold feet.

Confining me in this small hospital room where I could not even see out was like putting a wolf in a small steel cage. I could lie in my bed and hear the cheering when football games were played at Murray College. I could tell every time Murray made a touchdown or an extra point, and I tried to keep score by ear. I wondered how this football stadium looked, what kind of a building the high school was, what color clothes the people in the street were wearing. I wondered about the hospital I was in; I had seen but one room, Room 223, my cage, my world. I didn't even use all of this room. I still lay helplessly in bed.

When this tent was removed, after twenty-one days, Dr. Houston said I could write one letter a day, but I discovered that my hands were stiff and sore and that lying down in bed made it difficult to write. Instead I dictated more replies to my wife. I still wasn't out of the habit of thinking that I was lying here wasting time. Naomi read one of my seventeen-year-old unpublished short stories to me, and I dictated revisions. But before we got very far I fell asleep again. Next day I went back to this story, doing a little more each evening before I went to sleep. Months later this story sold to *Esquire.*

Now they let me have a radio close to my bed. On Saturdays big football games were broadcast from all over the nation, and I asked Dr. Houston if it would be all right for me to listen. "Sure, sure, go right ahead and listen," he told me. "Just don't root too hard for any one team." But it was very strange. On Saturdays I seemed to sleep more than on any of the other days. I would start listening to the games, but I never found out how any of them ended. I was always asleep by then.

Yet gradually I awoke more and more from my days and nights of groggy sleep, though my once-strong body still lay in perfect immobility. I was as long as my hospital bed and my shoulders were almost as wide, yet Edith McDougall could move me gently from side to side and give me a bath. Strange that I had to submit to helplessness and complete dependence on a woman I'd never laid eyes on a month before. I asked her all sorts of questions. I knew that her husband was a farmer and I asked her to find out from him if spreading lime on broomsedge would kill it. I told her about the dream I had had about working with my cousin on a steep hill spreading lime on the broomsedge. When she brought back her husband's reply, I got another surprise. He said liming the ground would destroy broomsedge.

On October 31, I was allowed to sit straight up in bed for five minutes. The very idea excited me as much as a flight to New York would have a few weeks earlier. But I couldn't take advantage of the whole five minutes, for everything started whirling around, and I was very happy for Mrs. McDougall to ease me down on my bed again. But the following day I sat up ten minutes with only a little dizziness, and the next day fifteen. On November 13, I was allowed to sit up fifteen minutes in the morning and dangle my feet over the bed. In the afternoon I was allowed to repeat the performance. On November 14, Edith McDougall and Naomi walked on either side while I made two faltering, shaky steps from my bed to a chair. I thought a thousand needles were sticking into my feet. But it was so wonderful to be able to move again.

There was one place that I wanted especially to go. I wanted to walk to the door of my room and look out into the corridor. For weeks I had heard people walk and talk along this corridor, until I thought it must be a wonderful, gay, and exotic place. Lying in bed I imagined the way it looked—its length, its walls and doors and lights.

While I was sitting in my chair on November 14, Mrs. McDougall told me that I would get to see the hospital corridor the next day, for I was to take a ride in a wheel chair to the X-ray room. That afternoon, after I got back in bed, I became excited about my next day's journey in a wheel chair. I would get out of Room 223, out of the cage that had held me for thirty-six days.

Only a sedative could put me to sleep that night to make me forget my glamorous journey to the X-ray room on the following day. This would be the greatest event of my hospital life—a ride in a wheel chair.

I used to travel thousands of miles every year on trains and planes, but it seemed as if I had less time to think then than I now had traveling a few feet from bed to chair. On a plane, if above the clouds, I could never take my eyes off the different cloud formations. I sat there looking out at a small fairyland of strange white mountains, wondering if this didn't look like the Heaven that the old people dreamed and talked about. And when there were no clouds and I could see down to the earth, I kept busy trying to follow rivers and cities and highways to know where I was.

I carried a notebook with me and a fountain pen, but when I tried to jot down a note I got ink all over me, because of the pressure. Often enough I had a pencil with me, but seldom did I take notes anyway. Once I wrote a poem in the air, "Up Silver Stairsteps," and it was published. There's hardly an airport east of the Mississippi I don't know, but you can't do much good thinking in airports.

Riding trains in forty-four states of this Union was something else. My fountain pen would work all right. It didn't leak ink all over my hands. I found more to see and write about in surface travel. Once I rode on a two-coach train almost a whole day across the state of Iowa. We moved fast over the flat prairie country, across endless cornfields and grazing lands, with the whistle screaming and smoke flying. This was one of the happiest rides I ever had in my life. I got acquainted with everybody on the train. There were not more than a dozen.

I enjoyed riding into a station in one of the big cities with the engine's bell ringing and the people rising and standing in the aisle with coats over their arms, briefcases and suitcases in their hands. I stood among them, trying to be first out. I never knew why. I wasn't thinking about anything except getting off the train. I had a clean notebook in my briefcase. Not even a note. Often I planned a peaceful ride, where I would sit down and write an article or letters. But I couldn't, not when there were people to talk to, fascinating people whom I'd maybe never see again but whose story I could take away with me...

And now I was excited by the prospect of a ride in a wheel chair!

Carefully I selected the pair of pajamas I liked best. Naomi bought me some new leather house slippers for the occasion. Edith McDougall wheeled the chair in, and she and Naomi helped me into it. Then we left the small cramped world of Room 223, where I knew by heart every piece of furniture, every spot on the ceiling, every scar on the painted walls. We went into the wide world of the hospital corridor, which had seemed like such a happy, bustling place while I lay on my bed. I had called it the Great White Way. Now, all dressed up and going some-place, I found the corridor very much smaller than I had imagined. Slowly Mrs. McDougall rolled me down the Great White Way toward the X-ray room, while Naomi walked along beside her. The patients in the rooms along the corridors looked out at the procession, many waving to me. But I could only nod, for my hands and arms were stiff and sore and heavy.

"Well, here we are," Mrs. McDougall said, as she wheeled me left through an open door.

"Not this soon!" I cried. "I thought the room was up on the second floor. This isn't far enough." I was bitterly disappointed. I actually felt cheated, as if there had been some kind of chicanery.

Mrs. McDougall and the tall, slender technician helped me up from the chair to a standing position. Quickly and silently they made X rays of my heart while I was standing up. Then I was helped down into my chair and wheeled back to my room and put to bed. I hadn't been gone ten minutes. I was as chagrined as if my flight to New York had been grounded in the first town out of the airport.

But that afternoon, late, Dr. Hugh Houston came to my room smiling, with the news that my heart was not enlarged. I didn't know it until then, but the X rays made of me while I was lying in bed had shown that my heart *was* enlarged. Naomi, Edith Mc-

Dougall, and Dr. Houston seemed overjoyed about the X rays. I wasn't as concerned. I had known positively for some days that I was going to live.

On November 17, I was allowed to ride to the end of the corridor, this time to the mail room. On November 18, I wheedled two rides in my wheel chair out of the powers that were, and in the evening, Dr. Ralph Woods, president of Murray College, came to visit me for fifteen happy minutes. He had introduced me the day I had spoken and had seen me collapse afterwards. Relief on seeing me alive was written all over his face, and it aroused a corresponding emotion in me.

On November 18, Naomi and Mrs. McDougall wheeled me out on the porch to see the sunset. In all my life I had never known anything so beautiful. Actually it was an ordinary one compared to others I'd seen, but to me it was the loveliest. The wind was a delight to breathe, too, after forty days in the hospital, the longest time in my life I had ever been shut indoors. My mother was an outdoor woman, and she carried me every place outside even when I was a baby. As a child I always hated to go inside a house at night to go to bed. Now I refused to go back to my room. I leaned down on the wheel-chair wheel so that Mrs. Mc-Dougall and Naomi couldn't push me back into the hospital. I wouldn't go. I'd felt the breath of new life stirring in me, and I wanted to nurture it.

"You must go back inside out of this wind," Mrs. McDougall said severely. But I shook my head, still watching the sun set, and she wasn't able to push the wheel chair. Then Dr. Houston came with an orderly, and they wheeled me back in. Actually I was physically helpless and easy to handle. But I savored my moments of sunset for days.

Dr. Troutman advised that I stay in Murray until I could ride home sitting up in our car instead of lying in an ambulance. Mrs. George Curry, my wife's sister, came down from Greenup to help us on the 500-mile trip home. In all it took us six days, and everything was carefully planned to the last minute detail. We stopped at a motel, where my wife had reserved a place in advance after Dr. Houston had recommended we stop only where I need climb no steps.

On our way to Cave City, our first day out, Nancy and Naomi changed places driving the car. I got out just for a minute, to look at the white autumn clouds rolling over Western Kentucky near Hopkinsville. The winds seemed to blow in toward me from all directions. I was their objective. They seemed intent on reviving me, on breathing life back into me. I stood on that hill a happy man.

Yet when Dr. Troutman visited me in my hotel room, just as soon as we reached Louisville, I fell into a deep gloom. He smiled when he examined me, but I couldn't return the smile. After seeing the countryside from Murray to Louisville, I was inside a room again, confined, imprisoned. Everyone who has had a heart attack will have these days of depressed moods, when he believes that the best is over for him, that he is through in his profession and in life. Such moods have actually taken the lives of some patients. I had a bad one at the hotel in Louisville. Nothing could coax a smile out of me.

Naomi went with me in search of a barbershop where there was an elevator to take me down and bring me back. We found one at a nearby hotel. I will never forget how the men in the shop stared at me with my long hair, my once-ruddy complexion now the gray color of burnt clay, and my wife helping me into the chair. They knew something was wrong, and pity and curiosity showed all over their faces. I hated it. For months it was to remain difficult for me to adjust myself to a world where trivial things like getting a haircut, or a taxi, had become problems.

Two days later we reached our native hill country of East Kentucky, and home. Naomi Deane's parents and my father were there to meet us. Our furnace had been turned on days before, and the house was warm and waiting. I was deeply touched to see my home again. I knew how lucky I was to be alive on this last day in November. I had been due back home on October 9.

My father, almost twice my age and half my size, helped me from the car. Inside, a bed was waiting for me. I went right to bed, gladly, while my brother-in-law, George Curry, was putting up a sign where our lane joins the W-Hollow Road that read, "No Visitors. Doctor's Orders." Another was placed on our front door. Dr. Troutman had instructed Naomi carefully and sternly to do this. Visitors, even your closest friends, those who love you most, can kill you. It had never occurred to me before I had a heart attack that it took energy to talk.

I was still inhabiting a strange world of cholesterol and pro-thrombin, high blood pressure and electrocardiograms, antico-agulants and diets and bedrest. But I was home.

I started writing this, my first journal, on January 1, 1955, for two reasons. As a result of my heart attack my hands had become stiff and sore. Dr. Vidt suggested that I gently squeeze and fondle a rubber ball to loosen them up. That sounded like nonsense to me. I'd rather gently tap the keys of my typewriter and maybe write a few stories and poems as a by-product.

That's what they were afraid of. They'd taken my old friend, the typewriter, and stowed it in the attic, where I couldn't see it and be reminded of my beloved trade. But they allowed me a pen and a sheet or two of paper a day. So I decided to work the stiffness and soreness out of my fingers by writing a journal.

The second reason was my wife, Naomi Deane. She urged me to write it. Later she told me why. For weeks she had watched me lying in bed, staring at the ceiling, sometimes refusing to talk, examining my bleak future and wondering if it wouldn't have been better if my heart had stopped beating altogether. Naomi is a wise woman and, like other lucky men's wives, she knows me inside and out. She knew that, with me, it was write or die. She started me writing this journal.

JANUARY

     This is the beginning of a new year. I am not making any New Year's resolutions. I have never believed in making them. Instead, I have always had dreams, counter-dreams and sub-counter-dreams. I have had high things to work for in these dreams. If I cannot reach my highest dreams, then I fall back to my second line of defense, my counter-dreams. If I cannot make these, then I fall back to my third line of defense, my sub-counter-dreams. I rarely have retreated behind this third position.

     But this year, I know, I won't be able to accomplish as much as in former years. There is a possibility, a very good one, that I shall not live through the year. But I'm not too much disturbed by this. If I die this year, I'll be doing a natural thing. I'll be doing something the plants, flowers, and trees, and all living things in this valley and upon this earth, including men, the highest and the lowest, have to do. The process of dying is as natural as that of being born. I shall not be alone.

25

But this year I plan to do something different that will not tax my limited creative powers. I'm going to keep my first journal. Now that I cannot travel, I shall be here at home. I want to keep a record of life, here in this room, this house, this valley, from day to day. On this New Year's Day, 1955, warm and sunny, I thank God first that I am alive. Life is the greatest thing that we possess. And now I have time not only to live it but to examine it.

I I

This has been another day like spring, except very early a white frost covered the carpet of dead leaves over these dark winter hills. Later, from my window, I watched the frost rise up in vapors toward the sun. This valley is very beautiful with the dark, leafless oaks on the hills stretching their bare arm-branches and twig-fingers above the floating, milkweed-furze mists. Sitting in our new living room, where there are windows on three sides, I realize how lucky I am to own these rugged, poetic hills around me. This soil has produced in two ways. It has produced grain, and it has caused my mind to produce thoughts.

This year I will not be driving over the highways at a rapid rate of speed, riding trains between big cities, flying through the blue skies by day and the starry skies by night. I will be confined to my farm. This must be my world. The winter sunlight making the barren black oak branches shine like the new spring skin of a blacksnake after he's shed his rough winter skin must be my beauty.

I I I

This morning I opened the kitchen door and walked around the side of the house. This was my first time around my home since early October. Just to think I could do this again made me grateful to God. I was never more humble in my life. The wind, beautiful and bright as polished silver, rushed from all directions for me to breathe. I stopped and laid my now soft hand on the rough bark of a dogwood I had set by the culvert that goes under our house. Here was a friend, a part of the winter's dark beauty.

At 10:00 A.M., Dr. Vidt and his nurse, Elsie O'Leary, were here, and I was dressed in my bathrobe, ready for them. My brother-in-law, Whitie Liles, had come from Riverton with our mail, just at the right time. Dr. Vidt and Elsie were trying to set up the EKG (electrocardiogram) machine, but were having trouble finding a place to attach a ground wire. Whitie took over and attached the wire to the iron pipe under the washbasin in the bathroom.

Then I lay back in bed while Elsie fastened straps over my ankles and wrists, and one around my chest. She arranged the wires, then turned on the machine. These EKGs had become a regular part of my way of life at Murray Hospital, but I was not used to such a routine at home. Dr. Vidt said I was too excited and was talking too much. He put everyone out of the room but Elsie, and made me lie still ten minutes before she ran the EKGs. Afterwards he solemnly took my blood pressure and counted my pulse.

"Very, very good, Jesse," he said. "You still have a good heart!"

"Yes, I have a good heart," I answered. "I tell my heart that it is valiant." And I did, too. Often I lay in bed, talking to my heart like that. My heart was doing the impossible for me. It was slowly repairing its injuries and at the same time sending blood to all parts of my body.

Giving blood from my arm was something I had never much appreciated. They had taken blood from me so often since October that there were little needle-puncture scars around the veins on my forearms. But it had to be done again. So I turned my head while Dr. Vidt drew blood for my cholesterol and prothrombin tests. They sure were fond of my blood, these people.

Dr. Vidt stayed until twelve noon, talking in the old living room to Naomi. I tried to eavesdrop on what they said. I cupped my ear and leaned toward the door, for surely they were talking about me and my heart. How unashamedly I coveted their good health!

I V

If a man continues to think in low terms, he will soon be living just at the level of his thoughts. Man should listen to a piece of fine music each day, he should read a good poem, story, or novel. And it will profit him to read a portion of the Old or

New Testament each day. These were the things I had time to do now.

One should look for the beauty in the daisy petal in the pasture field instead of looking over his fine breed of cattle and calculating how much a pound they will average. One should stop and listen to the spring winds in the April leaves. One should love the touch of the eternal dirt from which we are all created, and the beauty of a star in the sky, and the sad refrain of winter winds in the dead leaves.

One should see beauty in the fluffy flakes of snow falling in barren timber and, in another season, the aroma of different wild flowers, the lean shape of blossom and leaf. There is so much to elevate our thoughts in each of our private worlds that we should never stoop to thoughts of despising, hurting, cheating, taking advantage of our fellow man.

These are the kinds of thoughts I try to keep in mind. I must think only to build and never to destroy.

V

At an early hour I looked down from my window at the morning star, throwing its rays down upon this bleak winter earth. It seemed to light up the whole valley behind our house. I could not help but believe that this star was bringing a new light into our valley, into my life, at the beginning of this New Year.

How undisturbed it seemed as it looked down on the fretful scurryings of a billion men. We can fail or be successful at whatever we choose to do, but this bright morning star never fades. It continues to shine and to do the work its Creator bid it do. The Kingdom of God may be within us, but we do not have the steadfastness of the morning star. Our little human machines are more uncertain, our human ways more erring.

As long as I could see this star, although it was dimming in the morning sky, I could not go back to sleep. Light rays from the east were flooding the valley, and the winds were rising and bending the leafless twigs. The brown winter broomsedge was bending down when the wind blew over and rising again when the wind passed. It moaned through the branches of the little pine

I'd set in front of our smokehouse, and rustled the green leaves on the holly tree by the walnut stump. And mingling with it was the new winter laughter, after the rains, of the little stream that flowed under our house.

What if I could command the wind to stand still, the water to stop flowing, the morning star to dim its constant light? Even if I desired, I could not. I am human. I have no powers of command over God's world, and luckily so. If I did, I would make a mess of it. Look what I had done already to God's great gift to me— my heart.

I only wish, standing at my window, that I can be as steadfast as this morning star as I journey through this new year.

V I

I dressed in wool socks, heavy leather house slippers, pajamas, and robe, then got into an overcoat and put a hat on my head. I walked out the back door and over the ground where I had played when I was nine years old. Then I went along the walk and under the dogwoods to the yard by the well. My thoughts went back to this part of the yard in the years from 1915 to 1918.

Tall apple trees grew here then. I climbed these trees and shook the apples down for my mother to make apple butter. I remember well these tall trees with boughs bending under the weight of red apples. When I shook them down, the apple-tree leaves, gold-tinted by early frost, went zigzagging to the ground.

At the corner of the house I paused and looked down at the stream which runs under the house. In the early days when we lived here, Dad hewed a log and put it across this stream. We walked over this footlog on our way to the barn. On the other side, now our front yard, used to be the garden where my father, mother, and I worked together.

We raised fine gardens here. We had a June apple tree, currant bushes, gooseberry bushes, and grapes in this garden. Now it has a clean concrete walk and a broad driveway of white, thick concrete leading to the garage. I went down the walk remembering days when my mother, a young woman, wore a bonnet and worked over this ground with a hoe. At the graveled road I stopped and laid my hand on the trunk of the wild-plum tree, still standing, that once had looked down on this boy of nine helping his parents turn the good earth in a vegetable garden.

I turned back up the driveway, walked through the garage, which was chiseled out of the bluff of stone behind our house, and took the winding walk beside the retaining wall back to the kitchen door where I had started from.

I'd been gone about four minutes. This was the extent of my physical exertion. I was as tired as if I had climbed a mountain.

V I I

In the evening, about seven, there was a knock on our door. Naomi opened it and there was Gene Darby. He walked in with a big smile. Gene Darby, six feet two inches, 170 pounds, twenty years old, was a part of my valley.

"Well, I've come to tell you, Uncle Jesse, good-by," he said. "I'm leaving for the Army in the morning at four. I'll be on my way to Fort Knox."

He seemed more like a younger brother than a nephew to me. We just sat and looked at Gene. We'd heard that he was going. But it was something we didn't want to believe. It couldn't be that the last twelve years had passed so swiftly. That was when Leonard Darby and my sister Mary separated. Mom and Dad brought Gene home to raise. He didn't have a home, so Mom and Dad had given him one. And they'd given him love. Shortly after his parents' divorce, they got Nancy, his sister, too.

Dad slept in one bed with Gene, and Mom slept in another bed with little Nancy on her arm as if she were her own child. And many times I heard Mom say she wanted to live long enough to see both grown up and then she'd be ready to die. But Mom didn't live that long.

"After my basic training at Fort Knox," Gene was saying, "I'll go to Maryland. And from there to Germany."

My dad's health hadn't been too good, and Gene, even as a child, had gone out with him to work. Dad taught him to milk cows, plow, chop, saw—do all kinds of farm work—and we never had a better worker grow up in this valley. He worked, hunted, went to school, and grew, not only in physical stature, but mentally and morally as well.

"I've never raised a better boy than Gene," Dad said. He took pride in saying this, too. "When Gene leaves, and I leave, the hill will be different." Now Dad was gone, and Gene was leaving.

The years flashed back and told Naomi and me that we were older. We had pictures of Gene in knee pants. He was not a good student, and when he made his first "A," his grandmother framed it. His grandmother loved him, bragged on him. And he loved her. There's a little book I wrote about Gene entitled *The Beatinest Boy* (that's what we called him), which tells how he got her a Christmas present. In this book a little fiction is thrown in—very little—because you don't have to embroider the facts much with a boy like Gene.

Now he was going to Europe though he'd hardly been away from his home in this valley. Once Naomi and I took him, with Nancy and Jane, to Cincinnati and stayed at the Metropole Hotel for a weekend. We pretended all three were our children. Gene had been used to getting up at 4:00 A.M. and milking cows. So he was up at that hour in the hotel and he got us up. He was a little fellow, nine years old, in his first long pants, and he dragged us out onto the empty streets of Cincinnati at four in the morning.

Gene made his first money working for me. Fifty cents at first, then seventy-five cents, then a dollar, and a dollar and a half, and two dollars. I hired other boys, too, but it was Gene I could always depend on. And when I was away, in New York or on lecture tours, and Gene stayed here with Naomi and Jane, I never worried. He was practical and resourceful. Though he might not have made the best grades in school and had to work for the grades he got, he had horse-sense, willingness, and tenacity. He was a boy I always wanted for my own.

Here sat a man who as a child once entered a house. The law had had him, but my parents intervened. They took him into their home, which was a way of life, and now we looked on the man they helped him to become—clean-cut, no drinking, no smoking, hard-working, unafraid, handy with a fist—but only when it was necessary. And all because Mom and Dad didn't pretend their

Christianity, nor wear it on Sunday clothes. They lived it, taught it.

The little boy who used to cut our grass with the old push mower, sickle our weeds, set trees, was leaving the valley a man. There are so many ways we watch time's passing—the growth of trees, the building of new houses and roads, the coloring of hair.

"Gene, take care of yourself. We want you back here," I said. And come back he must, for he's left a part of himself in the valley.

V I I I

When I awoke this morning, I went to the windows in this house so I could see all three hills, and the two valleys. God had been here last night and left us one of His extras. This extra was snow. We didn't need it, we'd had plenty of rain last autumn and this winter.

Yet we didn't want to do without this exquisite beauty that God had zigzagged down on us from the heavens. As I looked from the windows and Naomi looked at brief intervals as she got breakfast, I could not help getting excited over a valley as pretty as this one. It was a damp snow, four inches on the ground, and hiding all the scars of the earth. Snow was piled on the branches of trees, fingers of pines, briers, twigs. It pressed the warm dead leaves down to feed and nurture the earth. The sky above was as blue as the shell of a robin's egg, and long icicles were hanging on the rock cliffs on the W-Hollow bluffs. Snow outlined every branch of every tree in the woods with soft white pencil markings.

I couldn't go out into this white world of softness and winter beauty that excited me so, but I could shuffle from window to window looking out in almost all directions. Finally I persuaded Naomi to let me walk onto the porch, check the thermometer (it read eight above), and take several deep breaths of winter wind. How much these few moments added to the lifting of my spirit.

I X

I doubted this day would come this soon, if ever at all. Two days ago, I got up and Naomi suggested I put on my shoes, shirt, trousers, and sweater and sit around in them. I jumped at this suggestion. I felt more like me again to get into them. Robes, pajamas, house slippers rob a man of his virility. Now on this Saturday morning Naomi and Jane suggested that I go to the post office with them.

The car was started and the heater turned on. In a few minutes we were driving down W-Hollow. Naomi drove slowly, and I looked at the hills again, the creek bottoms. I looked at the curves in the road and at the winding stream. I looked at the old familiar Daughtery house and barn. We drove over the road I'd walked over, driven a team and wagon over a thousand times. Now, after a brush with Death, I was going over this road again.

We reached the hardroad, turned and drove down State Route 1 to Riverton Post Office, familiar and the same. In the past I'd always come rushing to Riverton anxious to get the mail. A free-lance writer lives by the mail. Now it had been three long months since I was here.

In Greenup, in front of the courthouse, I saw the bundled-up old people and looked at their good, familiar faces. I sat awhile in the car, then went over to the drugstore, saw a few friends, stayed only a few minutes, was sparing in my talk, came back. I couldn't meet too many.

Here was the small town that I used to think was very large when my father and I hauled vegetables and produce here in an express behind a mule. How Dad loved this town. He should have been here now, on the courthouse square among the old men. I looked for him, but he wasn't there.

For years Greenup was the town where we knew the people, where we bought our necessities for living and sold surplus crops from our farm. But seeing the town had never made me happier than now. I was an excited little boy again, walking between my mom and dad.

Coming back we drove along the familiar road beside our much loved Little Sandy River, whose water in winter is summer-leaf green and in summer as yellow as autumn leaves.

We came up the winding Sandy River Road to Womack Hollow and the W-Hollow Road to make the circuit. This simple drive I'd taken thousands of times but never appreciated it as much as today.

Because no man loves life so much as he who comes back from
death.

X

      One lonely night under that oxygen tent I promised God
that, if He'd let me live, for His guiding my physicians, for His
giving my heart strength, I would thank Him in verse when I was
able. A small gift for His kindness. Today, I wrote that poem.

> I thank God that He granted my stay here
> To count the many songs in winds that blow,
> When April's spring returns again this year
> I'll walk with Him where rivers rise and flow.
> I'll stand beneath the graybarked sycamore,
> With softer hands I'll feel its scaly bark,
> Not any man will ever love life more.
> I'll pray as I walk in the April dark.
> Death held me prisoner 'til God stepped in
> And took me by the hand and gave me breath,
> And I was glad this heart was cleansed of sin,
> And that I followed Him from arms of Death.
> Back to my valley for the blooming spring,
> Back to my garden and the wild bird's song,
> To shadow, sun and multicolored wing,
> The land, God must believe, where I belong.

X I

      One of my great pleasures now is feeding the many species
of birds. Robins, snowbirds, bluebirds, sparrows fly in when we fill
the feedbox with grain and scatter it under the dogwoods. Some
of these stay with us the year round, especially the cardinals. They
roost in the barren vines under the outer rim of roof around
our house. In the spring they will build their nest there as they
have always done since we've lived here.

    From the windows Naomi, Jane, and I watch them eat. But our
birds have rivals, the ground squirrels that have been here two
years now, have raised families, and have enticed others from the
woods to join them. Early mornings, when the birds fly in, the
ground squirrels come from their dens under the dogwoods and

rock walls on the banks of our stream. They begin barking to scare the birds away, and wake us up in the bargain.

This morning I watched them and laughed. The redbirds left the scattered grain under the dogwoods near the ground squirrels' dens. They flew to the box on the smokehouse wall, fussing and roughing each other up. Then other birds flew in, stuffed themselves, and flew away, each according to the might of its species.

Meanwhile the ground squirrels gathered the grain down below. They stood on their hind feet and ate like little folks. Their appetites satisfied, these nimble, beautiful creatures filled the pockets of their mouths. Then they ran into their dens among the rocks somewhere underground. There they unloaded and stored this grain for a rainy day and returned for more.

X I I

Yesterday was exceedingly cold, but today the sun, a big ball of fire, arose and changed the weather. I watched from my window, and as the sky brightened, the snow melted on the south hill slopes and ran down the steep faces of the hills. The icicles hanging to our eaves began to drip, and I heard their steady tapping all the way around the house.

So, in this time of thaw, I put on my brown Canadian sports coat, my hat and gloves, and took a brief walk to listen for the sounds. When the soft wind blew, I heard the frozen trees creaking on the hills on both sides of me. On the hill slope on my left were tall pines, and their thawing needles sighed hoarsely in this warm January wind. The oaks on the steep slope on my right—tall, somber blackoaks, shorter and sturdier whiteoaks—groaned relentlessly, like old people rising up and their bones popping.

The drip-drip of the icicles from the cliffs made a soft rhythmical beat. The brown, hungry-looking broomsedge on the knoll was whipped down by a gust of wind, its sighing sounds pleasant to hear. In the time of thawing, the winds usually become gay and frolicsome, like cattle first turned from a barren barn lot onto a green, lush pasture in the spring.

One sound I heard struck a plaintive note in me. So many times in winters past, when I was walking from Greenup High School in the late afternoon of a short winter day, I had heard the same sound —that of a flock of snowbirds talking to each other. Now I watched them rise on a short flight, from the bluff to a dead winter weed field. Though their voices sounded plaintive, they must have been happy, for the snow was melting and they could get to the ground again and pick up the little seeds. These birds spoke to each other in their own language, I was sure of that. One or two would get into a conversation, and all would rise up in another short flight and alight again. Then they put their heads close to the ground and continued their search for food.

I listened to the sounds of the melting ice falling into the creek and the winter singing of cold stream water as it dashed over the rocks, a very different sound from the flow of warm summer water over these same rocks.

Most of nature's sounds in any season are soothing to the ear. There are exceptions, like the roll of thunder and the crack of lightning when it strikes. But there is something particularly fascinating about sounds in the time of winter thaw, something soft and whispering and songlike.

X I I I

This was the morning I was determined to walk to the tool shed beneath the bluffs. Outside I was surprised to see that a thin, blue-looking snow had covered all the dark places where the big snow had melted. It was as if the whole earth was under a strange uneven blanket. The thermometer showed two degrees below.

Walking up the road, I heard hungry birds and saw three pecking at seeds which I thought were frozen in the snow. As I walked on, I came to a rabbit's tracks, where he had come down the hill from under the pines and crossed the bottom toward the creek. I thought of the days when I tracked rabbits over these hills and bottoms to their holes and set traps and caught them for food. I thought about Januarys of long ago, the many rabbits and deep snows. Then I went on walking, for my objective was now in sight.

I went around a little bend in the road. This was my first time out of sight of the house when I was alone. It was strange to be this far away and by myself, yet on such familiar ground. I felt the earth to be my companion, the earth I'd walked and planted and cared for. Without a backward glance, I walked on toward my goal, the tool shed.

Here I stood and looked at a bluff that an outsider wouldn't give a second thought, a medium-sized bluff with the upper portion covered with trees while the lower was a ledge of rock.

Here was the water hole where I used to bathe after working in the fields. And here was the place I found a short story once, "Who Is Dollie?" My second cousin was taking a bath when Dollie came down the road, and he jumped out and took off running.

Here I'd gotten ideas for poems. At this spot my father used to rive boards. He rove them here to cover our house back in 1940. This place by the bluffs was always the center of things, a little spot we loved. My brother James and I had once raised peanuts here, where my tool shed stands now. And this was the place where we liked to scatter fodder for the cows.

But the best time of all was when spring returned and filled this spot with wild flowers, percoon, Indian paintbrush, violets, agaratum, mayapple, and sweet william.

Now, high overhead on the cold stairsteps of the wind, the crows slid over talking to each other.

I turned and started back. I felt wind from up the valley biting my face. My feet were getting cold despite the heavy wool socks. I heard the wind in the sedge and briers on my right, its lonesome sighing in the frozen pine needles on my left. This had been a good walk. But I was glad to get back to the house, sit before an open fire, and warm my feet and hands. For a long, long time I'd lain on a hospital bed and sat inside this house, dreaming of seeing again this little spot of earth where a tool shed sat under a bluff.

X I V

By now, the end of January, I dream, or it has become a fixation, that my circulation is better. I imagine that a part of the clot in my coronary artery is worn away. Now that the cholesterol (which makes for clotting) in my blood is normal, and since I continue to take one and a half grains of hedulin, an anticoagulant, each day, my thinned blood must be circulating better. For I feel less cold in the extremities of my body; my fingers, feet, ears, and nose feel warmer now than at any time since last October. Today I thought that color might even be coming back into my face. I looked hopefully in the mirror, as I had done yesterday and the day before and all the days before that, but my flesh remains a very pale gray, the color of burnt clay where a heap of logs has been piled high and burned for a tobacco seedbed.

I have a ways to go. I must work at it. I must be patient.

FEBRUARY

I attended church this Sunday morning. Up until this time, since my coronary occlusion four months ago, I've not been in any crowd. I waited until after the last bell before I entered and took my old seat again. I listened to the familiar hymns, soft organ music, a moving prayer, a sound, ringing sermon. My friends at church, remembering the "No Visitors, Doctor's Orders" sign at the end of our lane spoke quietly to me, with affection in their eyes, and moved on.

The Reverend Guy Coffman preached to about twenty-five or thirty in this little 110-year-old Methodist church, the oldest standing church in this county. Its red-brick walls heard the marching feet of both Union and Confederate soldiers. Mexican War recruits rattled their sabers in front of this church on the wilderness road which ran in front of our church door and is Main Street today. This church has withstood every great flood on the Ohio River.

When I came home from the hospital, it was only a matter of hours before Reverend Coffman was there. I looked upon his kind face, the thin white hair, and I felt better just to have him there. Lying flat on my back in bed, I looked forward to his regular calls, for they brightened my days. I needed spiritual as well as physical help. A man should not have to have a heart attack in order to draw nearer his Creator, but that is sometimes the way it happens.

At church this morning I asked God what I asked Him in the hospital and in my room at home, to aid my heart as it tried to repair itself and send blood to all parts of my body to keep me alive. Each day I thank God that my heart is doing so well. Although in our warm house I sleep at night with wool socks on and a hot-water bottle to my feet, though my feet still don't have much feeling in them and the tips of my ears get cold in the night, though I don't have the color in my face I once had and my breath comes short when I walk up the road, still I feel that God is on my side, that He has plans for me, that He is, literally, in my heart.

11

I awoke because I thought it was daylight. There was a broad strip of light running across my room from the window where the curtains were tied back. I thought Naomi had overslept and it was late. I got up from bed, switched on the light, and looked at my watch. To my surprise it was only 4:00 A.M. But the room was filled with light.

I went to the window and looked out at the largest moon I had ever seen. It was hanging in a light-blue sky directly over Shinglemill Hollow. And its bright light was flooding the earth.

Shinglemill Hollow is covered with timber, mostly oak. Looking up toward the big moon, I saw the dark leafless trees moving in a slow morning wind. Too many people, impatient for spring's warmth, discount winter as a season of beauty. But I was excited now by the dark, hard stems of trees clinging tenaciously to the crevices in the cliffs, reaching naked fingers toward the winter skies, asleep, their roots embedded in a frozen tranquillity.

Standing by my window, I saw something stirring in the yard. I watched the small moving creature—I knew it was a rabbit—hop down across the yard, playing in the moonlight.

When I scattered grain for the birds in the afternoon, they often left little heaps, but by daybreak the following morning these were gone. I had figured the rabbits or our three-legged possum from under the house was eating this grain. Now I watched the rabbit hop down under the dogwood within twelve feet of my window. Where I'd scattered grain, the rabbit sniffled over the ground gathering what the birds had left. When he was through, he hopped around into the kitchen yard, and I followed him.

I went into the kitchen and looked from a window. He played over the kitchen yard and went under the smokehouse and came out again. He ran back past the dogwoods toward the front yard, and I hurried into the old living room, following a beam of moonlight shining through the windows. After he ran, hopped, jumped, and had himself another good time, he went into one of the tiles that drains our front yard. And I went back to bed.

When we were sitting at the breakfast table, Naomi told me she had opened her eyes to find the room filled with light. She had gotten out of bed, switched on a light, and looked at her watch, and it was only 3:00 A.M. Then she went to the window and looked out at the most beautiful winter moon she had ever seen. I told her that the same thing had happened to me an hour later, but that I'd shared the moonlight with a rabbit.

I I I

When we awoke, rain was coming down. I'd awakened three times during the night, and each time I heard rain tapping the roof above and hitting the shingle walls. Once I heard a pair of redbirds that have roosted three years running in the vines outside my window, talking to each other about the night and the rain, or perhaps about a place to build.

When I walked out this morning, the streams were leaping down the small ravines on the slopes, pouring over the rocks, moving down to the larger streams in the valleys in a hurry. The air was saturated with moisture, but the rain soon stopped. Then clouds of mist rose up like white smoke from the morning earth. The whole valley seemed to be rising up. It was a beautiful, wet, cloud-rising February day.

This day I would have liked to put on my raincoat, but not a hat,

and walk over the wet, rain-packed carpet of dark-brown leaves
hugging close to the earth. This was the time to watch raindrops run
down the twigs on barren trees and drop to the ground. This was
the time to walk under the wet pines and breathe deeply of the wind
they had flavored—but for me such a walk was only wishful thinking. Instead I walked around the house and looked at each hill
bathed in the white mists, at the raindrops following each other to
their jumping-off places on the small twigs outside my windows.

I V

After breakfast, Naomi was in the kitchen working. Tired
of not doing anything, I came into the old living room and got busy.
I built my first fire.

Once I'd been an expert at building fires. I'd built enough of
them since we'd been married, and for years I'd watched my father,
who was more of an expert than I. Now I punched the ashes down
through the grate and, outside, loaded two empty coal buckets, one
with fire kindling and the other with coal.

I laid some paper in the bottom of the grate, then placed kindling
on top of this. I crisscrossed the kindling the way I used to build
a rail fence, so the fire could get air. On top of this fire kindling I
put heavier kindling, and on top of the heavier kindling I laid wood.
Then I struck a match and lighted the paper. The flame licked up
through the kindling, and soon I had a blazing fire.

I took coal from the hamper and placed it on the fire. I laid each
lump precisely where it ought to be, building up the coal so air
could come up from the bottom of the grate. By the time Naomi had
finished in the kitchen and had come in to build the fire, the one I'd
built was so hot it almost ran her from the room. She quarreled with
me because I had lifted a bucket of coal and carried it from the
garage.

But the only unforgivable mistake I'd made in making the fire
was the use of paper. Dad never would let us use paper or kerosene.
The way he built a fire, and I never saw him fail, was to have himself
a supply of rich pine kindling, dark and heavy, with plenty of resin,
that he gathered from dead pine logs and stumps. He sawed or

chopped these stumps and logs into kindling and laid it away in a shed for winter.

He used only a few sticks of his pine kindling, along with dry sticks of other wood, to start the fire. He took his knife and whittled shavings on the sticks, so that when he struck a match and touched the flame to these rich pine shavings, the fire fairly leaped up through the dry wood. But the use of paper and kerosene to build a fire my father scorned. He would have none of it.

V

During the cold spell we had one water pipe to freeze, the cold-water pipe in the bathroom. Naomi long ago said that if we didn't come to some agreement on the three-legged possum, who had left the tile in the yard and had gone under our floors, our pipes would freeze.

Our house has solid underpinning all the way round, except where pipes go under the bathroom and the kitchen. Here there isn't any underpinning at all, and we use dirt in the winter to stop the holes and keep the wind from blowing under the floor. The possum has found this out. When the ground is thawed, this wise fellow opens a hole under the bathroom, where the soft dirt is, so that he will be able to get out and find food when the ground freezes up. Now there is another way the possum could get out, and that's to go through a tile that leads from under the floor to the creek. But I suppose he isn't partial to taking this damp tile route.

We believe he has a bed by one of the hot-water pipes under our floor. When he opens a hole in the loose dirt, Naomi fills it up, and he opens it again. His opening a hole and her filling it up goes on for days. Then she comes to me and lays down the law. "Jesse, you've got to do something about that old possum. He's opened a hole under the bathroom floor and the cold air can blow up under there and freeze the water pipes."

Two weeks ago, in a cold spell, she noticed this hole under the floor the skinny old three-legged possum had made and she wanted me to have Lige carry dirt and fill it up. But I worried what the possum would do for food if he wouldn't go the tile route and we filled up his hole and the dirt froze. With only one front leg he couldn't dig through frozen dirt. I answered that I wanted him to have a way out even if we did get a little cold wind blown under the house.

Now I considered that we were lucky, with temperatures of twenty below and a possum hole big enough to funnel icy wind under our bathroom floor, that we only had one pipe frozen. I told Naomi we were lucky, but she just smiled and shook her head.

V I

In my peculiar life, climbing stairs has become an adventure.

Naomi and I drove to her mother and father's home this afternoon. This time I was determined to go inside. I'd seen Mr. and Mrs. Norris many times since my heart attack, but only when they'd been out home to visit us. I'd not been inside their house since last September. When we drove up and parked, I studied the back steps. I had planned to go inside this rear way so people wouldn't see me struggling to get up the front steps when a short time ago I was a strong man running up them three at a time. But after a few minutes' reconnoitering from the car, after counting the steps of both front and rear flights, I chose to use the front stairs because they were a couple of steps shorter.

A few weeks ago, in a magazine, I'd seen an ad for one of those one-person banister elevators that run up and down stairs. I had quickly turned the page. Now I was glad that I had no such aid but must depend on my legs, weak as they were.

I walked up and faced the steps. I wasn't going up backwards, as one doctor had suggested that I do. Nor did I want Naomi holding onto my arm and supporting me. I wanted to do it by myself. I made the first step by using the soft muscle in my right leg to support my weight as I raised the left one to the step above. I paused. Then I lifted my back foot up and planted it beside the first. I was on my way. I went slowly, carefully, a step at a time, until I'd reached the porch, breathing heavily, perspiring. This was my first flight of stairs. It might well have been Everest for the elation I felt.

V I I

The first time I learned to stand alone, to walk, to put food to my mouth I don't remember. But in my boyhood I had typhoid fever, my hair came out, and my legs and arms became flabby, weak, and useless. I had to learn all over again to stand alone and then to walk, finally to use my arms and hands and put food to my mouth. My hair grew back on my head. Thus, even before my heart attack, I had learned to do everything a second time.

Now I was having to learn to do everything over for the third time. In the Murray Hospital, after being in bed for thirty-five days, I just about had to learn to feed myself again. This didn't take very long, but I was clumsy at first. Then there was the slow and gradual process of leaving the bed and sitting in a chair. Later, there was the first time to get out of pajamas and robe and house slippers and back into trousers, shoes, shirt, and sweater. The first time to sit at the table and eat with Naomi and Jane. The first time to see a sunset, go to the post office, walk down the street in Greenup, go to the doctor instead of his coming here to see me.

The first time to walk around the house for months and to feel the wind against my face and to hear it blow—what a thrill that day was. But yesterday I experienced the excitement of first contact with the world beyond my bed, my room, my house. I used the telephone again. I called New York and spoke to friends there. The thrill of my growing world made my voice shake.

V I I I

Now that the snows have gone, that barren hills have thawed again, and the ground is soaked with snow water and rain, the birds have become very independent. I carried grain out this morning and put it in little piles, spaced about six feet apart on our back walk. But we didn't have many birds flying in to eat.

And the birds that did fly in for babychick feed soon got into a fight, not only with different species of birds, but among themselves. The snowbirds fought each other, the sparrows pulled feathers from one another. And the bluebirds had to rise in flight to avoid getting pecked and flogged by the others.

When snow was on the ground, and all seeds were covered and frozen, when the weather was subzero, all these birds ate from one pile of feed at a spot Naomi had cleared of snow. When they were cold and hungry, they had something in common with each other— need. So they ate together. You might call these birds "foul-weather friends." I guess that's why Noah was able to load two specimens of every kind of animal into the ark. But if they hadn't all been threatened by the flood, they'd have torn each other apart and then taken out after old Noah.

I X

Little blue berries hanging in clusters to the leafless sand-briers, each berry in each cluster with a drop of rain hanging to it.

Long fronds of the weeping willow, awakening with the new blood of another spring, slap the arms and thighs of the wind in playful greeting.

The dark, leafless iron tracery of a thousand trees on breadloaf hill, silhouetted against the low rain-laden skies.

Little drops of rain following each other down a slick plum branch and sliding off to the ground.

Dead tree, without branch or bark, standing stark and tragic amid the faintly green but still sleeping trees that will awaken to leaf and life again in a few weeks' time. Dead tree that needs no tombstone, that marks its own grave.

X

There is one man I miss. I watch the road for him to pass. It seems that something has gone wrong that I do not see him. I walk down to the bluff, where Lige is cutting sprouts, and he is not with Lige. He should be there, looking over the work and doing what he is able. He should have stopped and talked to me and told me what I should be doing in the fields at this time of year. I've looked for him all day.

Now that the snow has melted and the hungry crows are flying over the empty fields of later winter, it is time for him to be going over this farm, digging up dirt, smelling of it, sifting it through his fingers, and making plans.

He is a familiar figure in this valley, this small, wiry man who walks and talks like the blowing wind. He's made more tracks in this valley than any other man. His hoe and plow have turned over more scattered rocks in the fields. I shouldn't be looking for him, but I can't help it. I never needed him more. There are so many things I'd like to ask him.

I watch the road in front of the house, and I listen for his light knock on our door. I don't see him walking down the road, and there is no knock.

Although I feel, and always will, that he is ever near (for how could he leave this place he loved so well?), I will not see him going about his quick ways, working, sweating, laughing. For he is my father, and he sleeps eternally at Plum Grove, just one hill over from this valley he lived in all his life.

X I

The first people to walk in this valley, to own this land, to make houses of the big yellow-poplar logs, were the Byrnes. As far as we know, they and their relatives—the Sinnetts, Garthees, and Chatmans—were the first here to build homes, travel the ridges, and clear the little creek bottoms.

They were different from most hill families in that they didn't have family cemeteries on their farms. They didn't leave a grave-yard in W-Hollow. The mute evidence of their pioneering is five or six long graves, sunken places in the earth, outside of W-Hollow, where the headwaters of Shacklerun begin. But they were the first to own this valley and trap in these hills and leave their footprints on this prolific dirt. We've never seen one of their footprints. They've been washed away by time and the seasons. They came about 1800 and stayed until about 1850.

Then, about 1850, the Daughterys came. Their in-laws and rela-tions were the Collinses and Myerses, and they bought all this val-ley, farmed it, raised the best strawberries and sweet potatoes in Greenup County. A sweet potato raised by Win Daughtery, which my father saw when he was a young man, was nine feet long! It was

on display in a store window in Greenup for weeks, and other people saw it, too. W-Hollow, already famous for strawberries, became
famous for sweet potatoes.

These people preserved timber, kept out fire, protected their
land as if it were their own blood and flesh. And they loved
W-Hollow, I know. Because, my father, as a young man, worked
for them, and when I was a child, I worked for them, too.

But at the end of their half century, they died one by one
and were hauled from W-Hollow and buried on Three Mile Hill,
now grown up like a forest. With the death of W. W. Daughtery,
the last male descendent of the Daughterys was gone. In death they
gave up W-Hollow, this valley they owned and loved. They left
before the age of the automobile, but they had rubber-tired buggies, fringed surreys, and hugmetights. They made millions of
tracks over this valley, but like the tracks made by the Byrnes and
their kinfolks, they didn't last. The prolific dirt, good for sweet
potatoes and strawberries, couldn't hold their tracks forever. Time
and the seasons washed them away.

Then the Stuarts and their relatives, the Hiltons, took over
W-Hollow. They didn't own any of it at first, but later they managed to win practically the whole valley—all the land owned by
the Daughterys, Collinses, and Myerses, and some more. They
raised hay, cattle, sorghum cane, and tobacco, some sweet potatoes
and strawberries.

They've lived here from 1896 until the present. The Stuarts still
remain, but I am the last, and leave no sons. It is a half-century
valley for any one family, and our time is about up.

My father's plow and my mother's hoe turned over all the
pebbles and stones on hill and bottom in this valley. They lived
in eight different places in this neighborhood. They planted millions
of steps, more than any other couple who ever lived here. But
I cannot find one of them now.

X I I

Today Gene Darby returned from Fort Knox, where he
had spent seven weeks in an armored division. He'd written but
few letters home, and we were worried, since he'd never been away

from home before, that he was glad to be away and that he had forgotten us, forgotten W-Hollow.

But he came home, lacking fifteen cents of having enough to buy his ticket, at two-thirty in the morning. And when he came, everybody got out of bed. Whitie, his uncle by marriage, came down here to borrow flour to make biscuits, and this day was declared a holiday.

From two-thirty in the morning until four in the afternoon Gene never stopped. He went to the barn and fed his horses and spoke to them. He spoke to the cows he'd milked. He walked all over the hill and looked at the trees and tramped the fields as soon as it was light. He stood and listened to the streams as he had done all his life up until his twentieth year.

Now we knew that he loved this valley and that he couldn't escape. He was not any different from the rest of us. No one yet who has eaten the food from this soil, drunk water from this earth, and breathed this air, no one whose eyes have seen the beauty of the four seasons in W-Hollow, has ever wanted to leave.

MARCH

Before I got out of bed, I heard them calling. Naomi has always contended one says "Phoebe," but I maintain he says "Pewee." Our annual visitors were back to build their nest, and this was exceedingly early for flycatchers. I wondered where they'd get enough insects to sustain life.

It was good to hear their calling. Theirs were the voices of old friends. I got up and looked out the window. Daylight was breaking. And the pewees, though I couldn't see either one of them, were hopping in the vines. Their voices brought pleasant memories, and one unpleasant one, too.

When I was a child old enough to learn anything, I learned to respect these birds. My father and mother loved them. And, in the little house where I lived until I was nine, a pair came each spring. My father used to say, "Must be time to plow the garden, our pewees are back." They built a nest, a mudwall, fastened onto a log just above our front door, lining it with straws and feathers. Here they laid eggs and hatched their young. They were conscientious parent birds, flying over our garden and yard, snatching insects from the air. They built so high on the wall of this house, a cat couldn't scale up to the nest.

Then we moved from that little log house to the house where we live today. We lived here three years then, and over our front door a pair of pewees built each spring. We moved on to another house and another, and later I traveled in other towns and states. But when Naomi and I came back to W-Hollow, renovated this house, and moved in, the pewees returned. Unable to build in front, where we had added a porch, they moved to the rear of our house and built up close to the roof beside the kitchen door. Here the hen bird laid her eggs, and she and the rooster hatched them.

But Jane had a cat, Mollie, quick and clever at catching snakes, rabbits, squirrels, and even quail for her kittens. One night we switched on the back-porch light, frightened the mother bird, and she flew off, fluttering confusedly among the vines. Mollie scaled the wall and caught her before our eyes. We wept. We thought it would be disastrous for the four young birds.

But the father bird caught food, carried water, and hovered over these young birds at night. And each time he left the nest after food he'd alight on our smokehouse and cry plaintively for his mate. He said, so Naomi, thought, "Phoebe."

After Mollie, Jane's cat, caught this bird, I could endure her no longer. I gave her to a neighbor who loved cats. I couldn't kill her, yet I knew that Mollie—a cat, a killer by instinct—would be after the father pewee if we kept her.

But all four young pewees grew up and flew away with their father.

The following spring two pewees returned and built behind the house, up high, out of reach of cats. And since that time they have returned each spring. They are more accurate weather prophets than the bluebirds. When they come, we begin to prepare for spring. They are our birds of prophecy, and we rejoice at the thought of the warm weather that follows in their wake.

I I

This morning I saw something I'll not soon forget. I walked out, and the whole valley was a meadow of frost. But the sun was shining down from a blue sky, and the frost was melting and ascending in thin, white, twisting streamers toward the sun.

On the right bank of Shinglemill Hollow stream, between the stream and our garden, there was a city of white tents. I couldn't believe it until I walked over the footlog and looked. They were spider webs, spun since yesterday, but now they were empty of spiders. Could spiders stand freeze and frost? Where had they gone? Why had they built and deserted a city of white tents to show conspicuously in the sunlight on a winter morning? Maybe the spiders were staying under the dead grass, under the tufts of the creek banks, in crowded holes, under clods in our garden. But I didn't really know.

Their small city of tents held the moisture of the melted frost and shone brightly in the glow of early-morning sun, looking like an army of white pup tents pitched on a field where marching men camped for the night.

Not long ago the weather was twenty below. Where were the spiders then? I could ask where were the snakes and frogs, the terrapins and turtles. They'd soon be awake and stirring, too. The terrapins would certainly be stirring, for we'd had one thunderstorm and this was Nature's early trumpet that woke them. Something had awakened the spiders, too. They had quickly built a beautiful city, then they had fled. I couldn't explain it, for spiders have integrity. Touch a web and see. They are reluctant to desert their delicate homes.

I I I

As on a warm, soft day in early June, the sun came up, and a slow, soft morning wind blew. After all our cold winter blasts, I welcomed this sudden change of weather. I walked over the yard, looking at the knoll crowned with broomsedge that rippled in the soft wind like ripened July wheat. And on beyond the knoll was my pasture field, where broomsedge covered almost fifty acres.

Back inside, I was sitting by my desk, when I thought I smelled burning broomsedge. I hurried outside and looked up the valley. The orchard hill seemed a mass of high, leaping flames.

Whitie, my brother-in-law, hadn't told me that he was going to burn the broomsedge from this pasture. Naomi and I went up the valley toward the fire. By going up Sulphur Spring Hollow, we could see over all the broomsedge land. We could tell if anyone was firing it, standing by and watching. Now dark billows of smoke and red tongues of flame were swirling up sixty feet or more. But when we reached the field, we were relieved to see Whitie come leaping over the broomsedge like a deer.

"We're firing with the wind!" he shouted when he saw Naomi and me. "Linn Darby is up on top firing the ridge."

Then I knew that, with two men like Whitie and Linn watching over the field, we were safe.

"Leaves under the trees beyond this field are too wet to burn," Whitie shouted.

He fired the base of the hill, and flames went up to meet the flames burning slowly down from the top. No man could have outrun the fire racing up the hill through this dense broomsedge. We could feel the heat down in the valley below. The broad tongues of golden flames, expanding like water flooding out of control over a dam, leaped out and cleaned the broomsedge from the ground and left in its wake a dark land of charred stubble.

Since we were children, we had gathered to watch people burn their fields of broomsedge in the spring. The burning day was carefully selected by our fathers, a day when the broomsedge was dry enough, but not too dry, and the wind was right, sometimes in early March, sometimes as late as the first week in April. Strange, how everybody liked to watch the dry, flimsy, worthless broomsedge burn.

Men careful of wildlife and timber chose the right time to burn, and a number of them gathered to watch over the fire to see that it didn't get out of control. But a few in our community, who didn't have any regard for timber or wildlife or even farm-houses, set fire and let it go. Then we gathered in a hurry and fought the fire away from our timber. Many of these men set fire to kill the snakes. And with the snakes, they burned up nests of young rabbits, quail, birds, and terrapins.

But Whitie's fire wouldn't get beyond this pasture of golden broomsedge. The rabbits didn't have nests of young here, nor did the few remaining quails. The snakes, terrapins, frogs, and lizards were sleeping in their secret hibernations.

It was a beautiful spectacle to watch—the long red tongues reaching out and cleaning the land.

I V

Always we watch for the very first sign of spring. This morning Naomi and I walked down the lane while the warm winds blew and lightning cut across the darkening heavens. We were look-ing for places where we planned to set Easter lilies beside the road for next spring.

"Look here," I said. "First blossoms of spring!"

"Hazelnut blooms," Naomi said.

We had for many years gathered hazelnuts from these bushes beside our lane road. They had grown here, and we had protected them all the years we had been married. I'd gathered hazelnuts from these bushes many times on my way to and from school.

When Naomi and I were married and came here to live, she didn't know hazelnut blooms until I showed them to her on this bush, their soft yellow-green tassels, like spears on corn tassels, clinging to leafless little branches. Jane, born three years later, learned hazelnut blossoms from this bush. Actually it is not a single bush, but several large clusters, for the hazelnuts had ex-panded since we had protected this hill from fire and allowed trees to grow again.

But I'd seen fires race over this hill and kill the hazelnut roots tucked away in the deep loam. Three times in my lifetime I'd seen this hill cleared and farmed, and my father cleared it once before I was born. Each time the hazelnuts were cut down and dug up by the roots. But despite fire and clearing, a little piece of root remained hidden in this deep loam, and from this root they sprang again.

This family of hazelnut bushes fought to live and grow here just as a few families of men, the Byrnes, Daughterys, and Stuarts, had. Each family fought to survive, and did survive approximately a half century. But the hazelnut bushes had survived as long as all the families, a century and a half and maybe longer. They would not die. They clung to this same small portion of loamy land at the foot of the hill beside the road. And this year I admired the hazelnut bushes more than ever for their stubborn will to live. I felt we shared something in common.

V

More than sixteen hours of heavy rain have caused the streams to rise and sing down the little valleys. Years have passed since we have had a rain like this. It took such a rain to find twelve leaks in our roof.

The grass now shows signs of life in our front yard. Our big weeping willow is about to leaf. Dark rain clouds scoot over the wind just barely above the leafless sleeping trees on the hilltops. High above, the lightning is splitting these dark clouds, thunder following from one ridgetop to another.

"It's a scary time," Naomi said.

"It is that," I agreed.

And then I thought: I should mark every day we have thunder in March. It's an old saying, Thunder in March, on a corresponding day in May we'll have frost.

For the first time in days, the surge of the streams is louder than the March winds. Radio stations announce that everywhere in the Ohio River Valley a record rain is falling, that the Ohio River is rising again toward flood stage.

Shinglemill roars down the narrow channel between the rock walls by the redbud and dogwood trees and leaps through the large tile under our house like a bullet through a rifle barrel.

Water runs in thin sheets over the rocks on the bluff, in streams down valleys, in ravines, and in ditches beside the road. The earth has absorbed rain and melted snow water until it is saturated, and all the channels are filled. Everything that will hold water is full and running over.

And this is still winter. The fields are desolate and empty, the land still barren. For the wild birds flying in to the feedbox, this is a strange time, with all the streams and winds singing and with dark trees high on the ridges turned to a silver gray by a thin, gossamer sheet of ice over the hard boughs. Yet down in the valleys the barren trees are not sleet-covered but rain-dark, like a thick black beard on the earth's face.

What a fascinating world to return to from a hospital room and a brief meeting with the dark unknown.

V I

The first flood I can remember was in 1913. My father took me over the ridge and down Academy Branch to see *the flood*. That was the second highest in the recorded history of Ohio River floods, and I'll never forget the surging waters this child saw standing there on the bank. I watched a house go down the river too, then a haystack floating with some chickens on it. These things have remained with me all my life.

Since then I've seen floods come and go, and their victims go and come back. These people flee only to return to their homes again to await another disaster, probably next year. They like their small home towns along the Ohio. They view a flood stoically, somewhat like an inconvenient holiday. And they'll move back, clean up the filth, live for a time in discomfort, and run the risk of epidemics— either out of apathy, lack of alternative, or love for their property. Maybe a mixture of all three.

In this season of flood, I've seen the last road from town jammed with boys leading cows, men and women carrying belongings, pictures, and clothing, fleeing from high waters and looking for a home. Everybody in the county who lives in a higher, unflooded section opens his home to the refugees, large houses absorbing as many as six or seven wandering families.

There is a special hospitality among people during a flood. The flood is a common disaster they unite against. If the water keeps on rising, people will be out here asking for shelter. Empty houses will be opened and hastily aired out, food supplies pooled, old clothes collected, hats passed for money. Sometimes there's a "school's out" spirit of celebration about this annual "disaster"— though a true disaster it is for many.

V I I

Only one road leading to Greenup was open this morning. The water rose to a high level Sunday, Monday to a higher level. The river is a yellow-gold ribbon. When the sun breaks through the clouds, the river's surface appears to be almost on a level with the streets in Greenup.

People came to me this morning to get two empty houses to live in. They got them. They asked for a tool shed on the farm to store household effects in. They got it. They asked for an old smokehouse. They got it, too. Fortunately, the highlands around Greenup are so extensive in comparison with the flooded areas that the people without homes are a mere trickle to be absorbed, housed, and fed.

Before this day ended, the last road into Greenup was blocked off by state police. Only large trucks, moving vans, emergency cars, and ambulances were allowed through the rising water. Greenup is now a city of booted men, wading murky waters, working and sweating to save their stores, their merchandise, their homes. Predictions of another 1937 flood have forced them to take this one seriously. They are moving upstairs or moving out. Gas pressure is low. Furnaces are out. There is little heat.

My sister and brother-in-law's house has two extra families. The county's bookmobile has been parked full of books near our tool shed. The old Daughtery place has been taken over. The Collins' house has a family moved in. The narrow W-Hollow Road is filled with parked or slow-moving vehicles. Another major flood is here. But this one I can only watch from the side lines.

V I I I

Floods have come in December, January, and February. They have come in early March. They usually come in winter months. Warm winds blow up from the South, meet cooler winter winds from the North, and there are storm battles.

If Southern weather dominates, the grass begins to grow, flowers bloom. I've seen the white field daisy, percoon, even peach and apple trees bloom in late December and January. I've seen pussy willows, weeping willows, alder bushes, and sumacs leaf in these winter months.

All cold-blooded animals awake when the thunder and rain are heavy. We hear frogs everyplace, in the new-made ponds, in the streams, and beside the river. Terrapins and turtles crawl again. And it is amazing the number of snakes, more than we ever dreamed we had, that leave their hibernating seclusion when the flood waters rise. Instinctively they climb up trees for safety. In 1937, when I was marooned in the McKell High School in the worst of all Ohio River Valley floods, I rowed a boat under trees and reached up with my oar to knock down clusters of snakes hanging to the barren boughs of trees before I dared go under them. I saw thousands of snakes. They were in every tree where the backwaters had risen.

Rabbits came out in the open on that plot of ground around the schoolhouse, and a dog wandered there and had her litter of pups while we stood eating Salvation Army food. The dog didn't bother the rabbits. Ground and garter snakes were everywhere, so many we couldn't have killed them if we had wanted to. Instead we picked them up, played with them, put them in our pockets for the fun of it.

In a time of emergency all people, friendly and unfriendly, get together. In McKell High School in 1937, living side by side, eating together, and warming by the same fire were people who hadn't spoken to each other for twenty years. Instinctively, this same feeling was among the lower animals. They seemed to have suspended their urge to kill in this time of disaster. Their instinct had served them well in another way, too. They had known sooner than we that the flood waters would force them out of their natural habitats. When we humans sought the higher ground, we always found animals there first.

Water crested two days ago and started slowly receding yesterday. We drove to Greenup today for supplies and mail, and to see the town after the seventh worst flood in the Ohio River's history. We followed the Little Sandy River for two miles. Where the Ohio River had backed the Little Sandy River up, there were deposits on the trunks of the trees as if they had been painted with a yellowish, murky paint. It was hard for us to believe that the water had ever been this high along this river, six to eight feet deep in one place on the road we were driving over.

When we drove into the town a few of the streets were dry. But many of them were still wet with black, foul-smelling water or a thin, dark mud that stuck like glue. Along all the curbs were streams of brackish water, water pumped from basements and cisterns. Everywhere the large pumps were going, as many as four of them lifting water from a single puddle.

If you want to experience the essence of flood, go smell a city after one.

People were already back in business. In a matter of hours they had washed the muck and silt from their floors, and brought their stock down from upstairs; they were pumping out their basements while customers walked in and made purchases above.

Men walked the streets in boots. There was a thin gruel-mud running from the streets over the bank to the river. In the muck they found a boot, then another boot, then a man in a rubber suit. He was a well-known blacksmith and mechanic of Greenup whose boat had capsized three days ago. He was found not far from where he went down.

Trucks were rolling in, and men with big shovels, or scoops, were loading tin cans from stacks of debris higher than a man's head. These piles of refuse are all over Greenup, on the streets, courthouse square, front and back yards. In one front yard I saw what must have amounted to two truckloads of cans.

Our rivers and their tributaries have become arteries used for sewage and dumping. Instead of clean, flowing water, they have become troughs of filth. This is particularly true of the "Beautiful Ohio." Go to any small town along this river and take one look over the riverbank. Then see what you will see and turn back in disgust.

When the river rises up in anger, it gives back to the people what

they have given it. It is little wonder that many cities are required
to have garbage incinerators. But it *is* a wonder that other cities
have huge pipes into this river through which they pump such filth
and sewage—then they purify it with chemicals and drink it.

We have had more floods and higher waters as the years pass.
This is in part due to the disappearance of the trees in the Ohio
River basin, which once softened the ground with their roots and
leaves and absorbed the water. Now the ground is barren and hard,
and water drains off rapidly, racing down the eroded hills into the
valleys and then to the Ohio.

My father-in-law, Emmit Norris, a highly independent man,
grew so disgusted that Greenup never erected a flood wall, that he
figured out his own solution. His handsome street, with its two
rows of giant maples that shade the walks, is not on the river front,
but it is in a low area. His house was on a level with the others, and
when a flood came, water seeped into the basement and first floors
of these homes.

He asked others along his street to cooperate with him and do
the same thing that he planned to do, but they wouldn't. So he
went ahead alone. He jacked his house up so high that he could
build a basement under it from the ground level up to his first floor.
Then he filled in around his house with dirt and walled his yard in.
Today his house, towering over a row of houses, looks as if it sits
upon a small hill. And it does, a hill of his own making. When the
flood came this year, it didn't reach him. He was sitting upon his
hill, dry and comfortable, while his neighbors all around him were
rowing away from their flooded homes.

And in W-Hollow, we've had only the beauty and none of the
destruction.

The beauty of winter rain and singing streams that leap down
hills and run in silver ribbons when the sun pops through the
clouds—it is hard to believe that such beauty has gone toward making this flood.

Today I stood in our yard, now green with grass, and felt the
warm winds against my pale winter face. I imagine that I can see
the grass inch up in our yard, it has grown so fast, and the blossoms

on the hazelnuts, like brown-and-green strips of yarn, have appeared overnight. Young, tender leaves have come to the weeping willow, and now its long, green fronds wave toward me and swish in the wind like delicate fingers. The red buds have burst on the maple trees, the primrose and daffodils have blossomed in our yard.

But all this beauty is the other side of destruction.

I X

I had just climbed into bed for my afternoon rest when Betty Vaughn, my niece, who was forced from her home by flood and was staying with my sister and her husband up the road, came running down Shinglemill Hollow, almost out of breath, face flushed, excited. "A fire is out," she panted.

I ran to the kitchen.

"We saw the smoke rising from up at Glennis and Whitie's and I went to see where it was," she said now, her breath coming easier.

"Is it across the Seaton Ridge?"

"Oh, yes," she said. "It's in that old pasture field near where the Hilton House used to be."

This was my land.

"It's in my trees," I said. "Anybody fighting it?"

"I didn't see anybody."

"That ridge hasn't been crossed by fire in twenty years," I said. "It's our line of defense against fire. That fire will get our barn and house on the ridge. And all the trees we've set. It could get us."

"What can I do?" Naomi asked.

"Take the car and see if you can get help." I watched billows of smoke rise on the ridge. "See if you can get Glen Hilton. He knows how to fight fire."

Naomi and Betty jumped into the car. I walked the yard. I couldn't go back to bed. Dad, the old fire fighter, wasn't here. He would have smelled that fire. He would have been there hours ago. Where had it come from, I wondered. The Little Sandy was high on one side with flood waters and the Ohio River high on the other— and my land on fire between these seas of flood waters!

For two days, after all the heavy rains, the March winds had kept blowing. They blew at perhaps forty miles an hour, puffs of wind arising from nowhere and driving furiously over the empty earth and lifting thousands of leaves. The March wind was always dangerous. It dried the roads and the leaves in the fields, and it pushed fire. We called it the Road Drier and the Fire Driver.

Uncle Jesse, seventy-five years old, almost 300 pounds, came by for rakes and hoes and was on his way to fight fire. George Alexander, seventy-seven years old, came wheezing by to tell me everything was burning up and the barn and house were gone if I didn't get immediate help.

A car went up at full speed. Frank Hilton and Orin Nelson were in it. Both understood forest fires; they were skilled fighters. In a few minutes Glen went up with a truckload of boys. I learned later that Glen, on hearing the news from Naomi, had gone to Three Mile, where he had found a group of boys playing basketball and drafted them. We were lucky.

I walked the yard and watched the smoke. I watched the motion of the pine tops, and I knew the fire was driven by March wind directly north. Great clouds of smoke swirled upward. I could see the red tongues of flames now. I was quite sure our house was in danger, for the winds blew as I'd not heard them blow for days. I wondered how these men and boys were fighting the fire. How I wanted to be there myself! I knew how to fight fire. I had fought so many, I was sure of myself. But I was definitely out of it.

Helpless and out of it, an invalid pacing in his yard.

After a while the billows of smoke thinned in the skies. I didn't see the red tongues of flames any more. The first to return from the fire and tell me it was out were Whitie Liles and Betty Vaughn. Betty's legs were scratched by briers and bleeding, and she was tired. Whitie had lost his eyelashes and eyebrows and some of the hair on the front of his head. He'd been that close, but a good fire fighter has to grapple at close quarters with his enemy. I've fought fires with Whitie many times. Once in broomsedge he taught me to use a wet coffee sack. We caught the wind blowing from us and beat out a long line of fire.

"We've got it stopped," Whitie said wearily. "In fifteen more minutes it would have reached your barn."

Whitie and Betty got up from where they sat on the porch steps and walked slowly up the hollow. Then Orin Nelson came, looking as if he'd run through the flames, his face red and sweaty, his hair singed.

Later, Frank Hilton came with Dink Jackson, the firewarden, and the truckload of boys. They were a tired group. The boys had found fire fighting harder exercise than basketball. I talked to them for several minutes. Then Glen came down in his car. He was the last to leave the fire. It was out, he said, but he'd be back for another look tonight. The high wind might fan an ember they'd overlooked.

I couldn't go back to bed. Instead I asked Naomi to drive me to Womack Hollow. The fire had come from there, and I wanted to see how it had started.

Beginning at the first deep hollow on the other side of the gap, the fire had burned the top leaves, but only on the other side of the little stream. We drove on down to the "lover's lane" which is on this farm. Once the State Patrol asked me to close it, which I did with three huge locust posts. A truck drove up next day and rammed the middle post and pushed it over. I decided to let it go. I rationalized that it was better to have the cars hidden here than parked dangerously along the road.

This was where the fire started. Here were fresh car tracks. And where the car entered from the highway was a place burned off about ten feet square. A lighted cigarette had been thrown out a car window. Wind had whipped up the flames. They had leaped across the little creek and burned up from eight to ten thousand seedling pines we had set last spring.

But this was only one of the elements out of control. We drove a quarter mile down the road to Sandy River to take a look at the other—not a river, but a vast brown sea from hill to hill. The valley was a mass of brown, stagnant, and, out near the current, swirling water. What can be more destructive, and yet more helpful, than fire and water? And we have had our share of both. Our enemies and our friends.

X

The green grass returning to our yard was so amazing that I was up and dressed and outside with a ruler in my hand at the break of day. I measured the grass. It was approximately an inch high all over the yard. Not many days ago there were just green splashes here and there.

Green, growing, tender grass in early spring is one of the most fascinating things in the world. I think of the power of the legions of the grass. Hannibal's, Caesar's, Hitler's legions have been covered by the grass. All future dictators and military leaders, leading their legions, will not survive their inevitable battle with the legions of the grass.

Troy, Thebes, and Carthage did not. These little, fragile, tender, beautiful stems, one inch high, so soft to touch, so soothing to the eye, are the ultimate conquerors of every living thing. This grass is over all.

I cannot look at these thousands of stems without thinking of them as warriors. I have often referred to the grass this way in poems. Yet I would, if not forbidden for health's sake, lie down on this grass and roll. I would lie face down on it and touch and fondle these soft stems, feel their morning coolness against my cheek.

Grass is one of God's greatest creations. Grass is a food to animals and to man. Grass is a beautiful carpet to hide the scars of earth. Think of the living things that would perish without the sustenance of grass. Grass is a lovely flower. All of it blooms in one way or another. All of it seeds in one way or another. Even a few days before the official beginning of spring the grass had made my yard so beautiful that the cattle have already broken through fences to get in.

This grass is a poem. Each blade is a letter, a clump is a strong, selective, poetic word. This yard, an oasis of tender green, is a small spring lyric. Let the grass grow! Yet this grass will get me in the end, as it has the millions of people who have gone before. It covers them, and then their stones, with a soft green carpet. The grass will cover me someday.

X I

This morning I awakened at six o'clock with the pewees. I went outside to see if I could catch them eating their breakfast. I eased around the corner of the house by the dogwood trees,

stopping to listen. I heard my pewees. Across the creek, thirty feet
away, they sat in the redbud tree, each on a tiny sagging branch
only a few inches apart. These two were singing "pewee" to each
other as if there were food aplenty for them. But I didn't believe it.
I had stopped on the front porch and looked at the thermometer.
It was thirty-two degrees.

I looked over the green yard and up to the dark clouds for insects. I didn't see a gnat, mosquito, fly, bug, or moth. What were my
singing flycatchers going to have for breakfast, how could they
sound so happy? I could feed my other birds grain—cardinals,
ground sparrows, wrens, English sparrows, song sparrows, and occasionally a scarlet tanager. But I couldn't catch an insect meal for
my flycatchers. And I wanted these birds to stay. I wanted a nest
over one of my doors. I wanted to watch them build it, to watch
them feed their little flycatchers on insects. But how would they
tough it out until warmer weather?

They flew from the redbud to the walnut, and I followed, always at a safe distance. Then they flew to the vines around my
room. Suddenly one dove through the moisture-laden air with great
speed, snatching something from the dark, sunless, morning air.
Then the other left the vines and flew straight up into the air and
dove back, almost to the earth, rose up, and leveled off. They were
finding insects I couldn't see.

Birds don't divulge their secrets easily to men. I should have
known better than to worry. Birds with instincts unerring enough to
tell them when to fly south and when to return north and exactly
what direction to fly are too smart to miscalculate about food.

X I I

From the back yard I looked across our garden to see
white blossoms on the steep bluff under the tall gray poplars. Then
I knew spring must be here. The percoon was in blossom, and so
near to the house I had only a few steps to take to see the most
beautiful of all wild flowers.

I walked across the plank laid over Shinglemill Creek and then
across the garden. Where the garden ended and the bluff began, I

stood before the patch of percoon. The petals were white as snow and they fluttered in the wind of March.

My memory went back over the years as I stood looking at my favorite wild flower. Here was a flower that I had gone into the woods to find when I was a boy so small I could barely remember. I remember finding patches of the percoon when we lived in the three-room log house. We moved from there when I was nine. I still remember the places they grew.

When I was living elsewhere but returned to this valley over the years, I revisited these spots in the woods where I received such joy in my youth. I remember these visits more than my trips in later years to the castles of Europe, capitol buildings of our states, giant man-made bridges, the theaters of New York and Paris. This small flower had uplifted me in my childhood when I craved beauty and all that was to be had was nature's. I learned early from this flower's short season that "the thing most beautiful, the soonest goes."

In all the eight places I have lived in in W-Hollow, I have found patches of percoon. Whenever possible, I visited these daily in their short blooming season. For instance, where I stand now, I stood by this same patch of percoon in March of 1915, 1916, and 1917. That seems long ago now, and I have changed, but the percoon blossoms I see here are the same, as fresh and as beautiful to me now as they were to the small boy forty years ago who hadn't seen much except what nature created for him to see.

Then, in later years, when I went to college and learned percoon was really named *bloodroot,* a name I'd never heard before, I was ready to weep. *Percoon* was the name my mother, father, and grandparents knew. For me it was the only name that fit this beautiful flower.

I learned that the word *percoon* came from the Cherokee Indians of North Carolina. They called this flower, from whose roots they extracted red juices for their war paints, *puccoon.* Then the white settlers corrupted the Cherokees' *puccoon* to *percoon,* and that was the name I loved and grew up with. *Bloodroot* has always sounded harsh and heretical to my ears. How many poems I have written and published using the word *percoon* I don't know. I guess I have a vested interest in the word. Try using *bloodroot* in a poem.

Not much fragrance to these blossoms at this early time of year. Seldom is one visited by a butterfly or a bee. Their blossomtime is usually too cool. But their snow-white petals fluttering in the fickle winds of March have a beauty that is, for me, unexcelled by any other wild flower.

The chilly wind sends me back to the house. But I am happy to see the percoon blossom usher in another spring. I look forward to this event each year, for I feel lifted out of my dull winter-bound self after I've seen snow-white banks of percoon above the brown carpet of last year's leaves and under the still bare trees.

Last night, for the first time in months, I went to bed without a hot-water bottle to my feet. I wore my woolen socks and they were enough, they kept my feet warm. It is another step on my road back. My heart is stronger; it is pumping more blood down into my feet. I woke up this morning feeling elated, proud. For a moment I couldn't think why. Then I knew. My feet were warm, and I was proud of my heart.

X I I I

The rain first turned to sleet and then to snow. Cold winds of thirty miles an hour chilled my face, feet, and hands. The young green leaves in our yard and valley, and the blooming flowers, have been frozen and killed by this weather. Winter has returned and has killed spring. This earth lies in cold and sullen defeat.

The thermometer dropped to seven above. The ground is frozen, the fruit is killed, and the leaves on the trees are dark, crisp, and sere from frostbite and freeze. Spring came all right, but Winter pushed her out. Winter bullied Spring and took over and left devastation in his wake.

I took a brief walk up the road to the tool house and back. As I walked over the frozen ground, I realized how much a part of my own small world I had become. This is a world that I have made and, regardless of value, it is my world. Spring or winter, it is my world. And there isn't any use to grieve for flowers and leaves killed by the winter's freeze and frost. Nature knows more about perfection than man does. From old roots in the ground the flowers will grow and bloom again and the trees will releaf. Nature can reproduce parts of the tree, but man cannot reproduce another leg or a new heart. So, why grieve for all the flowers so beautiful in this yard a few days ago? They will bloom again.

X I V

Naomi came to my room and shook my shoulder.

"Jesse, Jesse," she whispered. "I hate to wake you, but I hear somebody in the utility room carrying away the fruit."

I rose up in bed.

"Listen, hear 'em!" she whispered.

"Yes, I hear 'em," I said. "Let's do something about it."

"We've heard things there before but couldn't find anything," she whispered as I got out of bed. "But I know this is somebody."

I got up fumbling for my shoes and snatched my robe on over my pajamas. From the corner of our bedroom I got the rifle and cartridges. I loaded the rifle and cocked it.

"Now, take it easy," Naomi whispered. "Don't get excited."

"I know, honey," I said, "but we can't let people come in and take the place over."

We had put the rifle with a box of cartridges in this corner for quick use after we had seen two carloads of strange characters drive up this lane, turn an old dilapidated car at our drive, look around, and then go back. I saw them twice, but others had come and turned like these characters, for we heard the cars, but by the time we got to the window they were gone. These were strange men, and I thought they might be bent on robbing us. I couldn't use my bare hands any more, but if I could get to the rifle, I didn't plan to be robbed.

Then, all of a sudden, this mystery of strange men was cleared up. Roy and Carrol Abdon, my niece and nephew who now owned Glen Hilton's home in W-Hollow, had rented the old log house on the place to a fellow by the name of Copley from Ashland. Roy heard that he was making moonshine. One morning as Naomi drove

us down W-Hollow to Riverton, we saw the high sheriff, Delbert
McKenzie, and three deputies closing in on the log house. Copley
was arrested, and the largest still, along with the greatest number of
barrels of mash and gallons of illicit whisky ever captured in
Greenup County, was discovered at this little log house where I
had spent my boyhood. The strange men who had come up our
lane were either the moonshiners or their customers on the wrong
lane. But the mystery of other noises around our place had never
been cleared up.

Stories had been passed down from generation to generation
that this place was haunted by ghosts. People had seen a woman
dressed in white jump from the upstairs window years ago. People
had seen a big red dog upon the roof tearing off the shingles. And
someone had seen a small child flying around the house one night
on a pair of white wings. It was true that an infant child had been
buried somewhere near our old wild plum around the turn of the
century. Dad vouched for that.

When we lived here between 1915 and 1918, we had heard things
that sounded like dishes falling out of the safe in the night, but
when Dad got up and went to look, the dishes would all be there.
Mom, as strong and brave a woman as she was, became afraid to
stay here when Dad worked late at night on the railroad. When
he didn't get home before dark, she barred the doors and kept us
inside. The people who had lived here before us—the Sinnetts,
Chatmans, and Deers, just to mention a few—all claimed the
noises ran them away. They told Mom and Dad that they had seen
and heard too much.

And right now, as we went tiptoeing through the old living room,
we heard plenty. Birchfield wasn't awakened by the noise, but he
was a cocker with long floppy ears and couldn't hear too well. I'd
seen him jump up and run the wrong way barking when he heard
hounds running a fox. Now we were tiptoeing across the porch, me
with a rifle in my hand and Naomi holding onto my arm, shaking.

"I don't know—I don't know whether you should be doing this
kind of exciting thing or not," she whispered just as I eased the
garage door open.

I never heard such a rattle of pans, fruit cans, and jars. Then I

stepped over and switched the light on real quick, holding my rifle
ready. We didn't see a ghost or a live person when we looked into
the utility room. We saw an old friend, who turned to make a fight
as Birchfield, finally awake, ran toward him.

It was our old three-legged possum, Graybar, trying to find
himself something to eat in a box of empty cans we had ready to
haul to the garbage dump. He had taken them out of the box and
had gone through each of them, rolling them about on the floor.

When Birchfield ran up to show us how brave he was, the
possum started grinning and growling louder than I ever heard one.
Birchfield stood back. This possum had bitten him once out in the
yard when he had tried to make friends with him.

"The ghost!" I said.

Naomi shook with laughter. I turned the bolt, and the cartridge
jumped from the rifle chamber.

"Well, he's hungry," she said. "We're not feeding him well
enough."

Our old friend didn't look too well fed. And he looked very
forlorn standing there with only one foreleg. I picked up Birchfield.
I didn't want his barking and fussing to annoy the possum. I carried him outside and closed the door behind him. Then I went
back where the possum already had his long nose stuck in one of
Birchfield's dog-food cans.

"Let's give old Graybar some real feed," I said.

"All right," Naomi said. "Fill him up and maybe we can get some
sleep then."

"Yes, ghosts don't operate well on full stomachs," I said.

I opened a can of Birchfield's dog food for him, and he ate it
greedily right there in front of us. We opened him another can, and
he ate it, too, but slowed down considerably before he finished. We
opened the back door, and old Graybar followed us on his way back
under the floor to lie down beside one of our hot-water pipes.

So March came in like a lamb and went out like a possum.

A P R I L

There is not a month in the year as fascinating as April. It is a month of bud, blossom, and leaf, and the awakening of sleeping life. I like to think I can put my ear down against the earth and hear the noises of growing roots. It isn't true, but I always imagined I could hear the swelling of fine, white-haired roots of flowers and vegetation taking hold in the soil and the giant oak's roots bursting through the crevices of rocks. I have heard sounds like the slow beating of a heart.

Trees that have been naked, dark, somber, and dreaming so long, awake and dress in soft robes of green. Though there is not a sign of life among the oaks along the ridgetops and on the summits of these cone-shaped hills, down along the rivers the elms, water-birch, and willows are beginning to awake. And along the little tributaries to the Sandy and Ohio Rivers, I have seen the broad green leaves on the buckeyes.

The winds now have the clean, new smell from leaf and bloom.

And April's winds have a different sound from any other winds that blow. I've listened carefully to them all. April's has a special lyrical tone.

This is the time of year I cannot walk a half mile without getting at least six ideas for poems—or rather, recognizing God's ideas for poems. This is the month of percoon white upon the bluffs, the month of trailing arbutus which likes to hug close to the rock cliffs, babytears, cinquefoil, violets, and whippoorwill flower. This is the month of dogwood, redbud, wild plum, and the multicolored blooms on the wild crab-apple trees that cover our hill slopes.

Streams, this year, are especially full. Bright waters spout from the steep slopes, spill sun-silvered over the cliffs, and flow under the blooming dogwoods and redbuds down the ravines to the rivers and the sea. Everywhere I hear the sound of spring waters, so different from the frozen mumblings of winter and the dry whisper of summer's slow, dwindling streams.

April is the month to plow the garden, plant seeds, test Nature at her work. When the seed in the ground germinates and a living shoot breaks up through the earth, this is a resurrection and a new life. The old husks return to the earth that bore them. Planting a garden in April and watching growing new life break up through the ground to mature in another season have always reminded me of the cycle of human life. We are born, we grow up, our parents spend their season and die; then we, like our own parents, give birth to young, nurture them, and go back to earth in our turn. April, this wonderful giver of new life, is a great reminder of birth, the first beautiful phase of the human cycle.

This year, especially, I am glad to be alive in April. I am more a part of it. Reborn myself, I shall watch more carefully the rebirth going on all around me. I shall go out on walks to all the wild flowers that grow near me, and there are many. I shall observe from day to day the clouds of green leaves that appear first on trees along the watercourses and gradually climb up the rugged slopes to the tough-butted oaks on the summits of these hills. But because every season has its hold on me, I shall look on the barren trees as long as I can, and the rock cliffs beyond, before they are hidden by April green.

I I

Many of the old people here say that every weed, tree, flower, shrub, and plant was put here by the Creator of this universe for a purpose. But does every weed have a purpose? I used to hear my father discuss this with his friends, particularly in relation to poison vine and a few other obnoxious weeds. Then there is old George Alexander, still alive and living on this place at seventy-seven, who is sure that every weed grows for a purpose. When I was a child, I used to believe what old men said because they were old. I still do.

At the same time I wondered what was the purpose of sandbrier, stickerweeds, Jimson, chickweed, and wild honeysuckle, which was taking our country then and almost has it now. I never could believe that any one of these had been put here for a good purpose. They were not beautiful to look at, they didn't have blossoms that would make you look twice, and, in its way, each was a detriment to man's progress, whether he was hoeing a garden or mowing a lawn.

The two obnoxious weeds my father detested most were chickweed and cocklebur. And he claimed that each worthless weed, after it was cut down, would stubbornly try to grow up and leave its seed to propagate its kind. And he stated a fact. Cockleburs would grow two inches high in a few days after they had been cut just before frost. And these two-inch plants would have small cockleburs on them; they would look to be top-heavy with seed. The same was true with chickweed. Cut it down and back it would come overnight, trying to reseed itself.

But no sooner does an honest man make up his mind about something but he has to change it right quick. Watching from my window this morning, after the rooster redbird had awakened me with his crowing at five-forty, I saw something that made me take the chickweed from this list. I looked down on our back yard and saw more than twenty birds, song and ground sparrows and an English sparrow or two, walking amid the chickweed, which was much taller than they, and stripping the seeds from the stems for their breakfast. The redbirds were in the feedbox filling their craws with our grain, but the others were settling for humbler fare.

At this time of year, before there are many worms and bugs and insects and after the old ragweed seeds are gone, the chickweeds are full of fresh ripened seeds. As I watched these birds devouring them to fill their little craws and satisfy their hunger, I knew that the chickweed does have a purpose after all. Now I wondered if the other so-called obnoxious weeds have some useful purpose we just don't know about—even the poison vine. Maybe the old men were right after all.

I I I

In the spring of 1916 Aunt Nancy Leadingham came to visit us. She was a large woman and built very much like Grandpa Hilton, her youngest brother. Neither Aunt Nancy nor Grandpa had ever gone to school, and yet they not only could read well, but read all the books they could get their hands on, which were not very many, and they read the Bible over and over. Both were people one would never suspect, just to look at them, of being booklovers. For Grandpa weighed about 220, had broad, square shoulders and the physical strength of three men. He worked until he was eighty-eight and died at ninety-two. Aunt Nancy, big and rawboned like Grandpa, didn't look like a woman. In the prime of her young womanhood she had lifted a barrel of salt up into a wagon bed. But the reason I mention all this is because of the story she told me in early April of 1916, a little story I remembered this morning as I watched Jane picking dandelions.

Grandpa, Mom, Dad, and Aunt Nancy were out in this back yard standing under the walnut tree. And while they stood there talking, I ran circles over the yard where there were hundreds of dandelions. This morning when I walked out into our back yard by the old walnut stump where Aunt Nancy had stood thirty-nine years ago and talked, I saw hundreds of dandelions, and I was reminded of that day in early April of 1916. It seemed as if they had all bloomed overnight. And that has to do with the story Aunt Nancy told me.

"Look at all these dandelions, won't you," Aunt Nancy said. "You remember, Nathan," she said to Grandpa, "when we were small the story Pap used to tell us about the dandelions?"

"No, I can't say that I remember it," Grandpa told Aunt Nancy.

"Well, I remember it," she said. "He used to tell us how the dandelions got here. He said his father had told him and his father's father had told his father. Once there was a family of poor children who looked up at the sky and cried for the stars. They didn't have playthings like the children have nowadays. But they cried and cried and they didn't get the stars. The stars were still up there in the light-blue evening sky, looking down from Heaven and winking at this big family of poor children.

"Then, Pap said, suddenly a stranger just came from nowhere, dressed in a high hat and a Prince Albert suit, and asked the children why they were crying. 'Because we want the stars up there so high and beautiful,' said one. 'And when we beg for them to come down, they stay up there in the sky and wink at us,' another child said. 'I want to see a star more than anything in this world,' a third child said. 'I would rather have a star for a plaything as anything I know.' 'Well, since you have such lofty ambition to look toward Heaven and want the most beautiful thing in the world, I will do all that I can to help you get the stars,' the stranger in the Prince Albert coat told them. 'If they won't come down to you, I will fix it so you can bend down to them.'

"Then, Pap told us, the stranger disappeared quicker than the flash of an eye. He disappeared the way that he had come. And Pap said the children were worried when the man disappeared. They stopped looking up at the sky and begging for a star to come down to them. They wondered about the mysterious stranger who had found them crying for the stars and had made the promise. Then one of the children looked down at the green spring grass, and everywhere there in the light of the stars they could see the shining lumps of gold. And these shining lumps of gold were the soft petals of dandelions, a flower never known before these children had cried for the stars.

"And then Pap told how happy the children were that they could bend over and pick up a soft golden star," Aunt Nancy continued. "The stars were everywhere at their feet, and the children sang a song that Pap used to sing to me, but I've forgotten the words. It was a happy song about wishing for the stars in the sky and looking for them at your feet and finding them there. And he told us that because those children wanted pretty things from the sky and cried and begged for something they couldn't get, children today have the dandelions that bloom like stars on the dark-green earth for children everywhere to reach down and pick."

Now every time I see dandelions in early April I think of this story that Aunt Nancy told me, that her father told her, and his father before him.

I V

With the coming of April, the season of resurrection, I am feeling lucky again. And around these parts, there's an old superstition that when a man is lucky he has knocked on wood. I've knocked on wood many times. Back at a time I don't remember, 1908, when my father and mother lived in a one-room shack near the coal mine, I was sick with something my mother called summer-complaint. Once when she went to the bed to pick me up, she thought I was dead. I was just a little over a year old then. She ran from the shack with me in her arms and started to the coal mine, where my father was back in the hill digging coal. Her youngest brother, Uncle Jiles Hilton, stopped her. Uncle Jiles took me from her arms and laid me on a table. He worked with me until he could see that I was breathing. Mom lost control of herself when she thought her first-born son was gone. But Uncle Jiles never got excited about very many things. He was back on a furlough from the Marines just at the right time to save my life. This was luck I don't remember.

I grew like any normal child, ran, played, tumbled, and had a better time than most. But once I ventured away from the three-room house we'd moved to down in W-Hollow. And I made the mistake of lying down on my belly across the roots of an old tree and drinking from a stream. It was cool, blue water, and I was thirsty. I got typhoid fever, was so weak I had to be lifted in a sheet, but after six months I finally pulled through. Later, but before I was nine, I had gone miles away from home in the woods and was thirsty. This time I lay down over a log and drank of water that bubbled from the rocks just a few feet away. It was typhoid for me

again, but it didn't hurt as much as the first time. In later years I've
been told by doctors in Scotland and America that my stomach was
slowed by typhoid fever.

In my senior year in Greenup High School, I started spitting up
blood. It was in the autumn, in football season, and I thought it
was caused by a fellow who broke through our line once and
roughed me up when I was trying to punt. He pushed me back into
the goal post from our one-yard line after I got away a wobbly punt.
After he smeared me, I got up and coughed. I spit up blood. First
I thought he'd loosened my teeth. But I felt of them, and they
were firm in my mouth.

After the game I learned the blood didn't come from my mouth.
I was hurt inside. And during most of my senior year I coughed
up blood. We didn't have school doctors and nurses then, and I
didn't tell anybody about it. I felt that I was going to be all right.
By the time I graduated I wasn't coughing up any more blood. I
knew what had been hurt inside me had healed by now. I knew I
was okay.

In Fort Knox, when I was seventeen, we were on the rifle range.
I was marking scores for a fellow in our company who couldn't hit
the target. He was afraid of a rifle. He turned around toward me and
squeezed the trigger. I heard the rifle snap. I grabbed his rifle and
worked the bolt which discharged the cartridge. I looked at it. The
cartridge had been snapped when the muzzle of his rifle was
pointed right at my chest. I put this cartridge back in his rifle, aimed
at his target, fired, and made his only bull's-eye. After this I was
too nervous to shoot when it was my turn. I was very lucky—
powder just didn't burn when I was the target.

When I was eighteen, I was taken off the air hammer in the
steel mill one night and put on a forge where I used a sledge
hammer. At the air hammer, when a big slab of white-hot steel was
brought from the furnace with giant tongs and laid down for the
hammer to pound and shape into a railroad-car axle or some other
large item, I had held cold steel bars beside the hot steel to keep
the ten-ton hammer from smashing it flat. This was dangerous work.
But I knew how to stand, and the right-size bars to grab and use
in a hurry. More than once I was lucky when the big hammer

knocked the bar from my hand and sent it across the blacksmith shop. I warned the fellow who took my place and showed him how to stand. He didn't last the night. He made the mistake of getting up in front of the bar he was holding. The mighty hammer came down and rammed the bar into his intestines.

An investigation of this accident showed that he was a careful man and that anybody who had been there on the job would have been killed. That was my first night off the air hammer in six months. I worked seven nights a week, too. When I carried shovels of dirt to put over the puddle of blood he left on the floor, I thought this could well have been my blood. He was unlucky. I was lucky. I often thought about this.

After working at the steel mills, I went to college. I finished college and came home and taught school. I taught a one-room rural high school. Then I taught in Greenup High School. Later I was made principal of McKell High School. Our county had a health nurse, and she wanted to test McKell High School pupils for TB. My pupils were a little reluctant to take this test. I walked up first because I knew there wasn't anything wrong with me. My pupils followed.

Three days later my arm was sore, red, and swollen. I couldn't figure what was causing the trouble until three of our pupils (out of three hundred) turned up with arms like mine. I went to the Health Clinic at Greenup to be examined. We four had all tested four-plus, as high a positive reaction as the test could show. The two doctors and four nurses let me see an X ray I'll never forget. It was an X ray of my right lung. I'd never heard of scar tissue before. Well, it showed in this X ray. My right lung was almost filled with scar tissue.

One of the doctors asked me if there was any time in my youth I could remember spitting up blood. I told him there was. I didn't tell him I had thought a football player from a neighboring town caused my trouble. Of the three pupils whose test was four-plus, the same as mine, two are dead; the other recovered after spending years in Arizona. The doctors and nurses told me I, too, had had TB when I was in high school but my system had been strong

enough to throw it off. I really knocked on the schoolhouse door
after this one.

I certainly didn't look like one who had ever had TB. I was
big and healthy, and there wasn't a man in this area who could
outwork me. Still, after my positive reaction to the TB test, de-
mands were circulated that I resign as principal of McKell High
School. One evening two men came to a McKell High School
musical program. They began using abusive language, and I asked
them to leave. The larger one called me a schoolteacher s.o.b.,
and wanted his money back. He got it back. Then I went outside
with him. Just as he rammed his hand into his pocket, I gave him
everything I had and placed the lick just about right. He slumped
against the schoolhouse wall. Someone phoned the sheriff, and he
arrived just as the man was coming to. There could be no mistaken
evidence on this one. His hand still gripped his .38. Mine was a
lucky lick. He lost three molars, and I only got stove-back knuckles.
But even with a damaged hand I knocked on wood.

In 1938 I started a newspaper and was hit over the head because
of an editorial about our schools. My attacker came up quietly when
I had my back turned and hit me with a blackjack made from a
piece of steel. He laid my head open to the skull in three places.
I got him by the neck, although I was dazed, and I had his tongue
choked out when I was pulled off him. Later, when he was tried
for assault and battery, the doctor who had cleated my scalp back
together testified on a witness stand that the punishment I had
received from those blackjack blows would have killed an ordinary
man. I suffered loss of memory for a while. But I pulled out of this
one, too.

Once, returning from California with friends—Mr. and Mrs.
W. A. Voiers—my wife Naomi and I agreed to go to Mexico City.
South of Villa Amada, when we were driving very fast, a rear tire
blew out. We left the road and turned over seven and a half times.
(I later counted the marks the opened door made each time the
car went over.) Mr. Voiers was thrown out and suffered a brain
concussion. When I came to, I carried Naomi, who was unconscious,
from the back seat through the small opening of the crumpled front

door. I laid her on a car seat. Then I brought Mr. Voiers, who
was unconscious, too, from the front seat. A Mexican farmer came
by, and the two of us turned the big car over on its wheels. Mr.
Voiers had bought it new for this trip. He later sold it for junk for
fifty dollars. The radio and steering wheel were still good. People
stopped and wondered how four people came from it alive. We
were lucky. I said a prayer on this one, as I watched over two
stretcher cases and one brain concussion on our way to Texas.

Then I spent two years in a place of the least danger I have
ever known. This was in the United States Naval Reserve during
World War II. But once when I was stationed in Washington,
D.C., where I lived with my wife and daughter, I got a furlough
to come back to Kentucky to see my parents. There were two
Chesapeake-and-Ohio trains that I could have taken from Washington, one at approximately six o'clock and one at nine, and my
ticket was good on either train. I must have knocked on wood. I
was eager to return to Kentucky to see my parents, but something
told me not to take the six o'clock train. I told my wife so. Later I
called a taxi and went to Union Station and caught the nine
o'clock train. The six o'clock train hit a rockslide, and I don't know
how many were killed or shaken up. Our train, which followed,
was routed down through Virginia via Roanoke and down the Big
Sandy River through Welch, West Virginia, and over the Louisville-
and-Nashville tracks to Kenova, where we got back to the Chesapeake and Ohio again. I got home sixteen hours late, but I made
it alive.

At the age of forty, I could do my share of hard labor. Old
George Alexander and I went to the timber woods and cut eighty-
seven logs in a short winter day. This was upon the highest hilltop
on my farm. An icy wind was blowing strong, and it was subzero
weather. He told me how men could take it in the old days. Coffee
froze in our lunch pails. But I enjoyed working in the cold. Up
until this time I was only in a hospital long enough to have my
head X-rayed and my scalp wounds cleated together after I had
been blackjacked. Only when I had typhoid twice was I forced
to go to bed in daylight hours.

In 1953, when I was writing a novel, I needed a typewriter

ribbon. I drove to Greenup and turned the town upside down
trying to find a new one. Then I visited three secretaries in the
town, thinking one might have an extra ribbon. Finally, wanting
to get back to my novel, I started driving in a hurry to Ashland,
Kentucky.

Just before one reaches an overpass into Ashland on Route 23, the
road goes up a hill, then around a steep bluff, where it was cut
from the sandstone cliffs. The great sandstones hang high above the
highway. I was driving pretty fast over this part of the road when
more than a thousand tons of sandstone tore loose from the cliffs and
dropped onto the highway right in front of me. The giant stones
completely filled the highway. I rammed my brake on and slid
into a big rock, and then I shot the car into reverse and backed
in a hurry. As I moved back, more sandstone fell where I'd stopped
and shifted into reverse. In another second at the most, my car
would have been flattened like a pancake on the highway. It was
a close squeeze, but I escaped, lucky man again. I couldn't wait
to knock on wood after this one. My steering wheel was plastic. I
knew substitutes didn't count.

On October 8, 1954, I pounded the lectern in an hour's talk
I gave to the teachers of Western Kentucky in the Murray College
auditorium. After this talk was over, I walked outside the auditorium
and collapsed.

Since this experience I have learned that a coronary occlusion
is one of the most often fatal of all heart troubles. With extensive
damage in two parts of the heart, I had, according to one doctor,
one chance out of a thousand to live.

Yet today I am able to take longer walks in the woods on my
farm. April is here as I am writing this. I walk beneath the bud-
ding trees. I examine bark, bud, and leaf on each shrub and tree. I
walk along and lay my hands upon the smooth and rough bark of
my old friends. I've known them since before they became giants,
since back in 1915, when I used to go after the cows in this pasture.
When I am among them, I laugh a lot. I never think about what
is going to happen to me next. This would be getting ahead of
schedule. I touch them and tell them I am a lucky man. I tell them
I am one in a thousand.

V

The idea of resurrection is a most fascinating one. I am glad that Christ's resurrection came in spring. It couldn't have happened in a more likely month than April, judging from the part of the earth where I was born and grew to manhood. I do not know about the Holy Land, where Christ was born, lived, and was crucified, whether there are four distinct seasons or not. I doubt it. I have been in Istanbul, Turkey, which is not a great distance away, and they do not have our four distinct seasons there. Yet this spring month of April is beautiful in almost every part of the world.

Since I have grown up in this valley on little farms, helped my father plow the creek bottoms and the steep slopes on the hillside, hoe the plants, and later harvest the crops in autumn, I cannot doubt resurrection. How can any farmer ever doubt resurrection? Though there have been periods that I didn't go to church, often when I was away a year or more at a time, there was never a time when I doubted the resurrection of Christ. He was the seed of God planted in the earth, the Son of God sent to show us the way. Only after death, the kind of death we know, He was called by God and came from the tomb and ascended into Heaven. It is a beautiful idea.

The man who has never planted a seed in the ground would be the first to doubt the story of the resurrection. One of the first things we have always planted in the spring has been our Irish potatoes. We plant them on Good Friday, the day of Christ's crucifixion. I have seen snow fall on our potatoes and the ground get cold. I have seen it freeze. The potatoes would lie lifeless in the cold ground. Then suddenly the crumpled dark-green leaves would peep up through the rough dark crust of earth. The potato seed had resurrected. And through the spring and early summer we hoed these potatoes and kept the weeds cut down. In autumn, after their summer's growing season was over and their vines had withered, we dug our potatoes. We put them in the cellar and the next spring planted from our own seed. Here was the process of eternal life—growing, living, dying, and rebirth.

In the same manner we have planted peas, sugar corn, beets, radishes, carrots, and lettuce. We have planted seed almost too small to see. But from that seed came the identical plant that gave birth to the seed. This is birth and rebirth. The month of April is the time of our greatest resurrection.

Before I ever entered a church, I had read the story of Christ's death and resurrection. I liked it so well that each year I read and reread it in early April before Easter Sunday. This is the time when God's world has resurrection going on every place.

Now there is another part of this resurrection. It is faith. Do we have faith and do we believe? I never had any trouble having faith. I know I have faith when I see one of the first wild flowers, trailing arbutus, emerge from the cold sod above the rock cliffs. When I see this exquisite flower and the little sweet-potato leaves on its stem, I know that this is trailing arbutus. I am sure of myself. I am positive. I know who I am, where I am, why I am. This is positive identification, and this is positive faith.

When I have sown Korean clover on a cold snow in February over fields I planned to pasture, I never had any doubt that these seeds would reach the earth as soon as the snow melted. I sowed them on snow because I could see how many of the tiny seeds I was sowing. And I knew, when the snow melted, that the seeds dropped down to the soft, warm earth and sank therein and that the late winter rains fell and buried them and that in middle March or early April, when warm suns and rains came, these seeds sprouted and grew. How can I possibly doubt the resurrection of Almighty God's Son when every spring I have seen the process of resurrection in the laws of Almighty God.

I have planted seeds in the garden and broadcast them on the slopes. I have planted seeds in the creek bottoms. I have sowed seedbeds to take up plants to reset again. Maybe this is the reason there are so many believers in resurrection among farmers and people who live on the land, who keep their feet on the ground and their eyes on the stars. In ancient times, shepherds with their flocks under the stars saw miracles come to pass, saw great visions open up. They dreamed dreams and wrote poetry. And why not? There are more true poets where people plow the land, work with animals under the sun and stars, feel the rain and wind in God's world, than there are in city apartments.

History records that for nearly 2,000 years there have been Easter celebrations in God's churches. If people have believed for nearly 2,000 years, then who am I, a small man from W-Hollow in the Kentucky hills, to dispute the greatest event of all times? Each spring I shall plant seeds into the earth and in a few days they will sprout and in a little more time I shall see the green bodies reaching up through the ground for the sun and wind. When I am no longer able to plant fields of my own, I shall have them planted so I can watch, or I shall watch others plant their fields.

In the woods the process is the same, but man hasn't anything to do with it. The walnut drops from the trees. Leaves fall from the same tree and cover this walnut. Then snows fall on the leaves and leaf loam is created. In the spring the walnut germinates and a sprout comes forth and a new walnut tree is born. The same is true with the acorn from the oak, the pine cone, the hickory nut, seeds from the berries, wild plums, crab apples.

Where God is Scientist, I see resurrection with my own eyes. I feel confident—I have faith—that when man, the seed of God, is planted in the ground, though his husk will go back to the earth, he will be resurrected into a new life, for this is the law of God.

V I

This evening I must write about one wild-plum tree. It is in the front yard and is very old. My father said when he visited Greenup County in 1896, a boy of sixteen, this wild plum was in bloom. He said it was an old tree then but much larger than it is now. When we lived here from 1915 to 1918, my mother made wild-plum jelly from this tree. Its white blossoms each spring planted seeds of poetry in me. I used to wonder how long this tree had stood and who had gathered its wild plums and made jelly before we moved here and where they were now.

Each year since I can remember, bluebirds have found a dead portion of this tree, a hollow limb or fork, that has made them a nice dry place to have their homes and raise their young. How many bluebirds I've seen in this wild-plum tree against a white background of soft, feathery blossoms. There is something about this wild plum that is specially endearing. It's like an old possession, a loved and dear one. Many people who have lived here in years past have come back to see it.

Each year I cut dead branches from it. I work to keep it alive. It would have been long dead had it not been for the care lavished on it the last few years. This year, once again, it is in bloom, but not with a cloud of white blossoms. It's more like an old man's white head when he has only part of his hair left. There is only a thin white layer of blossoms on its old and gnarled limbs. Nor will it produce many wild plums this year. Its spirit is willing to take on more life than its aged body can summon. All the wild plums it bears we will make into jelly, though it would profit us more to spend the time on another tree. How many glasses of wild-plum jelly it has set on our shelves and other people's over the years I would like to know.

Although this wild plum can't live much longer, I have done something to perpetuate it. From its gnarled root a young tree sprang, and I let this twig grow to a sturdy young tree, now large enough to have blossoms this year. And like the parent tree that towers above, its blossoms are filled with hundreds of butterflies. Talk about a chip off the old block! This tree is really an offshoot of the parent tree, not by seed, but from the big, gnarled, life-giving root. And it makes me happy to know this young tree will replace the old one when it goes.

People help themselves to the fruit of wild-plum trees. Somewhere on the little roads, byways, and lanes right now cars are moving along and the people in them are looking upon the slopes for the wild plums. These are people who like wild-plum jelly or who are locating the wild plums to pick and gather for summer sales. They usually drive in old cars, they are older men and women, and they have eyes like hawks. They can locate just about anything. They pick the wild blackberries, raspberries, dewberries, and strawberries, and they gather the wild plums. They hunt down the white walnuts and hickory nuts to gather and sell. Anything that grows in the woods they are on the lookout for.

There isn't any law, except the trespassing law, against pilfering a farm for wild plums. The trees grow wild and everywhere, and the finders are the keepers, regardless of whose farm these wild plums grow on. It doesn't matter if the owner of the land likes wild-plum jelly, too. It doesn't matter if he had it in his mind to pick and sell these wild plums. If the strangers who ride in these old cars beat him to his own wild-plum trees, then that is his bad luck.

V I I

In 1915 I bought some popcorn seed and wanted to plant it. I asked my father for a piece of ground that he had rented from W. W. Daughtery. I didn't need a very big plot for my popcorn. Though only a child of eight, I had to help my father most of the day in the field, and didn't have much time for my own schemes.

"Son, you'll have to find your own ground here," Dad said. "There is plenty of it. You'll have to clear you a small place. Select any place and go to work."

I didn't have an ax. So my father bought me a small poleax which I grew very fond of. I looked around and selected a place for my popcorn patch. It was a steep bluff about two-tenths of a mile down the road from the house. I started to work to clear the ground. When Dad learned of the place I had chosen, he said: "You couldn't have chosen rougher ground. You could have looked over a thousand acres and not have found a rougher place. But, Jesse, you've got to live and learn even if you are a child."

But I didn't let his words bother me. I liked this bluff. It was so steep that when I cut a brush with my little poleax it scooted down to the road. I didn't have to carry it. After I cleared the ground, I dug little holes in the soft dark loam and planted three grains of popcorn in each hill. I didn't waste a grain, for it had cost me a dime. My popcorn came up—three dark-green, healthy-looking stalks on a hill. That summer I hoed it myself. And in September I had grown some fine popcorn. My father was amazed, and also very happy with my yield. For three years I raised popcorn on this bluff. The third year, while I was cutting my popcorn with a knife, I laid my knee open to the bone. For some time I had a stiff knee, but when we moved away from this farm, I never forgot this ugly, rugged bluff. I always had a warm feeling toward it because it grew me such fine popcorn.

It was on this bluff that my eleven-year-old sister, Sophia, used to pretend that each mayapple was a little green parasol and a fairy was walking under it to protect herself from the sun. If it was a cloudy day, the fairy was under an umbrella, afraid it might rain.

There was not another family of children in this valley then for us to play with, and we lived in a world where we had to use our imaginations. We didn't have anybody to do our thinking for us. But nature was a great help. This morning when I saw these mayapples on my bluff, I thought of my popcorn and Sophia's fairies and the childhood years which now, like rains of yesterday, have moved swiftly over the rocky stream beds and out of this valley.

It has never been my level acres that have paid me the best dividends. It has been my bluffs, where the ground is poor and the wild flowers grow. This is the land that gives me ideas for poems and memories for happiness. This is the land that inspires me in the spring. I've let the struggling little oaks grow up on this bluff and the wild flowers grow under them. I have let Nature choose what should grow on this bluff and do her own landscaping.

V I I I

This morning I walked my first mile in 1955.

When I take an early walk, I look forward to it as much as I do the ending of a novel. I look forward to what I am going to see on my walk as much as I do to what I'm going to see in a fine movie. It is this anticipation that compels me to leave home before six and breakfast. I am always famished for food when I awake, like a bird or chicken. But my looking forward to the walk this morning makes me forget all hunger. Because I have plans. I have a journey in mind that I have lain on my bed in a hospital room and at home and dreamed of making for many days, weeks, and months. It is not only the journey itself but the land, the trees, animals, and birds that I will see again and the memories I will have.

I don't whistle, but I am happy enough to, as I walk over to the weeping willow and start to follow the stream. I can't waste my breath whistling. I'll need my breath. Now, walking beside W-Branch, I listen to its waters. At one place, where W-Branch spills over a rock for four feet or more, I particularly like to hear the water fall. And where the water flows swiftly over the rocks, it sings songs to me, old lullabies without words. I've heard these tunes before. I've heard them since childhood, when I walked over this same ground beside this stream.

Down in the little sand bottom under the beeches that Dad and I farmed until last year, I find a place where I can get across. This is a big leap for me, an extra two feet beyond a full stride, but I make it. Now I have left the singing stream, and I am in the land of the ground squirrels. They are talking to each other in their own language, which is familiar but not quite comprehensible to me. There must be a dozen or more. Birchfield, my cocker spaniel, has followed me, and he is the attraction. The reddish-brown ground squirrels with bushy tails and black stripes up and down their bodies peep from behind trees and rocks and speak to Birchfield and me. They don't know whether we are friends or enemies. They finally decide to fear Birchfield. They scamper into holes under rocks, into hollow trees, under old logs. They go underground in all directions. There must be a city of ground squirrels here, though this has always been the home for gray squirrels, this den in the tall beeches.

I start up the Byrnes Hollow. To my left, beside an old rotting stump, I see something growing which is very green—two nice holly bushes, and I know where they are now. I can come back for them any time that Naomi Deane wants them for our yard. I start walking up the dim path, one I used to follow when I went after the cow, old Gypsy, for Mom. I walk up to the little hollow, where the old sugar maple is still standing, and I stop for sentimental reasons. Then, I climb the bank, a gradual slope of only a few yards up to what once was our garden. Here the wild honeysuckle has taken over. The old sweet apple, where I used to eat as many apples as I could hold, is standing there dead. Its leafless body, the ghost of an apple tree, is filled with wild honeysuckle vines.

This country has changed since I was a child. Once there was only a tiny bit of wild honeysuckle here. Now it is everywhere. This is the land of wild honeysuckle and pine. I used to come to this field in early morning and late in the afternoon. I knew each foot of this land. I knew where each tree grew. I still know where they grow. These trees have never been cut down. I walk on to the gate between Dad's farm and mine. Dad and I put this gate here. I slowly open it and stand and look over the field that he and I so often cut sprouts on, plowed, planted, and farmed. Now it is growing up in small pines. He told me, not more than a year ago, it would grow up when he was gone.

In the south corner of this field we used to raise strawberries. And in the big field, which is about six acres, we farmed in corn and then we sowed it in pasture. Once I plowed and harrowed this entire new ground in five days with a span of horses, and Dad hired Charlie Sparks to plant behind me when I laid off the rows on Saturday. It was plowed, harrowed, and planted in a week, a record time for this type of land right after it had been cleared of trees. Mom, Dad, James, Mary, and I worked as a family in this field. Our working together welded us into a unit almost invincible.

I stop at the place where I killed my first rabbit, in a little ravine where chestnut oaks grow on the upperside of this field. It was on a winter morning, and the stars were shining. I found it sitting and shot it. And now as I walk in the warm winds of morning when April is in the air, I think of the many things that happened here and my many associations with this land. I walk to the pine grove where I used to write my high school themes for Mrs. R. E. Hatton. Here I stop and look the old grove over. It has grown considerably since my high school days. This is the earth I am attached to. This is the earth I love. Every square foot recalls a memory. Other people have lived and died on this land before I was born here, but not one was more deeply attached to it than I am.

I stop at the place where Dad and I set peach trees, and a few of the old stumps are here yet. Dad and I cut sprouts here when I returned from Europe and was trying to get myself in good physical condition again. I stop under a poplar tree this pasture fence is nailed to and look at it again. I think of the many leaves I've taken from this tree when I went after the cows. Each became a sonnet later published in *Man with a Bull-tongue Plow.* This place doesn't look the way it did when James and I were home and Dad was active. It was a beautiful, well-kept field then. Now the brush has started to take over.

I find a few clusters of flowers near the poplar where our dog, Don, once treed a possum. They are small flowers with a hard little stem like wire. I gather a wisp of these exquisite flowers. And then I stop and look at the mayapples. They have burst suddenly from the loam and are as tender as a percoon petal, beautiful to see, lifting their green parasol tops toward the light-blue sky . . . and less than six months ago I had to learn to walk again.

I feel pangs of hunger, and I am ready to go home for breakfast. I look down W-Hollow, and home is in sight. I have really done something this morning. I have walked completely around Bread-loaf Hill, which is at least one mile. This is the first mile I've walked since last September. I have accomplished my first aim, to walk a mile. And now I stand in sight of my home and breakfast, and I say to my heart: "Heart, you have been strong. You did it this morning. I forgot about you. There isn't anything wrong with you. You are a great heart! And I want to tell you so. You took me a mile over land I love. Heart, you used to take me over the cross-county runs from five to twenty miles. You used to take me over the two-mile runs for my college. But this morning has been your greatest mile."

I X

The ancient wild-plum tree beside our house has not only produced wild plums for jelly for hundreds to eat and blossoms for beauty that have made many happy, but it has housed each spring a family or more of bluebirds. Last year there were two nests of bluebirds in this tree, one in the box I nailed on the tree where it would get the morning sun. But this year I'd not seen a bluebird on it. I could clean it by unscrewing a bolt that would let me take the top off. This morning seemed a good time.

When I removed the bolt and looked in, I got a surprise. At first

I thought it was a blackeyed woodmouse that came out of a big nest and looked at me. Then she ran back. I called Naomi and told her that I had a nest of woodmice in the bluebird box. Then Glen Hilton drove up in his car. He stopped and I told him about the woodmice.

Glen walked over and thumped gently on the box. The big woodmouse ran out, only she wasn't a mouse. She was a flying squirrel. This was the first flying squirrel Naomi had ever seen, and I'd not seen one for many years. She was a beautiful autumn-oak-leaf brown, and her eyes were large and black. She ran up the plum tree and out on the very top twig. Then she spread the skin on her sides and glided downgrade toward the tall cedar tree. When she reached the cedar, her claws took hold, and she began to climb.

In the box I saw the furze from milkweeds, bark, and leaves in her nest begin to move. I was sorry we had scared her away from the little ones.

"She won't stay away from them long," Glen said.

"No, we must see that she gets back," Naomi said.

"We won't have to see that she gets back," Glen said. "If we stand away, she'll fly from the cedar to the wild plum and back to her young ones."

We didn't have long to wait. Naomi, Glen, and I walked away from this wild plum and stood near the garage to watch. The flying squirrel left the cedar and sailed down toward the plum tree. Her little claws took hold in the wild plum's bark, and she went up the tree in a hurry and through the little hole which I had intended only for bluebirds.

When we were boys, Glen, Aaron and Ed Howard, and I used to climb up trees in this valley and stick sticks back in the hollow places and chase flying squirrels out. We caught them for pets, and they made wonderful ones. They ate peanuts, mulberries, and pine blossoms, just like gray squirrels. We never killed flying squirrels or let anybody else kill them. We liked to chase them, make them fly.

I had to chalk up another credit to our old plum tree. Not only human beings, bluebirds, and butterflies but now flying squirrels shared her bounty. Tomorrow, before Naomi went to Greenup, I would add peanuts to her shopping list.

X

The boring bumblebee is so much like the real, docile, harmless bumblebee one cannot tell them apart unless he observes very closely. They are approximately the same size, have the same shape and color of wings. The boring bumblebee is much faster in flight, in fact the fastest insect I have ever seen on wings. And it will chase flies. Whether it will eat a fly or not I don't know, but I once saw a boring bumblebee go after a large, beautiful greenfly, which supposedly can fly sixty miles an hour, and pass it in the chase. This greenfly had made the mistake of alighting too close to the hole the boring bumblebee had bored into the rafter over our kitchen door.

Last summer I stood with a flyswat and tried, without success, to kill all the boring bumblebees. Though I killed a few, most were too fast on the wing. They bored into our house and left their little piles of sawdust beneath. When I stopped up their holes after they'd gone in for the night, they bored their way right on through the soft pine and out again. Then I squirted their holes full of insecticide, but this didn't kill these sturdy fellows. I couldn't get rid of them above the kitchen door, and I couldn't get rid of them on the front porch. They had moved in and taken over. Since insecticide couldn't stop them, I spent more time with a flyswat, just to reduce their number.

What rankled was how they had deceived me. First I thought they were the old friendly bumblebees and decided to leave them alone in the little holes they had found in our rafters. I didn't know they had bored the holes until I caught them in the act.

X I

I have looked for him all day, but I've not seen him. This is the time of year he liked to be going about. Always in April he was going with a seed bucket or a hoe or both. Sometimes he went down the road driving a team, a big black horse and a much larger sorrel mare with a flaxen mane and tail. There he'd be sitting upon the little seat over the wagon bed with the leather checkline in his hands. He was a little man, and he'd be sitting there on the creaking wagon with plows, hoes, mattocks, axes, and scythes loaded in the wagon bed.

He never drove or walked past that he didn't have from one to a half-dozen dogs following him. Only two were his dogs. But other dogs liked him, and they trotted in front of the big horses or followed the wagon. This small man, with a wind- and sun-tanned face, lean and spare with a big nose and blue eyes and a kind voice for horses and dogs, I keep looking for him to drive the horses by, but I don't see him. I often think I hear his wagon and I go to the door and look, but it's something else. I hear the winds in the oaks on the hill, the big weeping willow or the wild-plum trees.

And sometimes I think I hear his footsteps going down the road in front of my house. But I don't see him. It's a little trick the wind plays on my ears. Or, it might be a little trick my mind plays on me. I know he should be along at any time, and I feel sure that he will be. Because he's a part of this valley. He's a great part of it. He came to this valley when he was sixteen years old. And he grew up here. He was a young man before he was outside this county. He was almost sixty before he was 100 miles from home. He was never happy anywhere but on this little spot of earth. When he was away, he worried until he got home.

He had a routine in his home in W-Hollow. His horses expected him to be at the barn at four in the morning. His cows expected feed in their mangers at this time. And their patient soft brown eyes lit up, and the horses spoke to him when he reached the barn. And his hogs spoke to him from the pen until he fed them, too. They liked breakfast early, before the chickens flew down from the trees to help them eat their corn.

This was the way of life for this little W-Hollow man. For almost three-fourths of a century, he greeted his animals morning, noon, and night, fed them, bedded their stalls, and was kind to them. He loved animals, and they loved him. And in the spring of the year, especially in April, he got all his livestock onto the green

April grass. He put milk cows in a pasture, his horses in a pasture, mules in another, cattle in others, and he had a small pasture for his hogs. He gave animals range and freedom.

Sometimes, when I think I hear footsteps on the walk around the house, I go to the window. I expect to see him walking to my tool shed with a hatchet in his hand. Sometimes he uses all his staples or nails, and he just drops into my tool house to see if I have any. Then, too, he might need one of the tools in my shed. They're always there for him. His tools have always been in his tool shed for me. His tool shed is four-tenths of a mile away. I suppose his tools are in order. He has always kept them that way. This is the time of the year I expect him to be coming around to look over the fences to see if the wind has blown a tree across one or if a post has given way. We have miles of fences on this farm, and each April he has always gone over each fence, with his hatchet, wire pliers, and staples in his carpenter's apron, carrying along some extra pieces of wire and a pair of wire stretchers and staple pullers. He always went prepared to do a job.

So many times he passed here with a hoe across his shoulder. I knew, when I saw him coming with a hoe, that he was either going to the pasture to clean out the water holes in the spring or he was going to hoe one of his many truck patches. He had truck patches all over this farm, from the valley to the top of the highest hill. He planted potatoes on high hilltops in new ground to grow them good and big if the season had plenty of rain. And just to be sure, he planted some in the old land down in the bottoms, where, if the season was dry, he'd still have potatoes. He raised tomatoes in new ground so they would be soft and have a sweet taste. He set them in old ground to be sure of a crop. He planted corn, peas, beans, carrots, beets, and lettuce this way, too. He was the best gardener we have had in W-Hollow in my day and time, and he was always getting better. He studied land, plants, and seasons each year. He never could learn all he wanted to.

I saw a ditch yesterday on his land when I walked up the hollow to look at his pasture hill where he and I cleared the ground a long time ago. Now the cattle have so often walked in single file down the hill to the stream to get water that they have made a path, and water has flowed down the path and erosion has started. I wondered why he hadn't been there with some of last year's corn fodder and laid it in this ditch. Or why he hadn't cut sprouts and put their tips uphill to catch the wash of the next rain and stop erosion. That's the way he taught everybody around here, his sons and others in W-Hollow who came to his farm. He never let a ditch start. He couldn't stand to see a scar on his earth.

And he wouldn't let anybody hack one of his trees with a hatchet or ax. He wouldn't let any boy carry a beebe gun over his ground to shoot at his wild songbirds. He followed the stream through his farm to see if it was choked and had broken from its channel. If it had gathered sticks, brush, small trees into a dam, he cleared it out and let the backed-up water flow away. There wasn't anything on the ground, in the streams, among his trees, up in the air he didn't watch. He was the most alert man I ever knew. A fire could be two miles away and he could smell leaves burning and would come running with a hoe over his shoulder and be at the fire before anybody else. He always went first. He always got the jump on anything before it got the jump on him. He got control of weeds when they were small. He cut his corn before frost. He dug his sweet potatoes before frost bit the vines. He dug his Irish potatoes before autumn rains.

He was the first man ever to try new grass seeds on the W-Hollow hills. He was the first man to try to get a road built up the valley. He split blighted chestnuts for bridge flooring (because he wasn't able to buy flooring sawed by the mill) and built eight bridges so we could get a road. He was the first in this rural area to have electricity, for he had the first Delco system at his house. He was the first man to have a registered bull. He kept a registered bull for thirty years and charged only a small fee for his services to improve livestock here. I saw his young bull, a registered pole-Hereford, when I walked up the valley yesterday. It seemed that this sun- and wind-tanned little man without a trace of gray hair on his temples should be standing beside his stocky, curly-haired Hereford bull rubbing its shoulders and neck. But he wasn't there. It was terrifying not to see him.

I walked on up the valley to his barn. I could almost feel his presence there. In the mornings he always cleaned the stalls and rebedded them. Over there was his sweet-potato bed. Below it was his garden. This time of year I should be able to hear his laughter. It always rode on the W-Hollow April winds. Or he might be out somewhere in a patch of dogwoods, for they are in bloom now. He always liked them. He always liked to find a dogwood beside a stream where he could look at the white blooms and hear the water run at the same time. But I didn't see him beside the dogwoods up that way, and I didn't see him beside the stream.

It was not unusual for me to be looking for him. This entire valley was his beat. Exactly how many people have lived in this valley of W-Hollow since 1800 I don't know. But of all of them, not a one could have known more trees, wild flowers, cliffs, squirrel dens, hawk's and crow's nests, and groundhog and fox dens than the little W-Hollow man I'm speaking of. No one knew where more wild strawberries grew, more hickory trees that bore nuts, more black and white walnuts, than this man.

No man had ever plowed more miles of furrow than he. He must have plowed enough land for a single furrow to reach around the world. Men have said that his plowpoint has hitched on more rocks and roots than any other man's. Old men and young say his long-handled gooseneck hoe had turned over more gravel from year to year on every square foot of available W-Hollow farming land than had the hoes of any two other men. He knew this land. It was his land. It possessed him, and he possessed it. He was a part of this land, and it was a part of him.

Why do I keep looking for him? Why doesn't he come? Why do I think I hear him and his team go past when it is only the wind in the long green fronds of the weeping willow and in the strange durable half-leafed branches of the oaks on the hill above his house? Why do I hear him on my walks? Why isn't he here?

He must be here. He couldn't leave this valley. He couldn't get away from it. Especially not now, while W-Hollow is an array of wild flowers on every bluff. Wild alum, whippoorwill flower, sweet william, percoon, wild iris, wild plums, and the white sails of dogwood cover the W-Hollow hills. This is the most beautiful valley in the world in April when all the blooms are out. The small

W-Hollow man kept fires out of W-Hollow so wild flowers could grow and bloom and young timber could grow up sound as silver dollars. Only one fire ever reached his acres, and lightning set it. But he got this one out even though it was set in three places at the same time.

He had worked and laughed a lot up until the morning of December 23. In the afternoon, he sent for all his children but me. I wasn't able to be there. He lay on his bed and gave instructions. He told them not to sell his team of horses. He told them to keep his bull. He warned them not to forget to grease the wagon wheels, make a new wagon bed, and put new blocks on the brakes. He told them to be sure to put cup grease in the horse-drawn disk harrows and to plow and disk the garden early. He told them to clean up all the barnyard manure and get it onto the fields. Then he told them to spread lime on the meadow and to go over the fences and to check water holes in the pastures.

After he gave instructions, he said he must soon be going. He smiled when he told my brother and sisters his feet had tickled the skin of W-Hollow earth more than the feet of any man living or dead and now he was ready to move on. Then he smiled broadly and breathed his last. He left the community he had worked so hard to improve, protect, and keep beautiful. He had spent his lifetime in this valley, and now he left it a better place to live.

Knowing all this, I still find it hard to believe he is gone. This is why I think I hear him when it is only the wind in the willow leaves. I think I hear his hoe turning the stones over again in his corn row. How can he leave this world where his image is stamped so indelibly upon everything? He is still a part of this valley, just as it is still a part of him.

X I I

Once when I went down W-Hollow in April, John and Mary Evans' three small daughters were playing on the bluff beside the road. They were up on the steep, thin yellow bank, sitting on the warm, dry ground. The April sun was high in the blue sky, and the air was balmy. I wondered what they were doing. The winds were lifting their braids of long blond hair.

They didn't pay any attention to my being in the road below them. I thought they were eating something and I wanted to see what it was. Sure enough they were. They were picking the wild flowers that are so often called babytears here, though many people call them bluets. There was a small patch of bluets blooming where they sat. They were eating these flowers and making wishes, laughing and talking.

"Girls, what are you doing?" I asked from down in the road.

"Oh, not much," one said.

"I'm not going to tell you," the second one said.

"We're eating bluets," the oldest one told me.

"Why are you eating flowers?" I asked her.

"If you eat bluets in April and make a wish for a dress the same color, you'll get it," she said. "And I want a blue dress."

"I do too," said the second girl.

Their tiny sister nodded her head violently. She wanted a blue dress, too.

These little girls firmly believed they would get dresses by eating bluets and making wishes. There they sat above me, three slender little girls with long blond hair and blue eyes, in their very early springtime, just as the April bluets were in theirs. I was the only one out of season, old. But watching them there on the bank and hearing their gay chatter about blue dresses made me feel young as springtime myself.

X I I I

This morning Glen Hilton drove up in his little red truck and got out and came inside the yard.

"Well, Jesse, I figure there's not much use of going to the nursery in Ashland and getting the strawberry plants today unless you've got a cool, damp place to keep them over," he said.

"Why do you say that?" I asked him.

"Have you looked up and down the creek banks this morning and on the bluffs, bottoms, flats, everywhere?" he asked. "Look over there, won't you."

He pointed to the other side of our yard.

"Spider webs," I said. They were everywhere.

"That's it," Glen said. "That's what I am talking about."

"What do the spider webs have to do with setting the strawberry plants?" I asked him.

"There's coming a long dry spell," he said. "I have never seen it fail."

"But look at the overcast," I said. "It will be raining before this afternoon."

"No, it won't," he said, seriously. Then he looked up at the dark overcast, and he shook his head sadly. "No, it won't rain. The spiders know. The spiders are always right. You'll see."

"Well, if you think it's not going to rain, get the plants anyway. You can wet their roots and put them in the pump house," I said. "They'll keep for days, maybe weeks in there, until this jinx of the spiders is broken."

"You might make fun, Jesse," he said. "But I've worked out in the open, farming and cutting timber, all my life. And I've never seen it fail. Nature is smarter than we are. Nature told the spiders. The spiders know that it's not going to rain. I'll get the plants and bring them to the pump house and I'll wet their roots good, because we're sure heading for a dry spell."

"Nonsense," I said, looking again at the dark sky. "You won't have to wet their roots. You'll be setting them by noon."

He didn't reply to what I said, just got back in his little red truck and drove down the valley to Ashland to get the plants. But when he got back, I had taken a walk. I didn't want to see him. The overcast had disappeared, and the sun was high in the blue sky. The dew had dried from the spider webs, and everywhere I looked there were soft white tents flapping in the slow wind. I wondered who told the spiders.

X I V

Today, Naomi went into the back yard, where we have not mown the grass, to pick greens. She took a basket and a knife. She ignored the flowers—the babytears and cinquefoil and violets—that grow there in plenty. This morning she went out for food, and she brought back a delightful noon meal.

Here is what she picked. She picked willie britches, which

Mom and Dad used to call whitetop, though she didn't find too many of them growing. Then, near the Shinglemill Hollow stream, she found narrow dock, a slick green leaf, and very different in taste from sour dock. Of course, she couldn't leave the early and tender plantain out. And Johnny-jump-ups she picked to add flavor to our first mess of greens.

Naomi found pepper grass near the second walnut tree. Then the wild beet, a grass with a round, smooth leaf with just a faint resemblance to the beet leaf. She picked Sweet Annie from the yard for its very sweet taste. Near the chicken house, where the poke grows up each year into giant stalks the size of small trees and falls over, she picked the soft, juicy, tender young poke and added it to the variety in her basket. Then she found some pig ear, which grows very sparely here, and finally some of the rare ruffled lettuce and much more of the slick and common lettuce.

She brought her full basket to the house, filled the sink, and washed these greens through many waters to remove any particles of dirt that had beaten upon them in the recent rains. Then she put them on to cook, and the steam rose up with an earthy smell that was appetizing. I am always delighted with the first hodge-podge mess of greens. A hodgepodge cannot consist of less than ten different varieties. The more varieties the better.

Often we eat a mess of young poke, and it is wonderful. Someone has been telling us that young poke rolled in meal and fried is better than trout. We haven't tried poke this way. Not yet. We've cooked it as greens over all the years we have been married, and my mother did it before that. For just as long, we've gone to our creek bottoms every early spring, when there wasn't a leaf, to pick watercress.

I have read in several old English poems, one of them written over five hundred years ago, about the watercress in England. We have that same watercress here, and each spring we enjoy its earthy taste. But hodgepodge is so much better than either poke or watercress alone. There is more flavor to hodgepodge.

While Naomi boiled the hodgepodge and the good smell escaped into the kitchen, I fried bacon in a skillet. I enjoyed taking a long fork and turning each strip over carefully and, when it was well done, laying it on a paper towel on a platter and watching the towel become saturated with grease and then substituting another.

Naomi didn't cook any meat in the hodgepodge. If she had cooked meat, she would have used a piece of ham. But hodgepodge is better in the spring, we believe, cooked without meat. Whether to add pepper and salt, and perhaps vinegar, to a hodgepodge is left up to the individual when he takes it out on his plate. He can fix it to suit himself. He doesn't even have to have bacon with it. He can eat the combination of greens from the earth plain, simply boiled in water. Many a time I have eaten them this way, without salt, pepper, or vinegar. There is something about the taste, no matter what the variety of greens and regardless of how many, that reminds me of how fresh new ground dirt smells in the early spring. Many people like cornbread with it, Naomi for one. Today, I ate whole-wheat toast.

This is the meal we like to invite our neighbors to. We like to sit around the table for an early hodgepodge. Many, unused to the idea of eating what grows with the grass in the back yard, do not care for it and will not eat much. But there are just as many who will. What food could be of greater benefit to the human body than early tender greens just picked from the skin of the spring earth? What food could be more digestible? We have never heard of hodgepodge hurting anybody. And we do know that it is a weight loser. It doesn't add any fat but gives plenty of energy. And why shouldn't it? Hodgepodge is what early spring dishes out.

The greens Naomi picked today are very common varieties, but these are not necessary ingredients. As long as you know your greens well enough to tell what is edible from what is poisonous, you can choose from a hundred or more varieties. You can even put a few alfalfa, sassafras, and slippery elm leaves into hodgepodge. It is just what the name implies—everything that grows in the early spring that is good to eat cooked together in a big pot.

M A Y

Though I am still required to take bedrest every day, there was never anything said about the kind of bed I am to lie on. So instead of going to my room this afternoon, getting into my pajamas, and climbing into bed, I took a walk. Carrying a combination top-coat and raincoat and walking alongside W-Branch, I reached the mouth of Byrnes Hollow and stepped over the gnarled roots of the tall trees. Finally, I came to the right place. Here, I found a carpet of last year's leaves on the ground. Around me, in a small area, grew a variety of trees with leaves of different shapes and colors. This was Nature's room, and I had selected it for my bed. I spread my raincoat upon the leaves. I unlaced my shoes to make my feet comfortable, but left them on for warmth. I unfastened my belt, untied my tie, removed my hat, and lay down.

There was enough softness for comfort lying there on my back, which is the only way I can rest. The bed was not as soft as a good mattress, but it was what I wanted. If a draft blew over my body and I needed more cover, I could use half of my raincoat. I lay there and looked up through the green roof of leaves at the blue May sky. Everything was quiet on this Sunday afternoon, and I was at peace with the world.

I didn't go to sleep. Everything was so new about me and in such contrast to the plain, barren, and ugly walls of the hospital room that I had known a few months ago. This spacious room filled with trees, singing birds, and talking ground squirrels was highly decorated. Nature had used a varied color scheme here. Even if it had been possible for me to do so, I would not have changed a single thing.

The star-of-Bethlehem, which grew in white clusters at the foot of a tall beech tree, was not in a vase where it would wilt and have to be replaced with fresh flowers. And there were bluets and white violets growing here, too. My walls were decorated with leaves and flowers, and the ceiling above was the crazy patchwork of many green, gray, and red tints stamped against a deep, distant blue. I had found the perfect recuperating room. I knew that, if the weather permitted, I would be back here each afternoon for my "bedrest."

I I

The purpose of taking rest is to relax, to get away from stress and strife, which, though I have never been conscious of it, my doctors say is within me. If it weren't for these inner tensions, they tell me, my defective heart muscle and circulatory system wouldn't be forcing me to take bedrest each afternoon, something I hate violently to do.

Now, on my new bed of leaves beneath the beeches in this little valley between the hills, I don't hate it any more. I don't lie staring at a blank ceiling. I don't go back and recount my little accomplishments and failures, month by month, year by year, wondering what I could have done differently. Those days are as dead leaves of other autumns. That was life lived, life to be remembered for its pleasures and forgotten for its heartaches.

The mind is a most peculiar part of a man's being. It is a part that he should keep happy. The mind controls the body, it tells the body what to do. Put the mind in a hospital room with plain and ugly walls and it will go out and hunt for something beyond. Perhaps it will take one back through his lifetime to pleasanter scenes, or forward to bright hopes and plans. The mind has wings and it can soar.

But in the hospital, and even in my room at home, my mind recounted the past. And this was a renewal of the old stress and strife. I wanted to get away from worry. I didn't have a lot to worry about, but when I thought, *I will not worry, I will put worry away, I will not think of the old things that trouble me,* right then, the rebellious mind betrayed me. It did worry.

One has to control the mind gently by offering it something new, something better, to make it swing naturally and easily away from the old distressing thoughts.

Lying here on my bed of old leaves, with a new growth of soft green about me to shade my face from the sun, it suddenly was easy. My world was a different one. My thoughts didn't go back, they were of the present. My mind was not under strict control, but was pleasantly relaxed. It wasn't girding my body to fight some ambitious battle. For I lay flat on my back and looked up through an opening in the beech leaves at the afternoon sun. Then, when the wind barely moved the beech tree's branch of trembling leaves, the hole was covered over and I couldn't see the sun. It was a simple change, a soothing movement, and I loved it.

In my new resting place I shut out a past world. My present world became a very small one. I didn't think about ideas for poems. I didn't take paper from my pocket and jot down thoughts. I didn't sweat over lectures and trouble about the right end for a novel. I had much that was new to see in a new world of ground, tree, leaf, stream, flower, wind, and sky. And I was in complete agreement with my surroundings. I didn't think of the short stories I was going to write this month. Characters for these didn't start kicking up their heels in my mind.

Leaf and sky were only parts of it. When I was quiet, and when wild birds stopped singing and crows quit cawing and ground squirrels hushed their talking, I could hear the trickle of the little stream down the Byrnes Hollow. I had found the right bed for recovery, so much so that I hated for my period of afternoon rest to end. If I ever went to sleep, I was not conscious of it. There is a deeper rest than sleep, when the mind relaxes in complete harmony with the intimate, known world around it.

I I I

Resting in the afternoon under the beeches beside the gnarled roots where ants walked up and down as if on a busy street brought back to my memory the story of another man who found a new world beneath a tree. I was a student at Lincoln Memorial University then, and he lived in a house opposite the campus.

Each time I went to the store or walked in that direction, I saw this man sitting under the tree in his front yard. He owned a large eight-room house and his wife rented rooms to L.M.U. students. His wife did all the work and made all the money. Each autumn morning he would come out and sit under the same tree, where he had worn all the grass away. When the frosts came, he would sit out under this tree in an overcoat. Sometimes he would read a book, other times he'd sit there and look up through its leafless branches. Through the winter on days cold enough to be before a fire, he sat under this tree. In subzero weather, when it was just too cold to sit down outside, he would walk under it. This man and his tree were subjects of college jokes, speculation, discussions, and even annual themes.

In early spring, long before any flower bloomed or twig leafed on his maple, he was out in his rocking chair looking up through the barren branches watching for the first buds to appear. He was a handsome middle-aged man who had two sons in Lincoln Memorial University. As far as we knew, his hard-working wife never criticized him for sitting under his tree in the front yard. I remember there was talk among the students of going some night and wrapping a log chain around the tree to deaden the sound of a saw and cutting this tree down to see what the man would do without it. But we never did.

He repeated this routine through the circle of seasons the three years I was at L.M.U. He had done this for years before, it was said, and, I suppose, for years after.

Only his wife and sons knew then, though we learned later, what was the matter with him. He had survived a heart attack with damage so severe he had been given one chance in many to live. At his home, on his little lot, he had found new life in an affinity with nature. He had confined himself to this small world within the shade of this bushy-topped tree. He had been, before coming to Harrogate, a prosperous businessman in a large town in another state. He had driven himself too fast and too hard to accumulate wealth and prestige in his competitive world. Now he had come to Harrogate to try to let nature build back what he had so unmercifully destroyed. He finally succeeded in restoring his health, despite the limited medical knowledge of his ailment thirty years ago. Years later, he went back into business, more quietly, and resumed a more active life.

I V

While lying on my bed in this quiet world, I observed something I had not really noticed before—color. Within the imaginary walls were a variety of trees. The giant beeches directly over me had soft-green, lightweight leaves that fluttered with the slowest breezes. On my left, was a whiteoak with a light-gray-green leaf, not as fully developed as the other leaves.

Down over the slope below me, but still in the orbit of my little sphere, was the sourwood with red tints around the edges of its leaves. And near the sourwood stood a bushy-topped blackgum with many reddish-colored leaves. To my left stood two poplars (tulips) with large slick-bellied fan-shaped leaves that were very gray when the wind turned up their undersides. Near these poplars was a maple with light-green, ruffle-edged leaves. On my right among these hard- and softwood trees, stood a cluster of cottonwoods that appeared out of place. They didn't seem native to this valley, climate, and soil, but their leaves added variety to the canopy of soft May green above me.

The colors one sees, even the landscape around and above one, have much to do with a man's thinking. The human being is perhaps as sensitive to his color surroundings as the white rabbit that is protected by snow and the wild rabbit that changes its shade from summer gray to brown when autumn brings the hunting season.

The soft green on the beech trees had a very soothing effect on me. I could lie for hours and look up at these trembling leaves in the wind and never feel stirred in any way. The undeveloped, gray-green whiteoak leaf had a different effect. It made me want to rise up. I felt that something needed to be done, that something remained unfinished. The reddish-colored leaves stirred me, but not as much as a hundred sunsets that have prompted me to take notes. The gray-bellied leaves of the poplar left me unconcerned. I could watch them and lie perfectly still. The soft cottonwood, like the beech leaves, was soothing.

Nature has her ways of keeping one awake or putting one to sleep. If I wanted to be stirred a little, which I tried as an experiment, I looked fixedly at the reddish leaves. If I wanted to relax entirely, I looked upward at the feathery, misty clouds of beech leaves. And if I chose to remain just as I was, I focused my attention on the poplar leaves and watched their undersides turn up to the wind.

V

I have forgotten old ambitions. I have found a new small world that has subdued them. It has isolated me from a broader world that disturbed me. Just as the dry, parched lips of earth absorb the soft-falling spring rain, this little world has absorbed my thoughts and tensions, like a soft blotter absorbing ink. I am more relaxed in this green room, under this blue sky, than I have been since my first illness.

The beech leaves above and around me have made unnecessary the things I thought I had to do. They have destroyed the habits I thought I had to obey. They have taken away the ten pipes a day I thought I would never be able to do without. In their stead they have substituted clean wind for my lungs. These natural pleasures have been so satisfying that I am left to wonder why man is always burning with his ambitions, his desires to accumulate, his great competitiveness, his wild impulse to excel his fellow man.

Why is one so ambitious? Why have I been all my life? I have been a fiercely competitive person ever since I can remember. If I had two slices of bread, I wanted three. If I had completed my grade school education, I wanted high school, and after high school I wanted college, and after college I wanted graduate work, and then more after that. If I wrote one poem and published it, I could write the second one and the third and publish them, too. And the same held true for the short story and the novel. And as long as I was writing, why shouldn't I write the best?

Now, I wasn't thinking about writing in my new world. I had found one place where I could get away from it. I wasn't hearing about what others were doing, how they might be getting ahead of me. And they certainly weren't hearing from me about what I was doing. For no one knew.

I didn't worry because I wasn't working now and making money. Not when the soft beech leaves moved gently overhead and the May winds blew over me with the scent of burning brush. The winds seemed to whisper to me not to worry. Whether I made money or not I wouldn't starve. Maybe something I had already written would sell. Anyway, there wasn't any rush about it. Not any hurry to write something to sell. If I wrote anything at all, let it be for the joy of writing. Let it come from my heart.

I had been given artificial means of relaxation. Now, I wasn't taking anything to make me relax. Yet every limb in my body seemed rested when I arose from my simple bed. Doctors and others had tried to force me to relax. I had not been able to. But now I had stumbled into the right room at the right place and time.

V I

Not a bad idea Christ had when he went into the wilderness alone to fast for forty days and nights while He thought about many things. Why did He choose the wilderness, a wild country of trees, skies, winds, birds, and animals? And why did He go alone?

He had had a rough time. He was interested in formulating a new philosophy of life on earth. He had promised Man a reward of everlasting, eternal life.

Even one of His stature went into the wilderness instead of the tabernacle or the cathedral with ornaments of glittering gold. He climbed up the rough hillsides. He spent hours deep in the valleys meditating. His thoughts were higher than the winds were high, His soul as clean as wind-touched grass, His dreams big enough to encompass the entire universe.

And, yet, why did He choose the wilderness? Why did He cut Himself off from the small world that He then knew? Why did He get away from His disciples and His friends? There is something that is elevating in being alone with nature. Here is the peace of new perspective for men sick in an uncertain world.

And as I lay on my bed, I thought of the world known to Christ. I thought of Him as He walked away to be alone in the wilderness. What kind of a place was this wilderness that He visited? What did He do there? What were His thoughts? What were His decisions? What did He say in His prayers? Were His days there akin to poetry? Were the torment and anguish eased from His soul?

I know they were.

Because to lie under the green trees beneath an open sky upon a bed of leaves and feel the wind across one's face must summon forth the best in any of us. It brings out the man that is akin to God, the man that is one with nature. To see the beauty of a trembling leaf above one's head is to know that life has meaning. No wonder Jesus chose the wilderness to communicate with His Father.

V I I

This morning I went to the lilac bush in the back yard and stopped to watch the ground shaking under my feet. It was Old baby-handed Mole under our yard working on the roots of grass and flowers. For days now I'd noticed where he and Mrs. Mole had been tunneling in our back yard. They had left soft ridges where they had hooved the ground up with their snoots and baby hands.

I could have called Birchfield to the scene. Birchfield had killed mice, he probably would have dug down in the soft dirt for this mole. But I thought it best to leave Old Mole alone, even if he did threaten the grass and flowers and make the yard uneven for the lawn mower.

Old Mole had a pretty hard way of making a living. I hated to add to his problems. He'd not been endowed with the gifts of a ground squirrel, who had good eyes, or a flying squirrel, who had wings and could run and climb trees and gather nuts and fly. Old Mole had to fumble around down there in the darkness with a pair of little eyes, not much bigger than pinheads, created to face the dirt. I often wondered if he could see through them enough to know light from dark. I wondered if he once had big brown eyes like flying squirrels and woodmice. Because of so much work in the darkness trying to find food, had his eyes grown smaller over the centuries?

Now he was pushing very slowly toward Anthill by the lilac bush. Old Mole worked with his snoot and his little front paws that gave him the name of baby-handed mole. His hind legs were not as large and strong as his forelegs because he exercised his forelegs more by digging with them. He had small paws on his hindlegs, too, but he used these only to push himself forward as he dug underground.

I always had a lot of respect for Old Mole. He was the nearest to a coal miner of all the little animals, and my father had been a coal miner. I used to have fears about the mines falling in on my father and the men who worked with him. And I could imagine what a horror the weight of a mountain on a man would be. A coal miner could be buried in the middle of a hill. I never would go in a coal mine. It was not for me, back under the hill. Now I could have easily pressed the dirt down on half-blinded baby-handed Old Mole had I wanted to stop him from disturbing my lilac roots. But that would have been too much like a coal mine caving in on a man in the crushing darkness.

But at least I'd annoy him a little for ruining my lawn and disturbing my bulbs. I got myself a poplar branch, a small dead one, that the wind had blown down. When he started to bypass Anthill, I stuck the branch down in front of him and blocked his passage. He tried to go in all directions away from Anthill, and I blocked him. I made him go in this one direction.

The big black ants started running as if they were being attacked by Old Mole. The ants on top of the ground, who felt their city shake as if by an earthquake, moved about excitedly. What they did under the ground I don't know, but I could imagine the commotion. I had my stick behind Old Mole now. He couldn't turn back.

He shoved headlong under Anthill, which is about three feet in diameter. He went across in a hurry which is very slow for a mole. Yet his speed was positive evidence he didn't find anything he wanted under Anthill. On top of Anthill, the eternal city in our yard, ants gathered to attack and pursue this giant underground enemy.

Old Mole, his snout quivering, came to the surface just at the edge of Anthill, pursued by a host of big black ants. He moved over the yard, sniffling the ground. The ants followed him a few feet and then returned to their city. Old Mole found a soft spot of ground, bored in, and disappeared into the warm, yielding earth with which he was familiar.

V I I I

I wondered if something had happened to her this year. I kept looking for my old friend, but she had not returned. She had always come back before now, usually in the warm days of late March. I'd begun to wonder if someone had killed her while I had spent my afternoons in bed. There had been several people in the fields, even around the house, whom I had never seen before.

So far, over the years, I had protected her. I've had many high school youths grab a stick when they visited here and want to kill her. Once I grabbed a boy's arm just in time to save her, my old gray lizard that lives on the rock walls of our outdoor oven. I've had any number of guests who can't understand my attitude toward this lizard. And when one of them asks me why I protect a lizard, I have many answers. But I don't have and can't find a single reason why a lizard ought to be killed.

The high school boy who grabbed a stick of fire wood couldn't understand when I roughly caught his arm.

"What?" he said. He was surprised. "You don't want that thing killed?"

"I certainly do not," I told him. "It's a pet!"

Then he laughed! While he laughed I reached down and picked this fat old lizard up. I put her on my shoulder. She crawled all over me and finally rested on top of my head while we built the fire. She was even under my shirt. Often I had gone over the yard with her resting on my shoulder. She had caught flies from my shoulder. If this boy had killed her with the stick, I don't know what I would have done.

Each year she has come back to the furnace from her secret place of hibernation. When she is inside the furnace and I build a fire, she comes up the little chimney and goes down the outside into the grass and scampers over to the walls of my writing room. She understands about fires in the furnace. She's seen so many built there she knows when to get out of the way.

Now why was I so happy? She was back. No one had hurt her as I had suspected. She scarcely moved when I went to her in the yard. I welcomed her back and chided her for being late.

And this is what I have told so many people who don't know the value of a lizard. First, the gray lizard is harmless. I've heard that the smooth-skinned red-green lizard is poisonous. I have my doubts about this. But I know gray lizards are as harmless as frogs. Their skin is rough and scaly, and perhaps the people who have fears of these innocent little creatures who like to bask in the sun and catch flies are put off by their rough exteriors.

Watch the gray lizard at work and play and you will find him a fascinating creature. My parents taught me, when we used to work in the fields together, never to harm a bird, frog, or lizard and never to tear a hornet's nest down. All these are great flycatchers. But among these four, they said, the lizard and the frog are the cleverest of all. After watching a lizard at work, I believe they were right.

The mother lizard lays small soft tough-shelled white eggs in the dirt. Many times when I have snatched grass from around the furnace, I pulled up these small white eggs and put them back in the warm ground and covered them over. Later, I saw little lizards scampering over the furnace walls.

I have used the lizards in poems. The second article I ever sold was about lizards and hornets being great flycatchers. I received seven dollars for the article. That was long before I ever sold a short story or poem.

Now I inched over closer to my old friend and greeted her affectionately. Finally, I touched her with my hand. It had been so long since I'd touched her that she moved away very slowly through the grass. But she was back in her favorite haunt for another season, and so was I. I felt that she must feel warmly toward me, though I haven't had it from her directly.

I X

When Hubert and I burned the brush that he had cut and piled, we carried a five-gallon can and splashed the brush with oil. Then one of us struck a single match, enough to set a seasoned brush pile on fire. While this pile burned, we went on to another. We set more than a dozen brush piles on fire.

When we came back to the second pile to mind the ashes, I looked down and got a surprise. I waved my hand at a terrapin who had his neck stuck out of his light-brown, black-striped shell. His eyes looked straight at me. He was standing there with his legs out of his shell ready to go. But he didn't move. I reached down and beckoned him on. I finally gave him a little shove because I didn't want him to get burned. He still didn't move but stood stiffly there like a terrapin statue.

I called Hubert, and he came and looked. This terrapin was dead. When we had dashed oil onto the brush and fired it, he had tried to leave the pile, but the heat from the quick fire had overcome him. He stood there like a statue, one that is mute evidence of the destruction of forest fires.

Often in years gone by, after we had burned a clearing, the nauseating stench of burned-to-death terrapins stayed on the wind for days. Then, at a later date, their white shells dotted the dark, fire-burnt land. They were too slow to get out of the way of fire on their short legs. And their shells, good protection against other animals, were useless against fire.

I have always liked terrapins and have used them in verse, short story, and novel. And to see them destroyed saddens me. This state's Fish and Game Commission once gave orders to kill them. It was believed they destroyed wild game, but I never saw them bother anything but tomatoes. The Fish and Game Commission's theory about their destroying wild game caused people to try to hit them on the highways with cars. They did a good job, they smashed them flat—shell, blood, flesh and bone—on the asphalt.

Then the droughts came and water dried in the creeks, and the terrapins, who could roll down from the hills in search of water faster than they could walk, died in piles. But since I had plenty of water on this farm and kept fires out, I still had terrapins. And I welcomed them. I never saw a terrapin harm wild game.

X

I knew the pewees carried insects other than moths to their young in the mud nest over the kitchen door. This morning I watched them very carefully to see what their staple diet was. I watched them dive down on the grass, then come up with something and fly to the walnut stump holding these dark objects in their bills.

When the mother pewee came to the nest, I peered through the panes in the kitchen door. I got as close as I could without frightening the parent bird. She had carried in a grasshopper. And now I learned why she first went to the walnut stump after she dove down on the grass. She killed the grasshopper in her long, sharp bill before she fed it to her young.

I watched the mother pewee feed a dead grasshopper to a screaming little fuzzy-headed bird with a big mouth. Then the mother reached down into the nest and lifted up a long white dropping. She carried it out of the nest and dropped it in the kitchen yard. Thus, in a round trip, she carried in a load of food to satisfy the hunger of a young bird and she carried away a load to keep the nest clean.

The rooster pewee duplicated her flight—in with a grasshopper, out with droppings. They ran a constant shuttle service, feeding and cleaning. I timed them. In fifteen minutes each made six round trips. Once, in forty-five seconds each bird brought back two loads of insects for their hungry young.

X I

The sultry summer weather yesterday brought shimmering heat last night, and eventually thunder and lightning. This morning the sky was overcast, and we thought a storm was approaching. I sat on the front porch and watched the great green clouds of leaves. My father and Uncle Jesse Hilton always told me to expect rain when the leaves spiraled up toward the sky.

Now the oak leaves were twisting up from the strong, sturdy boughs, turning over and showing their soapy bellies to the wind and hot sun. Soft winds were blowing and the green leaves rattled as if their throats were dry and they were asking for water. Nature was getting out of time.

The winds came faster, and I knew there was something behind them. I got up from my chair on the porch and went down the walk. I looked north toward Ohio, the way rains come, and there I saw, very low on the horizon, just over the treetops, long, thin, racing clouds, their bellies as thin as those of fast-racing greyhounds. Behind these clouds was a smooth, gray storm cloud. This one would bring the rain.

I never knew a storm had color until now. The leaves, pressed by the forerunners, the messenger winds, were not their usual soft green, they had a pale, dry appearance. Many leaves with lighter undersides, such as the poplar, turned these toward the wind and the approaching storm. My father and Uncle Jesse had been right about the leaves and the storm.

Then I looked down the valley toward Moore's Hill. The great winds were carrying loads of rain across the earth in waves, as if they were using this water from the skies to mop the earth and everything growing on it. These waves of water, carried by the wind, one after the other, were gray like the clouds. They came into view and passed out of sight while the small and giant trees bowed to the breaking point for almost thirty minutes as the storm passed over.

X I I

We gathered flowers, and Naomi made bouquets. Then we filled our basket with wreaths. We got in the car and were on our way to Plum Grove. Naomi drove while Jane held vases of flowers filled with water so they wouldn't run over and I held the basket. We moved slowly over the winding, familiar road, around the side of the hill, down a valley and up a steep slope to the church and cemetery.

This was my first trip to Plum Grove since last July. This was my first time to see two graves side by side of people who meant so much to me in life. The two people in these long graves had brought me into this world.

I'd seen my father in bed in our home so many times. We lived in small houses and had little privacy. But we never needed it. I remember how he made all of us get in bed at eight and then he'd blow out the oil lamp and the house would be dark and quiet. How I resented this in youth! He always liked his night of sleep, and then he would wake fresh and rise early and feed the livestock. But now he was taking his long sleep. Mom had gone to bed a little sooner—almost three years before Dad. Beside them slept my two brothers. This was the way Dad wanted it. He had them moved from their graves on a pasture hillside to Plum Grove shortly before he died.

We had stones up to them. And Mom's and Dad's graves were green and well kept. All of Plum Grove looked clean and neat. The skies above were blue, and white clouds floated out to the horizon. All around in the distance were the low-rolling Plum Grove Hills. It was the best place I knew to lie down under a dirt cover when the time came.

In the little church not more than 150 feet away my mother and father met in 1901. They were married here in 1902. This hilltop was hallowed earth to them. Here they came to church. Not far away, in a running stream, they were baptized. Here they brought their children to church and Sunday school. And now they were laid to rest in this dirt they'd walked over so many Sundays.

Upon this very spot where their graves lie, the old Plum Grove School once stood, where four of their five children finished the grades. Here my father came often to see how we were getting along in school. He was an excellent man with a scythe, and he mowed paths so we would not get wet in the morning dew. He mowed a path every year for the teacher. This was his way of helping to have a better school.

As I looked at the new stones at my brothers' graves, I thought of Dad's advice. Years ago, my father used to say to Sophia, Mary, and me, when we walked three miles from here to the Plum Grove School, "Children, I want you to stay together. Stay together so you can help one another. Jesse, don't you ever get too far ahead or behind the girls. Look over them and protect them. If you are attacked, help one another. You must stay together." Later, when James, Glennis, and Mary walked to school together, he gave James the same instructions, to stay with the girls, although James was much younger than Mary. Even after we were grownups, he always hoped we would stay together.

Then in the summer of last year he talked once more about our being together. He believed in a strong family unit. We might fight one another, but if and when one of us was attacked by outsiders, we all went to his aid in a hurry. I often have wondered whether it has been this close family tie that has kept us from scattering to the ends of the earth.

This idea was very strong with my father the last year he lived. With his small pension, he saved enough money to get Oscar Sammons and Howard Riggs, our local undertakers, to take my brothers up from the pasture hill where they were buried on my Grandfather Hilton's farm. Grandpa was the only one among us who owned land at the time my brothers died, and Mom must have thought he'd own it forever. But he didn't. The land first went from my grandfather to an uncle, then to strangers who pastured this hill. The fence we built around this graveyard lot was pushed down by the cattle. To my father, it seemed his sons, my brothers, were not with us. My mother slept at Plum Grove, and her sons slept two hills and two valleys away due south. So my father had them dug up and brought to Plum Grove.

He made all the arrangements. He had to see the county health officer—had to get permission. Then he had the new graves dug at Plum Grove. They were reburied beside my mother. In the pasture there had been a stone up to one of my brothers, Herbert, but none had been erected for Martin. I don't know why.

After they were reburied less than a year, my father was buried beside them. Of the nine of us—seven children and two parents—four now slept at Plum Grove. They were together there as my father had always taught us to be.

And, in keeping with his idea, we got two stones for my brothers, the color and kind of the ones up for Mom and Dad. Only we got small, low stones for them. Herbert's old stone from the pasture we had remade and put up at Aunt Nancy Stuart's grave. We never knew Aunt Nancy or Uncle Bob. They were dead and buried before we could remember. None of Aunt Nancy's children ever came to her grave. So we had always kept it cleaned off, and now we had a stone up for her. We were following Dad's idea of staying together, keeping the close family ties.

J U N E

When I was a boy, I knew what a clock was. My mother had one which sat on the mantel and ticked the time away. I was glad I didn't sleep in this room so I wouldn't have to hear it. I didn't like the ticking of a clock. In those days I slept upstairs alone in this very house where we live today.

We had an alarm clock which my father set on a chair by his bed to wake him at four. He would get up, build fires in the fireplace and kitchen stove, feed his hogs, horses, and cows, and then eat his own breakfast and be off before daylight (in winter) to the railroad section four miles away. Dad often walked to work by lantern light or by starlight. Sometimes he went by bright moonlight. But when his alarm clock went off, we could hear the noise all over this house. After this clock's strange mechanical sound, I found it difficult to go to sleep again. I learned at the age of eight that an alarm clock can be an extremely disturbing thing in one's life.

Then Dad had a watch, which kept almost perfect time. He used to have me sit on his lap and show me this timepiece. He told me about what a wonderful thing this watch was, and he taught me to tell time by it. I learned how man measured time before I knew exactly what time was. Time was something to me, when I was a child, like wind and water. Time was flowing and eternal, like an invisible river. We could divide it into seconds, minutes, hours, days, weeks, months, and years, but that didn't bring us any closer to it. There were yesterdays, and time was with us now, and there would be tomorrows.

I had my way of dividing time. I didn't use a watch or a clock. My day started in the early morning when the sun came up. Then there were the hours of light, which were not long enough, and finally nighttime, which I loved for its beauty but hated because it sent me to bed. And there were the four seasons. These were my simple measurements of time. I didn't remember the day of the week nor the hour of the day. These didn't matter.

When I was a boy and played on the W-Hollow hill slopes and down in the valleys by the little streams, when I waded up and down the main W-Hollow stream and pinhooked minnows and killed water snakes with sticks, the only ticking of the seconds I heard was the falling of water over the rocks. This was the soft, rhythmical beating of time. This was the noise that time made. When I hunted at night and crept under rock cliffs to get out of a rainstorm, I would lie on dry leaves and listen to raindrops dripping from the rocks to the ground. This was another noise that time made. And when the winds blew, fast or slow, their rhythms recorded the passing of time. When the dark, ugly storm clouds raced across the sky, or when the white thunderheads floated out, lazy-like, across the blue, it was the passing of time. All my work and all my play in those days were measured by this sort of time. This was the natural schedule that I grew up by.

The dripping of rain from the rock cliffs or the falling of leaves through the bright air never hurried me. I took my time. I had plenty of it for dreams. The warm winds of summer made me lazy and detached. The autumn winds made me sad. The winter winds,

shrill and cold, made me hustle. And the soft spring winds stirred
me to awareness of life's reawakening. I didn't need a watch in
those days. I never was a clock watcher.

In fact I never owned a watch until after I began teaching
school. First I borrowed my father's watch. Later I forced myself
to wear one until I got used to it. Gradually my watch became a
natural part of my clothing which was hard for me to do without.
Minutes and seconds began to count. I was on a tight man-made
schedule. I couldn't escape it. I not only needed a watch, but I had
to have an accurate one like Dad's "railroad" watch. It had to keep
the exact time. For trains and planes were usually on schedule and
wouldn't wait for me. And at the other end somebody was there to
meet me. I had to lecture at a certain hour. I had to be out of the
hotel at this or that time of day. That constant tension of man-
made time gripped me in a vice.

This is the "tight schedule." It is one in which minutes are big
things, hours are actually precious. The watch that keeps perfect
time is on the wrist. A man flicks his arm up again and again to
keep up with the flow of seconds and minutes.

And then there was my heart. I treated my heart like a clock,
too. Not that I remembered it often. No, I never gave it a thought.
But I wound it too tight.

Now these tight schedules are fast becoming memories for me,
like the old clock that sat on the mantel, the alarm clock on the
chair beside my father's bed, and his watch that was inspected by
the railroad company so he would be to his work on time. I'm back
now on nature's schedule. My timepieces are rain, wind, and the
seasons. I can tell by the sun in the morning about what time of
day it is. I know the hour certain species of birds get hungry and
fly in for their breakfast. I know the time of morning the ground
squirrels make a noise about their feeding. I know the time the redbirds sing, for they awaken me at four-thirty each morning. Happily,
I listen to them and then go back to sleep. I would rather have them
wake me with a song at four-thirty than leap up at an alarm clock's
buzzing at seven.

I hear time dripping from the cliffs and bluffs to the leaves
below. I've about lost the habit of throwing up my arm every few

seconds to glance at my watch. I have other ways of telling time. I have the ways of my youth.

11

The time had come for me to do something about a large brown rat that had moved in. He was determined to share the cracked corn and bread and peanuts I'd given to the squirrels and the dishes of leftovers Naomi gave the opossums. But he wasn't going to move in uninvited on me. He would destroy the quiet life of all the other pets if he stayed on.

For three weeks or more, Naomi and Jane had seen him and called me. He would climb up on the shelf by the window, chase the ground squirrels away, and eat their corn. Birds wouldn't fly near him. They went without their breakfasts when he was around. He was the largest rat I'd ever seen.

I planned a way to exterminate this uninvited guest without harming a one of our pets. I put D-Con, a poison, in the woodshed, tool shed, smokehouse, and writing room. Ground squirrels, gray squirrels, and flying squirrels didn't visit there. I'd never seen one inside these rooms.

But Mr. Rat didn't visit these places either. Only a few little mice journeyed in from somewhere to bother this D-Con. Mr. Rat didn't range that far away from this house. Instead he moved under our kitchen. Somewhere under our house he had himself a den.

He had managed to go up the walls between the storm sheeting and the sheet rock, despite the studdings between these walls and the lining of rock wool. We heard him in the morning hours playing athletic games in the attic over my room and between the ceiling and attic floor in our bedroom. There is nothing quite like the noise of a large rat scurrying about overhead.

One morning I looked in the flowers under my window and saw a young bird, a ground sparrow. Beyond was Mr. Rat, playing with it as a cat plays with a mouse before he kills it. I tapped the windows above and scolded. But the rat grabbed this young bird and went under the kitchen floor.

I'd gone outside several times with my rifle to sit quietly under the dogwood and watch the place where he'd taken over the birds' feeding. But I never had a shot at Mr. Rat. When I appeared on the scene, he was always leaving. I saw him go under the kitchen floor into a hole that he had worn slick. I knew he had smelled me, and I could never slip up on him.

Then I went into my room and examined my window. I could see the shelf where we fed the birds all right, but it was a most difficult angle to shoot from. I could only get the top sash down so far and the bottom one up so much. Then the radio was in the way, and there was a screen fastened over the windows.

Naomi pulled the radio aside, I took the screen down, and we raised the lower sash as far as it would go. Despite the difficult angle, we arranged the ambush from my room the best we could. Naomi went to Greenup. Jane, who stayed with me, was to be my lookout for Mr. Rat. I loaded my rifle and laid it across a chair in my room. Then I went to my desk in the living room to write some letters. I'd been there about an hour when Jane came tiptoeing in and said, "He's out there, Daddy!"

When I got to my room, I went down on my hands and knees and crawled over to my rifle. There he sat upon the shelf shoveling the corn into his mouth. I'd never watched a rat eat before. I'd always gone after one in a hurry. Now, this old rat was beginning to get tame.

On my knees I leveled my rifle on him. I had to find a very narrow way to send a rifle ball after him, past the radio, over the window sill, and barely over the edge of the shelf he was feeding on.

I lined my sights on him and squeezed the trigger. He was facing me. At the report of the rifle, he fell over instantly, his life snuffed out. The bullet went between his eyes, through his neck, and lodged somewhere in his body. He measured fourteen inches from tip of tail to nose. I didn't have to worry now about the young pewees over the kitchen door, which I knew he would have eaten. For I had killed Mr. Rat with one little .22 shot.

For a shut-in this was Adventure. Why go to Africa? But I decided not to mount him.

III

At five-thirty this morning somebody fired a gun in our front yard. It was a strange-sounding gun—one with a loud roar. It sounded like a shotgun shell where there was only powder and not any shots. I jumped out of bed and ran to the front door. I looked up and down the road from the end of the walk, but no one was in sight.

It might have been the King Powder Plant, about five miles away, that had blown up. It had blown up before, and we had heard it here. I was sure now no one had fired a gun in our front yard. So I lay back down in bed and turned on the radio for the morning news. But the radio wouldn't play. Then I turned on a light. It wouldn't come on. Our electricity was off.

At six o'clock, Glen Hilton started his tractor in the field across the lane in front of our house. He woke Naomi and Jane. I was already up again, so I dressed without washing or shaving and walked outside.

"Jesse, did you shoot this crow?" Glen asked me.

"No, I didn't shoot any crow," I said. "But I heard a shot fired about thirty minutes ago."

"Well, it's dead. Right over there in the yard."

"Someone must have shot it from an electric wire. We don't have any electricity. Was yours off?"

"Not when I left at four this morning," Glen said.

Glen had brought with him a helper named Spraddling to drive the tractor while he sowed the beans. So I asked, "Does Spraddling carry a pistol?"

"No, I don't think so."

I went over and examined the dead crow beside the road. There was a break in the skin on its neck and a hole in the flesh—a very large one. It was a bullet hole all right, I decided. Glen agreed with me.

Naomi was up trying to get us some breakfast when Linn Darby drove down from my old home, where he was staying. I stopped him and asked if the electricity was off up there. He told me it wasn't. Then I told him ours was off and somebody must have cut the line in two shooting a crow in our front yard.

"Could be that a fuse has blown," he said. "I'll go inside and check." But the fuses were good. And there were lights above and below on this line. The fault, we figured, must be in the transformer on the pole in front of our house where the crow was shot.

This old crow and I were not close friends, but we understood each other. He came to my garden early, and I never bothered him. He'd been coming all spring. Now, someone had passed and shot him. It made me angry.

Linn and I went back to the pole. We were staring up at the transformer, where something looked strange, when Glen Hilton said, "I've got an idea about that crow. Do you think maybe he flew up there on the transformer and got electrocuted this morning?"

"No," I said. "He's got bullet holes in him."

"Electricity can break the skin that way and break every bone in his body," Glen said. "Let's look again."

So the three of us examined the crow once more. Sure enough, the holes were not bullet holes. The bones in his body were broken, too. He had been electrocuted. We had solved the mystery. It wasn't a shot fired. It wasn't the powder plant that had blown up. I asked Linn to report to the Kentucky Power Company what had happened soon as he got to Greenup. It was now eight o'clock, two hours later than we usually ate breakfast, and, crow or no crow, I was getting hungry.

At almost eleven o'clock a man by the name of Keaton came and fixed the transformer so we could have water, so we could cook, so the refrigerator and deep freeze would run, so our radios would give us news, so I could shave. Our place had surely bogged down in a hurry because of that dead crow.

"I've seen all kinds and sizes of squirrels get into the transformers and cause trouble," Keaton said, "but this is the first time it's ever been a crow."

"The world has changed even for a crow," I said. "He's got to be careful where he alights now."

I V

The English sparrow flew down from a pine to the tall cedar on the Yellow Bank. He alighted on a cedar limb and had just balanced himself when a hummingbird dove at him like a battling jet. The sparrow rose up in flight, and the hummingbird came back. The sparrow plunged at him, but he was too slow to get near the hummingbird. He missed by four feet.

It interested me to watch this fight. I knew the English sparrow was a quarrelsome bird able to whip most birds its size. But here was a hummingbird not as large as my thumb, really giving battle to the sparrow. I watched both birds leave the cedar and go up into the blue, sunlit air, battling each other. They went over and over and up and down in their battle.

I was their only spectator. I wondered if the hummingbird had a bill strong enough to peck the sparrow. I'd only seen him use it to gather sweets from the blossoms. Now I thought he was using it to ram the sparrow. I saw small feathers drifting on the wind about forty feet up from the ground.

The first round of this battle ended when the sparrow went back to the pine tree and rested. The hummingbird remained in the cedar, sitting up high in the tree smoothing his ruffled feathers and swaying on the bent twig with each little motion of the wind.

But the sparrow was a determined fellow. He came back to the cedar. Just as soon as he flew in, the hummingbird dove down from his topmost branch and hit the sparrow on the back. The battle was on. I never saw birds maneuver like these. They went up into the air and then dropped almost to the ground. But the little hummingbird was too fast, and finally the sparrow went back to the pine again to rest and smooth his ruffled feathers. The hummingbird never left the cedar. He sat on a twig and waited.

The sparrow went back for the third time. He didn't even get to the tree this time. His small enemy met him between the cedar and pine and flogged him unmercifully. He routed this English sparrow. He pursued him across the valley to the hill. Then the hummingbird returned to the cedar.

This made me suspicious. I knew birds didn't fight unless there was a reason. Perhaps both had nests in the cedar. So I climbed up the steps and, while the hummingbird sat on a twig and preened his ruffled feathers for the third time, I looked this cedar over. I couldn't see a thumb-sized little nest swinging from a cedar bough, neither could I find a sparrow's nest. One part of the cedar was old and had a hollow portion where the sparrow could have built. The hummingbird might have a nest up among the dark boughs. High in the tree there was a sourwood vine in bloom. But surely the hummingbird wasn't fighting over it.

The two birds may simply have been fighting for the mastery of the skies over our yard. Anyway, I enjoyed this bloodless battle, even if I didn't understand it.

V

When the pewee parents weren't dropping food into the nest over our kitchen door, the young birds sat up and flexed their little wings. They buzzed them as bumblebees and hummingbirds buzz their wings, exercising them, by instinct, for that first flight soon to come. Today as we watched them, Naomi and I agreed that we didn't want them to leave because the clouds were rolling over and it looked like rain. We didn't want them to fly out and meet their new world in a storm.

Lately, when the parent birds flew in, they often sat a few seconds and looked at their young. Since they were such conscientious parents, I figured they were counseling their young about leaving too soon and about rats, cats, chicken hawks, snakes, and foxes, all enemies to young birds.

I got my camera and climbed up on a chair in the kitchen door. This would be my last chance to photograph them before they left our house. I prodded the basket to get them to lift their heads. I wanted a closeup of their heads hanging over the basket rim, their hungry mouths open.

My prodding the basket had the wrong effect. The little bird that was flexing his wings at that moment left the nest and passed right before my face, flying. Then another passed, and another, until all five were gone in a matter of seconds. The last bird to leave didn't fly very confidently. He was the weak one in the family. There is always a weak one in a large family of birds, or of children for that matter. And in the field, there is always a young quail to linger timidly behind, and somewhere a hawk, fox, polecat, snake, or owl is waiting. The last young pewee flew weakly across the yard and alighted on a walnut stump.

"Jesse, why did you run them off their nest when a storm is coming up?" Naomi asked me.

She was very upset about their leaving the nest. We had watched the parent birds closely since they had returned in a cold spell early last spring. In the soft spring days, we heard them calling and we saw them mating. When the nest was finished and the eggs laid, they took turns sitting on them. When they were sitting, we rarely used our back door but went around the house to get to the writing room, tool shed, and smokehouse without disturbing them.

Now we heard thunder, and this disturbed us more. I put my camera away and went out to find the pewees. The parents were not as excited as we were. They were flying from one young pewee to another, carrying food and noisy advice. Two were in the valley and one was on each hill slope. The weak fifth one was still sitting on the stump in our back yard.

Then a shower of rain came. We waited in the kitchen impatiently. Just as soon as the cloud had passed over the third hill to the south, we went out and found the fifth little pewee sitting on the edge of the birdbath, dripping wet. Raindrops ran down his back and dripped from his tail feathers.

"Let's put him back," Naomi suggested.

I picked him up and reached him back into the nest. But it was like trying to keep one child at home when four others are out in the world. That fifth one wouldn't sit still. He stayed long enough to get warm and dry, and then he flew away on wings much stronger.

V I

We call the durable daisies with the golden eyes and white petals mountain daisies. They grow on the rugged slopes anyplace in any kind of soil, up high and down low, and I have found them blooming after frost. I once found them blooming, I believe, as early as February. They bloom over a season of half the year.

We say so little for the mountain daisy. Maybe it is because we have so many of them. Right now our hill slopes, our pastures, the strips alongside our road, along the banks of streams, are white with mountain daisies. Everywhere I walk I am in the company of the daisies.

Of all these millions of daisies, an unusual thing happened to one. This made me think about the millions of people upon this earth and yet the great value in one individual. This one little daisy has the average beauty of its kind and the same durability of stem, sap, and petal. But it has the special beauty of one little flower that should have died and didn't.

The slope above our garage is reserved for iris, yucca, and shrub. We have restricted areas of earth for some of our plants and shrubs only because others, like the daisies, grow so prolifically that they'd take over the whole place if we let them. We pull them out, toss them in a bushel basket, and pile them on a wall of brush and vegetation scraps, weeds, and trash that has been raked from the yard.

Today, I walked over to have a look at the wall. On top of the decayed vegetable matter, a beautiful mountain daisy bloomed alone. This flower had been pulled up with the weeds, and we had expected it to die with the weeds and be decomposed with the weeds. Yet this daisy had the durability and the ruggedness to live. Somehow its roots reached down into the decomposed vegetable matter, and perhaps a rain came and revived it as it lay bruised from someone's hands pulling it up. The tall weeping willow shaded it from the hot sun while it struggled to take root, gather sustenance, and live.

There are human beings born in one-room shacks, without anyone to love and inspire them in their younger days, who fight to live and give beauty to the world. Here, under this willow, growing on top of a brush wall, I had found such an individual flower, one of millions, that showed the will to live and the durability of its species. This is my favorite mountain daisy.

When we are very young and growing into the world, we
have a feeling that we are going to live forever. And this is the
greatest feeling I know. The world belongs to us and we're going
to stay on top of her and be alive forever. It wouldn't be healthy
for the young to believe otherwise.

But when we reach, say, thirty-five, we know we're not going
to turn the earth over and see what is under it. We have already
tried many times, unsuccessfully. We have failed even to turn over
a small hill to see what is under it. We have had great strength. Yet
our ambitions have been greater than our strength. We are beginning now to see that earth and time will whip us in the end. This
has a tendency to sober each of us, make us think. We are mellowed
by this thought, and we put away frivolous things, such as trying
to outlift one another, trying to do more work in a day, run a faster
race.

When these things happen to us, we are no longer growing into
the world, we are growing out of it. The world is not leaving us, as
so many who pine for "the good old days" are inclined to think, but
we are leaving the world. The thousand and one things we had in
mind to do, many of these we discard. We don't see any point in
doing them now. We wonder why we ever thought it was important
to do them in the first place. In this way the mind protects the body,
now weakened in certain parts. And as time moves on, the body
weakens more and more and the mind has more to do. Actually, we
are watching our own selves die by degrees. We are watching ourselves go slowly out of this world.

It took a great physical disaster to slow me, to make my stubborn mind realize my strong body wouldn't last forever. Now, I
know. If my mind had been alerted earlier, this wouldn't have
happened. The same is true of thousands of others.

Yesterday, when I went to the old Kilgore house, I realized I
was over the halfway mark physically. I tried to carry some tobacco
stalks from the front yard up a gentle slope to put them on a fire.

Though I carried small loads, I gave out. I felt weak and I had a little hurt over my heart. This was enough to give me a warning, so I sat down to rest. But think of it! Here I am still physically strong except for my life-giving muscle. A year ago, when I wanted to remove the stiffness from a leg, the soreness from a muscle, to free myself of a headache, I would do physical work. But when the life-giving muscle doesn't function properly, all that becomes impossible. A man must work with his ear, not to the ground, but to his heart.

I looked over the hills that I had cleared and saw them growing up in brush again. The earth was whipping me. I looked at the pasture fields where I had cut brush, year after year. They were on their way back to tall timber. The roads I had built through this farm had been deeply rutted by rain and snow. Tiles were stopped and ditches filled. Once my mind would have turned over restlessly at such a sight. It would have driven my body day and night until the brush was cut and the roads repaired. Now, it was different. My mind told me to sit and rest.

I must finish my remaining time working with my mind and not my hands. I love working with my hands. But my mind tells me that I am lucky to be able to work at all, lucky to be alive.

In a way this is true of everybody. As we live, we die. We grow into the world and we grow out again. We watch ourselves slowly die.

V I I I

Today was my first trip back on the ridge since last summer. Hubert Ross brought his car, and we put our tools in his small trailer and drove slowly up the long hill. We drove past the cabin and over the meadow to the barn, where he parked the car and started work.

Hubert was mowing with a scythe around the barn. I couldn't do much work, except to use a broom rake in the barn entry, where there were many tobacco leaves left from last winter's stripping. While gently raking up piles of old tobacco leaves, I saw something move down near the partition in the barn. It was close to the color of the tobacco leaf and a little hard to make out. I had almost stepped on it.

When I looked more closely and saw that it was a copperhead, I grabbed a tobacco stick in a hurry. Some of the old fight came back. I couldn't help it if my hands and arms were stiff and sore. I lost some of that soreness when I saw a copperhead. There is only one good copperhead, and that's a dead one.

This copperhead wasn't running from me or anybody else. Copperheads don't run from human beings, animals, or even forest fires. They fight until they die, but they usually don't die. They usually do the killing. There is not a more dangerous snake anywhere than the copperhead. He doesn't give any warning when he bites, and he can strike twice the length of his body. No other snake that I know can do this.

That is one reason we were never without a good dog for snakes. Jerry-B-Boneyard was one of the best. He ran any kind of snake the same way he ran a rabbit or fox, but he enjoyed a copperhead most of all. The smell of one, like cucumbers on a hot day, fascinated this small belligerent dog. I couldn't count the number of copperheads he killed in his lifetime. Now I didn't have a dog like him. I had to depend on my own eyes and on what quickness was left in my own body.

I came down overhanded with the tobacco stick but broke it on the partition. The snake was lying coiled, ready to strike. I grabbed another tobacco stick and struck again. This time I addled the copperhead.

One had bitten my Uncle Jesse Hilton when he was a young man. One had bitten my mother when she was a girl hoeing tobacco. One had almost gotten me one night on this same ridge. The moon was high and bright that night and the spring world was flooded with light. The copperhead got his fangs hung in my pants leg and old Jerry-B-Boneyard closed in and took care of him. There had been many copperheads killed on this ridge.

Now he struck at me once, but halfheartedly. My third blow with this tobacco stick killed him. I made sure he was dead by pounding him a few more licks. He was not two feet in length and the color of an old penny.

I X

When a June day is done and the sun starts down behind these hills, long gray and purpling shadows begin to lengthen across the creek-bottom meadows and the slopes planted in corn. The quietness of a June evening, the mystery of lengthening shadows on field and meadow, and the flaming sunset colors in the sky make this a world of deep peace and quiet beauty.

Before the sun is down and shadows are blended into one great shadow of night, the nighthawk begins his flight. He is fresh from resting all day in a hollow oak, a cliff, or even under a canopy of green leaves, where the sunlight cannot filter through to make him squint his eyes. Now he flits over his native haunt of earth, happy to be alive, and proud of his agile wings. His boom-booms reverberate over the shadow-filled valleys. He cuts through the air and circles and crisscrosses his trails on the silver wind, careful to avoid the chimney sweeps that dart here and there, uncertain of the direction of their flights.

Upon the creek-bottom meadows, the fireflies dance a slow, dreamlike ballet. The pewee sounds his last call for the passing day as he settles down on a nest of mud and feathers. The whippoorwills begin their lonely singing. June is the month in which the young whippoorwills grow big enough to leave the leaf on the ground that has been their home. The parent birds, whether in melancholy or relief, always sing more in June than they sang in April.

An evening wind has arisen that is fresh with dew. The damp leaves and flowers have combed this wind for dust and have scented it with their perfumes. Earth now begins to radiate her heat. One can feel it. One can smell it. One can taste it. There is not another month in the year like June for beauty of an evening.

The whippoorwills are beginning to get noisy, but they can't compete with the crickets. The crickets are too close to us, and the whippoorwills are high on the hilltops. The crickets chant under the floor and near our porch. The sound of their drowsy singing softly scratches the silk of evening.

All these sounds and the passing of the heat and the dew

underfoot suggest that June is a maturing month. This is the time when the growth of corn is prolific. Tobacco grows while we sleep. The June sun ripens the oats, rye, barley, and wheat. June is the month when nature gathers its forces for the final big push to produce bumper crops of corn, potatoes, and hay. June works hard now and plans summer's conclusion, the harvest.

June assures us that we will be fed. June is not only beauty, but she is life and growth and the promise of abundance.

X

I had my hoe in hand cutting a few weeds in the flowers that border our front walk when I saw him. He was crawling slowly up Shinglemill Creek. He had just left the big tile that is under the lane road and was crawling toward the tile under our house. He didn't see me, but I saw him. I figured that he was hungry and looking for something to eat. So I tiptoed across the yard with my hoe raised above my shoulder, careful that he shouldn't see my moving shadow. When I reached the creek bank, I saw that his eyes were fastened on something else. He began to slow down so that his skin wouldn't make any noise as it slid over the ground.

This big water snake did not know that he was crawling on forbidden ground. Slowly he slid along, sticking his forked tongue out to catch the sound. At the edge of the water on a little patch of sand and gravel lay a water dog, about the size of a lizard, sleeping in the sun. He was a pretty old water dog, his body reddish colored with white dots. Around here you see water dogs of many beautiful colors—black and white, red and white, blue and white, green and white, and even some that are polka-dotted in many shades.

When the water snake got closer, he slowed down and eased up on the water dog. I wondered if he had smelled the water dog, because a snake is so low on the ground he has difficulty, surely, getting directions and locating objects. Water snake came almost to a stop. I knew what he was going to do. I stood on the bank watching, my hoe poised and ready, but I knew I couldn't save the water dog.

Suddenly, water snake made a quick dash. The old water dog wasn't as fast as a lizard on a tree. These two, the water dog and the lizard, must be first cousins, only one lives in water and the other on land. They are built alike and crawl alike, they have similar bodies and legs and mouths. But the water dog, through the years, hasn't had to run and hide like the lizard. He could slip into a hole along the stream or plunge into the water and go down under a rock.

But this water dog didn't have a chance to get away from this fast old water snake that slipped up on him while he slept in the sun. He had left himself unguarded. He hadn't dreamed of an enemy's coming up this stream. Before he could even move, the water snake had opened his big mouth wide and swallowed water dog.

Now came my time. While water snake was in the ecstasy of swallowing this delicate red polka-dotted water dog, I ran down the bank with my hoe, which I had just filed a few minutes before until it was as sharp as a razor. When old water snake saw me, he tried to get away. He wanted to get to the tile under my house and he took off in that direction, his skin rattling over the gravel up the little creek bed as he crawled. But I came down with my sharp hoe and severed him not quite in the middle.

I barely missed old water dog's head. But water dog must have thought a miss as good as a mile, for he came out of the front portion of the snake in a hurry. There wasn't anything wrong with him. He was more alive than he had ever been, and the way he ran made me laugh. He ran as if he had just learned how. Perhaps he wasn't sure of what had happened to him. So many things had happened in so little time. He hadn't had time to be smothered inside old water snake. He hadn't had time to be digested. The lick I'd struck with my sharp hoe was a mighty lucky one for him.

Now I chopped the forepart of the snake in two again so as to make him die sooner, while the water dog scooted over into the fresh water and went down and under the tufts of green grass that hung like a curtain over a small cut in the bank. This might be old water dog's home. Or anyway, a good hiding place.

I went to the woodshed to get a bucket and a shovel to pick up the pieces of old water snake. Something bothered me as I walked along. I knew I couldn't be friendly with water snakes, blacksnakes, copperheads—not any kind of snakes. Still, I was sure that I had interfered with nature. Nature had everything worked out pretty well without man's interference. Man's interfering with nature had proved destructive more than once. With my killing this old water snake, I had broken one of the links that formed nature's perfect circle.

In the first place, this old snake ate only a few water dogs, minnows, frogs, mice, ground squirrels, and anything that lived in the water or denned in small holes along the creek. If it were not for water snakes, perhaps, minnows would clog the holes of water in the creeks until they died of starvation. Water dogs might over-populate them, too, and the water would become foul with their decomposing bodies. As I shoveled the three pieces of old water snake into the bucket and carried him toward the brush fence under the weeping willow, other links in nature's chain kept occurring to me.

The chicken hawks caught songbirds, and the owls caught the chicken hawks. The copperheads killed the water snakes, and the blacksnakes killed the copperheads. The rabbits ate grass, and the hawks and owls came down from the air and caught the rabbits. The snakes crawled on the earth and caught young rabbits and swallowed them. Foxes, dogs, cats, minks, weasels, and man also killed rabbits. It seemed as though the rabbits had a lot of enemies. But rabbits multiplied so quickly that they would soon take over if it weren't for the balance wheel of nature. Nature was tuned to a perfection no mere man could achieve or even begin to understand.

Through the years not any species of bird or animal I know of in this area has become extinct. Not a single one has caused the extinction of another by preying upon it for food. This is nature at her best. And I had interfered with nature when I used my sharp hoe on old water snake.

X I

Spring is gone, and with it the peach blossoms, but tonight I fell to thinking of springs long gone and a game we used to play.

One of my finest boyhood memories is of running fleet-footed as a deer over these hills in the early spring, hunting for wild-peach trees blooming in the dark, leafless woods. This was back when Big Aaron and Little Ed Howard and Cousin Glen Hilton and I ran wild in the woods together. We hunted at night and roamed the hills on Sundays.

We played a game when we looked for blooming peach trees. A blooming tree counted ten points. And when one of us found a tree he shouted so he could lay claim to the points and to the tree. He would return later in summer and gather the wild, sweet, delicious fruit grown from the sustenance of new ground in a deep forest.

I remember I loved this game of finding wild-peach trees in bloom. I can't ever recall losing a game on points to one of the others. I liked to think I ran faster than the wind blew.

First, I liked the sight of a blooming peach tree in the spring, the pink blossoms blowing in the cool winds of late March and early April. They looked so beautiful to me then when there wasn't a green leaf on the peach trees or any of the other trees in the woods. I liked to run ahead of my friends and hear them following me, breathing hard with their tongues out. I liked to hear myself shout, "I've found another one. Small. In a cove near a whiteoak. Filled with blossoms. My tree."

Then on I'd go. I'd never stop for a second look at this wild peach. My brogan shoes would rattle the brown, dead leaves of last year that carpeted the dark land under the winter trees. Often my shoe soles would get slick running over dead leaves, and I would fall, jump up in seconds, and be on my feet and away.

Later, when I went out to find wild-peach trees for my orchard, I knew where to go. We had played this game in the early spring near all these old houses and on these ridges. We had run over all these hills from Seaton Ridge to Buzzard Roost, as far as five to six miles away.

When peaches ripened in summer, we took baskets and went back to these trees. There were peaches aplenty for our four families. Though I found most of the trees and laid claim to their fruit, I shared it with my friends. We gathered these small but tasty wild peaches and carried them home for canning and for jelly.

When forest fires broke out, I never knew boys, or older people either, who fought them harder than we. For there were so many things in the forest we wanted to protect. But most of all we wanted to save our wild-peach trees. Sometimes the fires were too much for us, and they got our peach trees. But there were always seeds under these trees that had been trampled into the ground by our feet. The fire didn't burn these seeds, and they grew into trees again. The dirt saved the roots of the old trees, too.

Nature didn't grow wild flowers with blossoms any prettier than our wild-peach blossoms. Perhaps the percoon blossoms were prettier, but percoon didn't bear fruit. After percoon blossomed, it was through. But our peach trees were just beginning with their spring blossoms. Among these wild-peach trees in one patch of woods we found two October clings. These peaches ripened about the time of frost, and their flesh was as red as a sumac leaf.

When I was searching for young trees for my orchard, I went back to this hill where the two wild October clings grew, but I couldn't find a wild peach any place, for the forest fires had since ravaged this area many times. Yet I hope that among my young trees still to bear fruit I will have a wild October cling.

When I think of my wild-peach trees on this bluff, I can still feel the sweat on my brow and the night air in my lungs as I raced on through the dark, leafless woods, shouting when I found a wild-peach tree with pink blossoms on its naked boughs.

J U L Y

Lazy me.

This afternoon I walked slowly down W-Branch. The sun was beaming down. Weeds and bush leaves were wilted. They hung in limp clusters. But this didn't bother me. I took my time and walked slowly along. I didn't see any birds overhead in the lazy air. I looked up a time or two and saw only a few lazy white clouds resting high in the blue sky. They didn't have any props under them, not even the slow, lazy July wind.

Not anything bothered me. I wasn't even thinking. That took too much effort. All the energy I had I used to hobble slowly along over the stubble where the creek bank had been scythed, then down into the creek and along its smooth rock bottom. The water was low now and I could do this. I went over the dry rocks clippity-clop down around the cliff ledges toward the Byrnes Hollow.

On either side of the creek the wild phlox grew tall. The pink blossoms were filled with lazy bumblebees, and honeybees, and once a hummingbird dipped down from the skies to work over a dozen or more stems. I stopped to watch. Even the hummingbird had slowed down to a slow whir in this hot weather. I looked at the trickle of water that whispered lazily between the rocks. I didn't care what the water said. I didn't want to know. Whatever it said took too much guesswork to translate.

I walked on a few more yards to a little spur of sand that the high water of another season had washed behind a log. Here the bullgrass and the wild phlox had taken root and had grown. Just below was a pool of water filled with a swarm of silver minnows. They were huddled together, breathing water through their gills and coming up to the surface every few seconds for a drink of hot air. Even the water over the rocks was hot for them. But they had a nice place. They didn't need my pity. They were about as well off and as comfortable in their little world, breathing water and drinking air and waiting for a fly to drop down from the skies, as the average person who breathes air and drinks water and lives in a little house and waits for a gift from the gods.

I was as well off as the lazy bees and the slowed-down hummingbird. I was as well off as the minnows in the pool. I sat down on this little spur of sand. It wasn't the most comfortable seat, but it would do. My feet felt warm because my shoe soles were rubber, so I pulled off my soft summer shoes, then my socks, and put my feet in the warm water.

Back up in the Byrnes Hollow I heard a gray squirrel barking. He was, I suppose, lying out on a limb in the summer heat. He was barking because he wanted to bark. He might have just been happy. Or he might have been talking to the other squirrels. He might have wanted to listen to his own voice. What he was doing and why was his business. I didn't care what he did. I didn't care if it rained or if the sun continued to beam down unmercifully on all of us.

I was the only human near this spot. Twelve men could have guessed where a man was hidden in this valley, and not one would have hit on this out-of-the-way place. I was under the high bullgrass and wild phlox that grew on the banks of W-Branch, away

from everybody. It was a good place for a man to be on a lazy
afternoon.

The minnows knew I was a stranger. They swam up as close to
me as they could in their hole of water. They rested, breathed
easily, and drank a little as they looked this giant of a stranger
over. But I didn't throw a pebble into their pool. I left them alone,
let them take life easy in their little world as I was doing in mine.
They could go up or down, depending on the water in the stream.
They had to go where there was water for them to breathe. Breathing air, I could go in any direction, but not far.

These minnows were content in this big hole of clean, warm
water. There was a sand bottom to most of their domain. I saw
some kind of a bug tumble from the air into the water. I didn't get
up to see what kind it was. I wasn't that much interested. But the
minnows were interested, for it was food for them. I saw them
wrestling and pulling at this big bug. Some got a wing, others a
leg, and the biggest minnow in the group finally swallowed all of
the bug that was left. Then they swam around, silver minnows in a
silver pool in the sun, looking for something else to fall. This seemed
a nice way to live.

Their flashing about didn't disturb a hundred butterflies of all
sizes and colors that sat around the edge on the warm sand and
drank up the warm creek water. I enjoyed watching these butterflies,
they were taking it easy, too. I couldn't remember when I had ever
been lazier and more contented. The air was a little close down
under these creek banks, where the slow currents of July wind
didn't reach. But I sat motionless, not exerting myself in any way, so
I stayed comfortable enough.

A row started among some crows up in the Byrnes Hollow. But
they didn't bother me either. I wasn't interested in their family
quarrel. I heard the young crows screaming as if one of their
brothers or sisters was getting all the food. Perhaps they had found
a blacksnake lying up in a tree and were feasting on him. I used
to hear these rows among families of crows and slip up on my tip-
toes to find out what it was all about. Usually it was over a blacksnake. Crows often fussed over this wonderful delicacy. But I

wasn't interested now. I listened to the parent crows trying to talk peace to their young. Finally they got the dispute settled. They calmed down.

Then I watched an old water snake crawl out on a dead limb that stuck over the water. I watched as he coiled around this dead branch to take himself a summer sun bath. I don't know whether he saw me or not, but I left him alone. There was a time when I would have jumped up with a rock in my hand and he would have been a dead snake. Or I would have come up with a club and rapped him before he could slip off the branch. But he wasn't bothering me. I wasn't bothering him. He was enjoying the sun. And so was I. I was even glad that he was so comfortable, coiled that way around that limb.

I looked down into the water hole, but the minnows had gone into their little homes up under the roots of the bullgrass and wild phlox. They had seen old water snake up there above them. They had seen his shadow down in the water. But old water snake wasn't going to bother them. This was the kind of July afternoon it was too hot to eat.

Not a butterfly flew up from the sand bar. Our little world down beside the creek was very still. Even the crawdads lazed around on the rock in the bottom of the hole. They didn't bother to exert themselves for a good swim. I watched a white and red polka-dotted water dog crawl down the bank into the water. He too was taking his good-natured time. Water snake didn't see him, and I was glad. I didn't want to have to rise up to old water dog's defense. I might have. I am not certain. I would have had to shake off the lazy hour quickly. I didn't want to be put to the test.

I didn't want anything to happen among us to disturb our world. I sat here until the sun went down. I didn't hear another crow's cawing or a squirrel's barking. Lazily I dried my feet with my socks and then put them on, slowly. Next my shoes, slowly. I got up slowly from this spot whence I hadn't moved for an hour. No one seemed to notice my departure. I walked back up the creek for home.

I I

When we left the Hunter Theater in Greenup after the movie, I beat Naomi and Jane across the street. I had made up my mind I was going to drive the car home. I had to be there first and get possession of the steering wheel. When Naomi reached the car, I was behind the wheel, and I asked her for the key. She didn't say anything right then, just looked troubled. But she gave me the key. As soon as Jane got inside, I started the engine, switched on the lights, and started backing out.

"Do you feel up to it, Jesse?" Naomi asked me.

"I certainly do," I replied. "Don't you and Jane be afraid for me. I'm going to get you home. I've driven a little down our lane and on the W-Hollow Road, but never at night. I want to drive at night again." Yes, I wanted to feel strength and power in my hands. I wanted to be myself. I wanted to feel the old confidence again. I was going to drive this car home.

This was my first time behind a steering wheel at night since last September. I couldn't explain to Naomi and Jane how alive this made me feel. I had always been a happy night driver. I had liked to drive a car at night for long distances across the country on trafficless roads, or to drive a car at the break of dawn when all the world alongside the highway was beginning to wake and stir. To see the lights come on in the houses . . . to see the hogans in the desert all lit up at four that morning when Naomi and I drove across the Mohave.

Now I was driving up my own valley. The leaves were wet with dew on either side, and they glistened brightly where the moon's slanting rays touched them. Even the little stream beside the road, filled with water from recent rains, was a white ribbon in the moonlight. The gray-barked sycamores looked as if they'd been freshly whitewashed. My car lights flashed on the mountain daisy, the yarrow, and butterfly bush blooming beside the road.

Little by little, each little pleasure was becoming mine again. I had been patient. If anybody had ever told me that driving a car at night could have excited me this much, I wouldn't have believed him. But the little things we do, the small pleasures, only seem important when we are forced to stop doing them.

I I I

This morning when I took my walk up W-Hollow, I left the valley and went up on the hill to the tall big timber where years ago I used to come and sit under the oaks' shade and write poems. I used to come here in winter, too, just to hear the wind's lonesome sighing in the barren oaks. Not all the oaks lost their leaves in winter. The tough-butted whiteoaks kept theirs. I visited this grove whenever I had the time. Now I had the time. Plenty of it. So I went back to see my old friends and to lay my hands on their rough bark. I thought about how long they had been growing in this soil and how nature had planted them here.

Years ago there were no trees here. This ground was probably cleared by our early settlers. But land in this area will never stay cleared very long after it has been turned back to nature by the people who have tried to conquer it. In very little time trees begin to grow again. Where do they come from?

Trees in this part of the world have two main ways to multiply: either they drop their seeds and young trees grow up from the seeds, or saplings spring from the roots of the parent trees. One tree that seeds prolifically is the pine. Small wonder that we see such large groves of pines over these hills. The tall pines that have many branches, each filled with cones, we call seeding or mother pines. One of these can set a pine forest. Another that seeds prolifically is the oak. The ugly blossoms appear on the oaks in late spring, and the acorns grow in summer. By autumn the ground is covered with acorns, and where one of these acorns is buried under leaves dampened by rain a young oak will grow.

There are many other trees here that seed prolifically—black and white walnuts, wild plum, mulberry, and sugar maple, the beech from beechnuts, pawpaw from the long black seeds that look like pumpkin seeds, hazelnuts from the sweet kernel of the hazelnuts, honey locusts from the honey-locust beans, persimmons from the little brown seeds in the frost-ripened mellow-golden fruit, buckeyes from the big poisonous buckeye seeds. And all these trees will produce saplings from their roots, too.

But how do seeds get planted in the forest when there are no human hands to do the work? Well, Nature has mighty big hands. All the trees that all the people in the world plant would seem only a toothpick compared with the great forest planted by Nature's big hands. If it were not for Nature's hands, the earth would have long ago been barren of trees. Of course, the trees hire much of their work out. They hire songbirds and little wild animals that live in the woods to work for them.

In the autumn the seeds ripen on the trees and fall to the earth, usually after the first frosts. Then, after more freeze and frost, the leaves ripen on the trees and the wind blows them down. Then the rains come down and pack the leaves over the acorns, the black and white walnuts, the honey-locust beans, and the persimmon, pawpaw, and mulberry seeds. Dead leaves soon are converted to rich loam by nature's own methods. In the spring these seeds will germinate and sprout and trees will grow.

But what about the fields that men have farmed for years and then turned back to nature when the soil has lost its fertility? Somehow seeds reach these fields, for the old cleared places grow back in briers and little trees the first year they are left fallow. One answer is the birds. The birds eat wild blackberries, dewberries, raspberries, and strawberries, then drop the seeds upon the fields as they fly over them. Possums, and even dogs, thrive on ripe persimmons and leave the seeds on the fields. Winds blow the seeds, heavy rains wash them downhill. Deposited in new ground, they grow when spring returns with its soft, warm days and gentle rains.

One of the ways many of the oaks in my grove were planted sixty or seventy-five years ago was by ground squirrels and gray squirrels. Ground squirrels are great nut gatherers. They carry acorns, walnuts, and hazelnuts long distances and store them in shallow holes in the ground for winter. After these nuts are stored, the ground squirrel may be killed, or he may die of old age. His underground storehouse of acorns and walnuts is left to germinate when spring comes to sprout all the seeds Nature has planted.

Gray squirrels hoard seeds in dead trees and hollow logs, and since squirrels are hunted in this valley, many are killed every year before they use up their vast storehouses of food. In spring some of these old trees fall and go back to earth with all these stored seeds. Preserved inside the trunk or branch, the seeds grow and are fertilized by the rotted substance of the old trees.

Walk in a forest of giant trees someday and speculate when and how each tree was planted by Nature's own invisible hand, and whether she employed bird, animal, wind, or rain to assist with her spring planting.

I V

The three of us, Naomi, Jane, and I, had just come from the laboratories of the General Hospital in Ironton, Ohio, where blood had been drawn from my arm for a prothrombin test. At a little combination newsstand and canteen on the ground floor of the hospital, we ordered coffee and doughnuts from a short, stocky man with black hair and blue eyes, dressed immaculately, standing behind the counter. He was very busy cleaning the case in front and going over cups and saucers with great care.

It may sound like a little thing, but here was my first cup of coffee since last October 8, when I had had coffee in the morning. I couldn't recall when I had last eaten a doughnut with coffee. And the man behind the counter seemed to sense that this was an occasion. He didn't ask if there was anything wrong with me. Perhaps he could tell by looking, I thought.

I held the cup under my nose and smelled the coffee. I didn't want to make myself obvious to the man behind the counter, but he did look up, I thought, to see what was going on. Then he looked away just about as quickly, for after all we were his customers and he didn't want to offend. He didn't ask any questions, and that was fine with me. I gave him a dollar bill, and he gave me back seventy cents in change.

This man behind the counter had been particularly friendly to Naomi and me, handing up the pot of coffee and telling us to serve ourselves. While we were pouring, he explained how good coffee was brewed in a larger pot. Then he went over the glass

counter with a clean rag again, after which he went down the
hall, opened a safe, and brought candies back with him which he
placed neatly on the showcase. Naomi opened her purse and took
out a piece of paper and her fountain pen. She wrote on the paper
and showed it to me: "That man is blind."

A shock ran through my body. I looked at him again. He had
fine-looking eyes. It didn't seem possible that I could have been
wrong about him, I couldn't believe he was blind. I watched him
continue to lift things, place something else in another spot, wipe,
and clean. He did everything with the greatest precision. He never
made a mistake. Then I realized that he had memorized his entire
place. The only thing he couldn't do was pour coffee. This would
have given away the secret of his blindness. I didn't want him to
know we knew he was blind. I motioned Jane over from the
newsstand and let her read what her mother had written on the
paper. She couldn't believe this either and threw up her hands.

I have talked about my little world of five miles in diameter. Now
I had met a man proud of a much smaller world. His world was
only a few feet in the corridor on the ground floor of this hospital.
Here was a man who was making a living. Perhaps he was even
happy in his way. At least he wasn't grumbling. And thousands of
his corner worlds could be put in my valley.

Before seeing this man, I had once said that the only person
worse off than I was one with cancer. Now I changed my mind about
this. Here was a well-built, able-bodied man who couldn't see. If
my sight were taken from me, it would certainly alter my world. I
felt, after watching him, that I was so much better off than he. My
world was so much larger than his, and I could see mine. I didn't
have to memorize it. This man's cheerfulness in his corner-cupboard
world made me ashamed.

And he made me think. It matters little what we have done, where
we have been, what we have seen, and what possessions we own,
when and if something drastic happens to us. If we can make ad-
justments, then we are worth our salt. What matters most is whether
an individual has passed the place of readjustment. If he hasn't
and he is willing to work at it, then he can find himself a corner
in the world again.

I sipped my first cup of coffee down halfway and nibbled at my doughnut. But I appreciated these luxuries so much that I didn't want to destroy my second chance of having both. I drank only half the cup of coffee and left a piece of the doughnut. Watching this industrious man behind the counter, I felt suddenly very lucky. Perhaps sometimes he felt lucky too, because he didn't have cancer or because he had a good heart and a chance for survival for many years. Perhaps his mind worked that way.

Outside the hospital, happy to be on my way back to my world, I saw a well-dressed man, driving a large Cadillac, who was apparently in the best of health. But the way he was scowling and cursing and carrying on he was out of sorts with the rest of the world. He had two good eyes and the wild way he was acting he must have had a good heart. I wondered how long he'd have it.

V

This morning I noticed for the first time signs that my weeping willow was in trouble. A few branches were dead in its top, and closer observation showed leaves thinning on other high branches. It had begun to die at the top, a bad way for a tree or a man to start dying. I was grieved to see this happen to our weeping willow. I would do anything to relieve it of its trouble.

I have always felt a deep attachment for this tree. I brought it here, planted it, nurtured it, and then watched its quick growth with admiration. In 1941, shortly after Naomi and I were married and moved here, I stopped over at Three Mile and went up into Tink Brown's yard. There I got a handful of weeping-willow switches off a large willow that grew in the lower part of his yard near a stream. This willow had grown to a great size and was admired each spring by the many people who passed this way. I was one of this willow's admirers, and I coveted one for my yard.

I came home with the switches and stuck them into the ground on the banks of the little Shinglemill branch. In a few days, after more spring rains had fallen, I looked at my weeping-willow switches stuck in the ground and all were growing. I hadn't lost a switch. But I had always had more than my share of good luck with trees. I had set out whole orchards and never lost a tree. It seemed as if I just had to wave my hand over a few damaged roots I'd stuck in the ground and they would grow into a healthy tree. The year I planted my willows I was told that if the weather turned dry in summer I would lose them all. It did turn dry, but I didn't lose a one.

My willows grew so fast they blocked my view from the house down the valley. Although they were beautiful trees, I had to cut them all down except the one on the bank where Shinglemill junctioned with W-Branch. This beautiful young willow growing on this neck of fertile, well-watered land I let stand. This single tree couldn't block our view down the valley.

I never saw a tree grow like this one in the ten years that followed. My weeping willow shot up toward the sky. Had it kept on growing a few more years it would have been as high as the hill on the other side of W-Branch. Since its growth had been so fast, I feared it would be too tender to stand the windstorms in spring that swept up this valley. It lost several of its branches after they had leafed in the spring, but it stood.

When we cut the grass in our yard and pulled weeds from the flowers, I put all the rakings around the roots of my weeping willow. Such a fast-growing tree needed special sustenance from the earth, and I wondered if the dirt around its root base could provide enough. On two sides of the tree were streams, but where this tree grew was fertile bottom soil. I added green fertilizers over its entire root base. My tree drew enough sustenance from the land to become the largest willow in this area.

We must have about a million trees on the 750 wooded acres of this farm. Yet this weeping willow, the only one of its kind here, has a special place with me. Each spring it gets off to an early start to get leafed. So often we have rejoiced when we have looked from our windows to see the long, green weeping-willow switches swaying in the late February wind. At this time of year, the leaves are so small these branches look like green winds trying to escape into the bright sky. A little later, the whole tree looks like a green cloud on the wind, ever in motion, ever trying to depart. There never was a tree that brought as much enjoyment to this family, hungry for spring to arrive after a cold winter.

Almost every spring, it has leafed too early, and its leaves have been frozen dark and seared by a late frost. Yet this hasn't mattered. It has shed these leaves and leafed in a green cloud a second time. Our willow blooms even earlier than the percoon and trailing arbutus, two of the earliest wild flowers, that grow on the bluff above it. The millions of barren trees in spring must be jealous of this green weeping willow's early beauty.

Now that something is wrong with its flowering top, I am grieved. I have seen too many people get something wrong at the top. I know what happens to them. This is a quick way for this tree to go. Each year this weeping willow gives springtime to our world before springtime is here. This is the reason it is especially loved. This is the reason I will do everything possible to give it renewed life.

V I

Tonight I walked down the land to the W-Hollow Road. A few minutes earlier I had been sitting on the front porch in the cool of the evening, looking down the valley at the fireflies over the soybean field. Each one seemed to invite me with the golden glow of his little lamp in the twilight. So I accepted the invitation and walked slowly along this road.

There were millions of golden lights flashing on and off in this valley. I thought of the dark-green soybean field as being a sky spread over the earth and the thousands of fireflies as twinkling stars at my feet. This was the night of the fireflies' intricate dance in honor of the land in its season of fertility. They were trying to light up the whole dark-green, prolific, teeming earth.

Their jubilant dancing was of a pattern. They came from under the soybean leaves and lighted their way from two to four feet up. This is all the higher they got, except for a few wild ones who wanted to soar as high as the tall oaks across W-Branch. What strange calling possessed them to leave the others in their beautiful ballet over the warm, soft earth in the time of its greatest growth?

I stood watching the spectacle over my soybean field. Many of the fireflies lighted their way down among the soybeans. They probably had their wings wet and couldn't rise to any height. Perhaps that was the reason the whole dance was so close to the earth. Only the few dry-winged fireflies could rise to the tops of the giant weeping willow and oaks.

In the background was the orchestra for this ballet. Everywhere along the W-Branch the bass of the singing frogs blended with the lyric tenor of the stream, now full from a recent rain. I heard other musicians—crickets and cicadas and a far-off whippoorwill. Overhead a nighthawk screamed, for a moment interrupting the soft music coming from all over the valley. This was a summer night of music and dancing that a man could share with the creatures upon this earth.

Sitting on a fence railing, I watched a world I had not made. I took a notebook from my pocket to scribble down a few notes. But I didn't want to do this. Why work when all the world about was playing? I wanted only to look and listen and feel something within.

The whippoorwills came closer. One flew down from the hill and alighted on the W-Hollow Road not far from me. He sang a solo with the orchestra. My valley was the stage, and I was the only human spectator. I sat on the railing, spellbound. I would have applauded except that it would have disturbed the players and frightened them into silence. So I sat quietly, listening and watching, until minutes linked together into an hour.

I walked slowly back up the lane road, turning often to watch the ballet in its magnificent sweep over the drowsy soybean field on this summer night. A wind beginning to stir was filled with the night aroma of wild flowers, growing corn, tobacco, and soybeans, a good wind to breathe.

This was one of the unexpected joys that come suddenly upon one in the country. I had purchased no tickets, made no plans. I had merely stepped off my porch.

V I I

Yesterday Naomi and I were driving two Texas friends of ours, C. E. and Flossie Bryant, around the valley when Flossie suddenly pointed to the hills and shouted, "Look! Look at that goldenrod. Isn't it beautiful! I've never seen so much!"

Now this was strange talk to us. I guess we don't think much about our goldenrod, there's so much of it. But the talk got even stranger when C. E. said, "Yes, Flossie loves it. How much do you pay for goldenrod in Texas, Flossie?"

"A dollar twenty for a dozen stems."

Down in Texas they *paid* for goldenrod! Naomi and I roared with laughter at the idea. That was like paying for dandelions, or cut grass. Naomi and I decided we'd export goldenrod to Texas and make a million. We all had fun with the idea.

Goldenrod has always reminded me of Robert Burns, and for a good reason. Years back I laid a sprig of Kentucky goldenrod on Robert Burns' grave, near Dumfries, Scotland.

In the spring of 1937 I received a Guggenheim Fellowship to travel to Europe. I was delighted. Not only would this be my first time to travel on the ocean and to be away from my native country, but it would give me a chance to pay tribute to Robert Burns. Although he had been dead for 141 years, he was the man who had made this trip possible for me. I had read the prose and poetry of hundreds of other English, Scottish, Irish, and European writers and I had made friends among them, but the writer who meant the most to me was Robert Burns.

When I entered Greenup High School, I had never heard of Robert Burns. But my English teacher, Mrs. Robert Hatton, whose maiden name was Hattie MacFarland and who was of Scottish descent, grew up reading Robert Burns. Her father always kept a volume of Burns' poems close by and read them aloud to his family. And when Mrs. Hatton loaned me her book of poems by Robert Burns, I was so delighted I put everything else aside to read it.

Robert Burns' poetry caused me to make low grades in high school. I read his poems and neglected to work at my math, history, science, and even my English. But now this thought was often in my mind: If this man, Robert Burns, a Scottish plowboy who was born in a poor home and never had many opportunities, could grow up to write poetry that would endure, why can't I? I am of Scottish descent, I was born in a one-room shack in the Kentucky hills, and I, too, plow the soil. Why can't I do it if Burns could?

This was the way I felt about it. Mrs. Hatton and I discussed Robert Burns during the noon hours and after school. I told Mrs.

Hatton that Robert Burns' River Ayr was my Sandy River and his River Nith was my Tygart. My father's farm in W-Hollow became Robert Burns' father's farm at Alloway, and there was a Highland Mary in our Greenup High School. Robert Burns was within my reach. We were born under the same circumstances. His language, once the dialect was removed, was the simple language we spoke in the Kentucky hills. Robert Burns was a peasant poet.

Not only could I understand him, but I could move him, his house, poetry, everything from the far country of Scotland, to my Kentucky hills. I could do this though he had been dead over a century. For I understood Burns better than I did many of the native American writers I was forced to study. I told Mrs. Hatton how I felt about this poet, Robert Burns. I never got through thanking her for the book she loaned me.

"Since you like Robert Burns so well," she told me one day at noon, "I want to make you a present of this volume of Burns' collected poems."

This book changed my life. On my way to school in the mornings, five miles over rough terrain, somewhere along the path I would sit under the autumn trees and read Robert Burns. Even in winter I'd sit on a stump, log, or stone and read Robert Burns. I liked to read "The Cotter's Saturday Night" in winter. I liked to read "The shortning winter-day is near a close," and then look around at how dark it would be getting. Darkness came early, and I had work at home to do. I'd jump up, put my book under my arm, and take off running to get home before dark. I had wood to cut, water to draw from the well, and milking and feeding to do. But now I was usually late doing these chores. Sometimes I'd get mad at myself, for I had once been industrious. I had been until I got acquainted with Robert Burns.

It was in the springtime of the year that Burns did most to me. He made me forget to cut wood and carry water and feed and milk. For I walked along the road with Highland Marys and Bonnie Jeans. We had the Holy Willies and the Highland Harrys, too. A century didn't separate Burns and me. He spoke in a fresh, close voice to me from the pages of his book.

I was never by myself. Though my dog might hunt away to

find a possum, Burns was always with me. He hunted with me, plowed near me, and walked over my hills with me. I had found a literary man, although I didn't think of him as such, who was shaping and making a new life for me. For I, too, was writing poems. If Burns could sing of his neighbors, I could sing of mine. I wanted to write poems like his though, poems that sang. He didn't have to struggle to write them. They wrote themselves.

Burns was with me through my early years, and he went to college and various universities with me. By now I had found other literary companions, older fellows compared to Burns. Burns was always young. He never grew old. And I would have to grow old indeed, senile in fact, before I turned away from the youthful living of Robert Burns. There might come the time when we would part, but it wasn't in sight yet. To be young and happy and full of life, love, and sorrow was to be like Burns. Burns woke the song in me, he made me write *Man with a Bull-tongue Plow*.

Because Mrs. Hatton had given me a collection of Robert Burns' poems in high school, I was riding an English ship across the ocean in 1937. Two published books had earned me a Guggenheim Fellowship. Robert Burns could never come to my country, so I was going to his. And I had the idea that if Burns knew how many writers he had inspired, how many people he had made happy and made love poetry almost a century and a half after his death, he would surely be a happy poet where he dwelled in the skies. Once when I was a junior in high school, I dreamed that I died and saw Shakespeare in the clouds. He and Milton were talking together, aloof from everybody, and I couldn't reach either. But Burns had a whole crowd around him, and he wasn't any trouble to meet. He was a regular fellow with a good sense of humor.

Scotland was a cold, green, beautiful country with stone houses and fences and sea gulls gliding over Greenock and flying mists floating low over the grassy hilltops north of the Clyde. Robert Burns' Auld Reekie was still Auld Reekie. Smoke clouds scooted over the housetops and the stacks which protected the homes from downdrafts. Smoke clouds scooted on the low sea winds out to the Firth-of-Forth. This was Robert Burns' land. Robert Burns had once walked these streets of Edinburgh. He had once been wined and dined the hero of the hour here. Now I was going to pay to Robert Burns my simple tribute from the hills of Kentucky.

After getting used to Scotland's temperamental weather, its foods, currency, tobacco, language, and people, none of whom I knew as well as Robert Burns and not a one as friendly toward me, I set off by rail to Glasgow and by bus from there to Alloway. This was midsummer, and tourists were arriving by the thousands in the Burns country. Now I learned that a poet who had never made more than 3,500 American dollars in his whole lifetime, who died penniless, was the greatest earning power for the poor people of Southeast Scotland. People were coming from all over the world to see the land of Robert Burns, from America, Canada, South America, from all over Europe, Africa, Asia, Australia, New Zealand. Robert Burns had spoken to others besides this plowboy from Kentucky. Robert Burns was universal, he spoke to and for all mankind.

I waited my turn to see the inside of the house at Alloway where he was born. I was deeply touched by the barnlike structure, with low doors and small windows, framed with stone. This house had sheltered a great man. And at the same time one portion of it had housed the cattle and kept them warm on that night of his birth, January 25, 1759. I visited the remains of Alloway's Kirk, which figures in "Tam O'Shanter," and I saw the Auld Brigg. I saw the graves of Burns' ancestors buried around Alloway Kirk. I visited Mount Oliphant, Kirkosweld and Lochlea, where Burns lived seven years of his life.

Everywhere I carried his volume of collected poems. This was not the one Mrs. Hatton had given me. I had worn it out. I had worn out a second volume, for I had carried Burns with me even when I plowed in the fields or drove the team to Greenup. I had carried Robert Burns to the steel mills, to the army camp, and to college. I kept Robert Burns in my own library and in all the high school libraries where I had taught. I had the brief journey of his life well memorized. Now I was visiting his places and taking my time about it. The land Burns plowed was sacred earth. The crude old stone houses where he lived and the taverns where he drank and the fields where he walked were what I had traveled far to see.

I went to Mossgiel, where he had spent four years of his brief life. It was here he failed as a farmer, but not as a poet. Here he wrote many of his finest lyrics, including "The Cotter's Saturday Night." Then I went to Mauchline, where I spent a week. Here Robert Burns and Jean Armour went to housekeeping. And in the churchyard, many of Robert Burns' contemporaries slept, their graves pointed out now because Burns immortalized them in his verse. There must not have been any libel laws in those days. Maybe some people living today would have greater prospects for immortality if the possibilities for libel against writers were reduced.

In Kilmarnock, where I thought I found the poorest people in Scotland, Burns was as much alive as he was in his lifetime. In every home and shop, regardless how poor the family, there was always a picture of Robert Burns. He was on the walls. He was on the dishes.

From Mauchline I went to Ellisland, where Burns again failed as a farmer and again produced some fine lyrics, but here he made the fatal mistake of leaving the land. He became an exciseman, at fifty pounds a year. Then he moved to Dumfries. This was the last city for Burns. I spent most of a day visiting his last home. In the afternoon I went to the churchyard to see the Burns monument in St. Michael's.

I had traced the life of Robert Burns, except for his brief trip up into the highlands. Now, at this beautiful mausoleum, finer than any home Burns and his family had ever lived in, my quest to find the man who had so influenced my life ended. A well-worn path among the stones in St. Michael's led to his tomb. In my judgment, and apparently that of others, Robert Burns was more than a poet. Robert Burns was Scotland. I hadn't thought of Scotland when I had planned to come here. I had thought of visiting the land of Robert Burns.

That night a full moon came up, high and bright. By it I walked back to St. Michael's a second time, only to find the iron gate locked. But I climbed over the gate and walked up the winding path among the stones until I came to the Burns mausoleum.

Here was a white statue of Robert Burns standing at his plow with one hand on the handle, looking up at the guardian angel above him. At his feet grew a tuft of mountain daisies, and beneath his plow was a field mouse. I remembered the mountain daisies I had plowed up on my Kentucky hills. From now on I would never plow up a nest of field mice or brown woodmice that I wouldn't think of Robert Burns. I had come over three thousand miles to find his country and the place where he slept. So I spoke to him in the Scottish night while a bright moon looked down on St. Michael's.

Now was my time to pay tribute to the man who had stirred the blood in my veins with his lyrics and had caused me to write. From my third battered volume of Burns' collected poems, I took a pressed goldenrod I had carried all the way from Kentucky. I dropped this goldenrod on Burns' grave. This little tribute I could pay the man who had changed my life.

V I I I

My father taught me the art of conservatism. I saw him, when I was a boy, stretch a dollar and get more from it than any man I ever knew. He was forced to do this by necessity. He wasn't a stingy man. He didn't hoard money, for he never made enough to hoard. He had a large family and made a little wage, and it took every dollar to sustain us. The highest he ever made in a month was once when he got a lot of overtime. He drew $103 for that month on the railroad section.

As a boy growing up, I earned my money the hard way. I walked five miles to my work and back when I was nine, ten, and eleven years old and worked for a quarter a day. I don't know how many hours we worked. I know I went before daylight and got back after dark. At the end of the week I had six silver quarters. These quarters I carried in a little Bull Durham cloth tobacco sack. Later I made fifty cents, seventy-five cents, and then a dollar a day. I also hunted and trapped wild animals and sold their pelts. I have since come to believe they need their skins more than I need the money. I have always regretted making money in this manner, though I used it to buy books and clothes when I was in Greenup High School.

Later I worked in the steel mills, ten hours at night for forty cents an hour. I got a lot of overtime, and one summer I saved three hundred dollars, which I used for college. In college I worked, too, for twenty cents an hour, and afterwards I taught school for sixty-eight dollars a month. Though I held some important teaching positions in this state, the highest I ever made while I was teaching was two hundred a month.

My first lecture paid me two dollars. Then I worked up to three dollars and five dollars. I wish I knew how many times I got five dollars for a talk. More than a hundred times I was paid twenty-five dollars for a talk. I did a lot of speaking before I was booked on a trip that took me from Kentucky to California and back for twenty-five, fifty, and seventy-five dollars per talk. I lost on the first trip. But soon there was another one, and I didn't lose. My father always taught me to hold on to something, not to give up easily. Finally I was paid a hundred dollars for a talk, and my first time to get two hundred was in Dayton, Ohio. After this I treated myself to a good steak. When I quit speaking in 1954, I was getting five hundred a talk and more. At the same time I was speaking for twenty-five dollars or for nothing if the cause was good and there was no money to be had.

This same pattern applied to my writing. First thing I ever sold was a theme I'd written when I was in high school on keeping back yards clean. I sold this to *The Family Circle* and was paid two dollars. Next I sold a piece on hornets, trying to protect these valuable flycatchers, for seven dollars. I sold a piece on lizards and one on frogs for five dollars each, and one on trying to cultivate wild strawberries for ten dollars. My first poem sold for twenty-five dollars and ran three pages in *The American Mercury*. My first story sold to *Story Magazine* for twenty-five dollars.

I was slower than other authors in getting high prices. I would rather have more stories accepted and get lower fees. I believe in my father's philosophy never to overcharge but to work hard and long to accomplish one's aim. He believed in starting at the bottom. He said that if a man began at the top he had only one way to travel and that way was down.

Like Dad, I've tried to make my money count. I have never

squandered it, I don't believe in gambling. There isn't anything creative about gambling. I simply run the risk, when I gamble, of taking what the other fellow has earned. And he runs the risk of taking what I have earned. The part that isn't trickery is luck. It simply doesn't pay. In my early youth I traced my ancestors back for three generations and learned not one of them had ever gambled. They just didn't believe in gambling, though they were rough men, some of them. My father couldn't even play cards. He regarded them as a waste of time and would never allow a deck in the house.

Since I don't drink, I have never spent money on liquor. I've spent my money for things that I thought counted: books, music, land, and travel. And I've used a portion to help other people, not much because I haven't earned very much. When I lost a dollar, I grieved. If I could have given it away, could have known that it counted for something, then I would not have grieved. This conservatism springs from my ancestry, my training, and my experiences in life, but in particular from my father.

My father used to rant and rave about how our neighbors treated their most valuable possession, land. He always told me that, if I made money and could get enough ahead, I should buy land. This is what I have done since I have been twenty-two years old. For the last twenty-five years I have bought adjoining farms from one acre to 263 acres, until I now have 758.5 acres of hill and bottom land. I have combined several small farms into my one big farm. Now people criticize me for owning so much land. Some say I'm greedy, others that I'm foolish. But I let them criticize, I think I know what I am doing. I am taking care of this land for those yet to be born.

People around me butcher timber, burn land over to kill snakes, and let their soil erode. I cannot tolerate their collective wisdom, which produces such waste and destruction. I have wished a hundred times that our timbered areas were under the supervision of the state Forest Service. Someday we're not going to have anything left.

My father taught me so many things about conservation of land. He taught me never to let a ditch start in one of my fields. If one did start, he knew how to stop it, though he didn't know how to measure how much topsoil went down that ditch. He said, "While you try to measure, I can have it stopped." And it was true. He plowed with the contour of the slopes long before our modern conservationists began to write essays advising it. He wouldn't let us draw a plow downhill. His fields were never hurt by erosion.

When I bought my "worthless" acres, the timber had been cut and these acres were considered wasteland. My father said I should buy them while I was a young man and hold onto them, for before I was very old, they would be covered with timber and would be considered valuable. He told me to let trees and wild flowers grow, keep forest fires away, work to prevent erosion, and wait for the timber to build a new topsoil. This is what has happened. People drive out here from the cities to get my leaf-rot topsoil for their flowerpots. I let them have it, for there is so much of it now.

I didn't collect these acres for profit. But right now I could sell them for three times as much money as I have invested in them. My father had good judgment. He himself didn't make enough money to buy many acres. If he had, he would have taken care of this land for posterity. My father and I often talked about the future of this land. He had me look up the population of the United States when his father, Mitchell Stuart, was born in 1832. The census taken two years before his birth showed there were 12,866,020 inhabitants in this country. In 1880, when my father was born, there were 50,155,783. In 1907, when I was born, there were almost 90,-000,000 living this country. From my grandfather's birth to my daughter's, the population of this country had multiplied almost thirteen times. In 1950, when my father was seventy years old, the population was approximately 150,000,000. It had multiplied three times in his life, and at his death, when he was almost seventy-five, the population was near 165,000,000.

My father always said land didn't grow but populations did and we had to save our land for the generations to come.

Then he would walk or ride with me over this community, pointing out the old worn-out fields, worthless and in broomsedge and highly eroded now, where there had been big trees when he was a boy. "I remember when this field produced a hundred bushels of corn to the acre," he would say. "I saw tobacco grow here higher

than my head. I've cradled wheat here that was shoulder-high."
Then he'd shake his head and point. "Now look, won't you!"

Never let fire burn over your land if you can prevent it, he advised. Everything on the soil should rot and go back to rich dirt,
not to ashes. He spoke about all the lizards, birds, and frogs—nature's
great flycatchers—killed by fires. He spoke of the quail, young
rabbits, and possums that were usually killed, though the snakes
often crawled away. He spoke of the young trees with scorched
sides which, in later years, when they grew up to be saw timber,
would have rotted butts where the fire had scarred them as saplings.

My father had seen his own father cut giant saw timber, pile
it up into log heaps, and burn these trees. Now when he returned
to his native Lawrence County, Kentucky, and looked at these hills
which my grandfather cleared and farmed and on which he raised
wonderful crops, he saw ragged slopes with deep ditches, dwarfed
seedling pines, and the yellow dirt showing through the thin coat
of summer grass. "Look at that hill, won't you," he said once when
we visited his old home together. "It should never have been cleared
in the first place. It should have been let grow in timber and the
large trees cut about every twenty years."

"A man doesn't have to read about these things," he would say.
"All he has to do is to keep his eyes open to see what has happened
to the land. It gets thinner each year. Don't you care what people
say about you! Go on and buy more land, and conserve it."

And this is what I have done. I have lived in this valley all my
life, and I own these acres in my heart. Man can never own them as
securely by deed, for the land belongs to the people who love it
and to the future generations of Americans. Every man should be a
conservationist. We who pass this way once do not have the right to
destroy what belongs to others yet to come.

I X

Poison vine never would poison me. It would never poison
my father or my brother. My father was one of the two men in a
railroad section crew of eight to sixteen men it wouldn't poison, so
he was selected to mow through the poison vine along the section

right of way. Poison vine wouldn't poison a one of the boys I used to run with in my early days. Big Aaron and Little Ed Howard, Glen and Frank Hilton, Aubrey Greene, Kenneth Brown, or any of the others on a long list. A man that was bothered by poison vine we looked upon as weak. We always thought poison vine was something which affected women. Yet many of the women I knew it wouldn't poison either, including my mother and one of my sisters, though it would poison my two other sisters.

Over the years I have seen so many people poisoned by poison vine that I have developed a theory. It is simply that few real children of nature are poisoned by the vine.

By children of nature I mean people who live and work on the outside with growing things. I mean people who love the great out-of-doors and like to touch plants with their hands. These are the ones immune to poison vine. These are the children of nature.

My mother, for one, worked on the outside in her yard and garden more than she did inside. In addition, she went to the cornfield and the tobacco and cane patches, where she used a hoe and pulled weeds like a man. Mom liked the out-of-doors, the earth and sky, the winds blowing over her. She liked to hoe up a crippled plant to see if she could make it live. Poison vine never meant anything to my mother. She pulled it up with her bare hands as the rest of us did, and she was never poisoned in her whole life. My sister Mary, who also worked in the fields and garden and yard with us, never had any kind of vine or weed poison her either.

Not a one in our family ever had hay fever, though some of our friends in town had it so bad they had to change climates for relief. Hay fever is caused by the dust from ragweed blossoms, and we lived among fields of ragweed. It grew up on the wheatfields after wheat was cut. It came up in the potato patches after we had worked them the last time. It grew along the paths, and we knocked the sulphur dust from its blossoms as we passed. All our lives we grew up with the ragweed, season after season, and breathed its dust. Perhaps this is what made us immune to it and why we were never bothered with hay fever. We might have sneezed a few times, but that was all.

Those of my people on my mother's side who moved to the

factories in Ohio now get hay fever when they return. They come
back to W-Hollow and get poisoned by poison vine. They have to
take shots for poison vine and go to a cooler climate away from
ragweed to get rid of hay fever. But not one of the boys I grew up
with who has stayed here in the valley has ever had hay fever or
been poisoned by vines. They remained children of nature.

I had to do some thinking on this subject when I married Naomi
Deane Norris, a girl who had grown up in the small town of Greenup.
She had spent most of her time indoors, studying and working in
her home and in the schoolroom. When we started housekeeping
in W-Hollow, where we live today, she was poisoned by poison
vine by just looking at it on a hot day. She sneezed and sneezed
when she inhaled the pollen dust from ragweeds, hay, blossoms,
and the ripened seeds of almost any tree, flower, or plant. She
seemed to be allergic to everything that grew. When she touched a
flower, grass, or plant, she was poisoned. We went to doctors, and
she took shots and medicines. Some even suggested that we might
have to move out of the valley. But I told her to continue her work
on the outside and predicted that soon she would be immune to
most of the things that plagued her.

Today she works in the flowers from early spring until late
autumn. She is never poisoned by touching a flower. The sulphur
dust from the ragweed never bothers her. Though she is not ven-
turesome enough to show how she can handle poison vine without
its poisoning her, I truly think she could.

Since my heart attack, I have not been out with nature as much
as I like. My face is still pale, my hands soft, since I am not allowed
to do manual labor. I wonder what all this will do to my immunity.
Will I sneeze at the weed and be poisoned by the ivy? Another
thing—for fear of the copperhead, I no longer go regularly to the
blackberry field in season and pick wild berries. If you're in good
physical condition when you're bitten by a copperhead, your
chances of living are better than fifty-fifty. But if you've suffered
permanent heart damage, as I have, then your chances of surviving
a copperhead bite are more limited.

I used to like to wade into a patch of poison vine on the hottest
day in July and pull it out by the roots with my hands. I've scratched

my initials on my arms with it to show my friends it wouldn't poison me. Then I'd explain why. I had worked among poison vines from morning until night during the summer growing season. I'd become a brother to them.

But now I wonder how long I can stay indoors and still continue to be one of nature's children.

X

The noise was louder than a fast-blowing October wind in the crisp brown autumn leaves still clinging to the whiteoaks. But on this hot July day there was no wind blowing. On the high hill facing our house a rain crow croaked for rain, and somewhere among the water-lily leaves in the creek that flows under our house bullfrogs grunted hoarsely to each other now and then. But these had been the only sounds until Jane and I, sitting at the picnic table under the shade of our dogwoods in the back yard, heard this noise like the wind in the sear brown autumn leaves.

"What is it, Daddy?" Jane asked as we jumped up from the table.

"Listen," I said. Then I saw it. "Look!"

"Oh, Daddy," she screamed, "don't let it do that!"

I had had the bushes, weeds, and bullgrass scythed in my young peach orchard on the steep slope just across the stream. The July sun in the past three days had dried the leaves on everything scythed until they were as sear as October's frostbitten whiteoak leaves.

"Stop it!" I shouted.

I clapped my hands to make more noise to prevent what we were about to see. Jane screamed and turned her head in the opposite direction.

The noises we made didn't stop the long blacksnake. The lean bullfrog was coming down the steep slope faster than a bowling ball, and each time he hit the ground the snake tried to grab him. I'd never seen a frog jump for his life like this one was jumping. Each time he landed, I thought the snake would get him. But the frog would rise into the air faster than a June bug.

"Don't let it catch the frog, Daddy!" Jane cried.

Since the blacksnake hears with his tongue, this one didn't hear

Jane's screams and my shouting and hand clapping. He kept his tongue inside his mouth, determined to get the frog. He was going to chase him all the way to the creek. But just as the frog reached the foot of the steep slope and started to hop across the little bottom to the creek bank, the blacksnake caught him after one last long hop. Jane turned around just in time to see it.

"Don't cry any more, Jane," I said. "Help me, and we'll save the frog."

I hurried for the footlog that lay across the little stream. Jane was at my heels. We crossed the broad-hewn log and in a few seconds were standing over the big snake lying there in the grass swallowing the frog. We saw the frog's hind feet go in just as we got there. When the blacksnake saw us, he started crawling back toward the hill. But the frog inside him made a big hump in his long, trim body. And this big hump served as a brake and slowed him down.

Part way up the hill, he found a hole in the ground made by a baby-handed mole. He stuck his head inside and crawled in up to the hump in his body. But this hump again served as a brake.

"Goody, you can't get away," Jane said. "It serves you right. You swallowed poor little frog!"

I reached down and caught the snake by the tail and lifted him up. He was almost as long as I was tall, big enough to swallow the frog easily. And he would have enjoyed his meal had Jane and I not come running to disturb him in the first stages of digestion.

"Poor frog was trying to get back to his home in the water lilies," Jane said. "What are you going to do to that old snake, Daddy? Aren't you going to kill him?"

"Not if I can help it," I said.

The snake squirmed in the wind as I held him upside down and shook him. I hoped he might lose the frog, but he didn't.

"But, Daddy, he's killed the frog," Jane said.

"No, he hasn't," I said. "Not yet."

"But the frog can't breathe."

"Frogs stay under water without air over a minute sometimes. It's not dead yet."

I laid the squirming snake on the close-cut grass in our yard.

Like most blacksnakes, he was a big fellow, but not dangerous. He'd crawl away from a person any time. He didn't want trouble. All he wanted was something to eat—a mouse, bird, frog, young rabbit, or baby-handed mole.

"Get me three forked sticks, Jane," I said. "Get them in a hurry if you want to save the frog. Up there where they scythed over the peach orchard."

"How big?"

"Big enough to fit over the snake's back and fasten in the ground," I said. "Hurry!"

Jane ran as fast as her legs would take her up the steep bank while I held the snake by the tail. Even if I had turned him loose, it would have been difficult for him to crawl away with the big knot still so near his head.

Jane came running with the three forked sticks. One I put over the snake's body near his head. I pushed it down into the ground far enough to hold him. Then I placed the second fork over the snake's body on the other side of the frog. By then I had my knife out of my pocket and was figuring the right place to make the incision. I put the third fork over the snake to hold the rest of his body in line. I knew he would squirm when I went to work.

My knife blade was sharp. I keep it that way for farm use. When I applied the sharp blade to the snake's tough skin, he flinched. I'd seen so many snake skeletons on our farm that I knew a little about the blacksnake's anatomy. I'd have to cut through his ribs to get to the frog, and I would have to be careful not to go too deep and cut the frog. He'd already had enough punishment. Jane stood by and watched me cut through the skin, then the ribs. Slowly now I opened the snake until Jane could see the frog. But my incision was not big enough to get the frog through, so I had to make it longer.

In a matter of seconds, I got the frog by the hind feet; carefully, slowly, I pulled him through the incision. I did as little harm to the snake as I could. He was squirming about wildly until Jane had to push down on the forks. Then he pushed the third one all the way up, but Jane quickly reset it. When I laid the frog on the close-cut grass stubble, he seemed lifeless.

"You're too late, Daddy," Jane said. "The frog is dead."

"Maybe not. Go to the spigot and get some water and pour it over him."

Jane ran to the spigot for a dipper. She poured the cool water slowly over the frog while I worked on the snake.

"Daddy, he opened one eye," she shouted.

"Pour more water on him," I said. "He'll open both eyes."

When Jane returned with more water, the frog had both eyes open and was sitting up. Jane poured the cool water on him and he moved off a few inches.

"He's going to be all right, Jane," I said. "Don't worry any more about the frog. But think of this poor gentle blacksnake. He worked hard to get himself a meal. Now we've taken it away from him and cut him up to do it. We've got to save the snake."

"Let him die, Daddy! Snakes are killers."

"So are frogs," I said. "So are birds and moles. They kill each other, plants, insects, flies, worms, bugs, for food. Each kills to survive."

"Not anything will eat a snake, Daddy."

"Snakes kill each other," I said. "And chicken hawks and owls kill snakes."

Jane stood looking first at the frog, which was taking short, slow hops toward the stream, then at the incision in the writhing snake.

"You like the fireflies in the evening, don't you?" I said to Jane. "You refuse to catch them and put them in a bottle like other boys and girls. You say, 'Daddy, I like to watch them light their own way through a dark night world.' Well, the frogs sit down there on the water-lily leaves and reach up and catch the fireflies when they turn on their lights at night. That frog was up there in the peach orchard, wasn't he? He was up there on top of the hill because there are plenty of greenflies in the hot sunlight. He was up there getting his dinner, and the snake was up there hunting his. So, this happened."

"Daddy, what can we do now to save the snake?"

"Run to the house and ask your mother for the turpentine bottle," I said. "Look in the toolbox in the shed for that role of adhesive tape."

I had to set the forks deeper into the ground. The big blacksnake didn't like his wound, and he didn't appreciate being held close against the ground so he could barely move.

When Jane returned with the turpentine and adhesive tape, the frog had hopped down to the creek. He was back home. When night came, he would be singing with his friends and catching the fireflies from a lily leaf.

I poured some turpentine on the incision, and the snake bounced right off the ground.

"Now, hold these forks down real tight, Jane."

Jane held the forks down on each side of the incision while the blacksnake writhed as if it were in much pain. The turpentine must have smarted some. I unrolled the adhesive tape and cut several short strips in a hurry. Then, down on my knees, I fastened a piece of tape on one side of the incision and drew the wound closed before I clamped the tape to the other side. I used the tape from one end of the incision to the other. I had made the cut high enough so that when I used the tape, it wouldn't wrap too low around his body and interfere with his crawling. I wanted to be sure I'd done a decent job—one that would give this big harmless snake whose dinner we had robbed a chance to live.

"Now take the forks up," I told Jane. "Let's see if he can't crawl away quicker than when he had the frog inside.

Warily Jane remove each fork, and the big blacksnake crawled away, very slowly at first. He held his head high in the air, his tongue out to catch the sounds. He wasn't taking any more chances.

"The frog got back to the creek, and he's going back to the peach orchard," I said. "Back home to the sunny south hillside."

"But, Daddy, why did we do all this to save a snake?" Jane asked. "And come to think of it, after your telling me about the frogs catching my fireflies, I wonder why we saved the frog."

"They're both our friends, Jane," I said. "If it weren't for the frogs, I don't know what we'd do about bugs and insects. If it weren't for the blacksnakes, the moles would eat our garden. That snake tried to get into that baby-handed mole's hole up there. He's been in it before, probably made a meal there once on baby-handed moles. Blacksnakes are friends to the farmers."

But Jane wasn't listening. She was watching our big blacksnake, who had reached the steep slope. He turned and looked back at us.

"I don't believe he holds anything against us, do you, Daddy?" Jane asked.

X I

Where the gray bodies of sassafras, not much larger than my wrist, grew from a sterile W-Hollow hill slope, I stood looking at the red and yellow leaves that had already fallen to the ground. This was hard for me to believe, that the sassafras had started shedding leaves this early. The yellow and red leaves that lay on the ground were drops of blood which had passed through the veins of this tree. These leaves had been created from the sustenance drawn from a soil too thin to grow anything but sassafras, scrubby pine, green brier, and sawbrier.

I walked up closer to the sassafras thicket and picked up a small handful of leaves from under one of the trees. I squeezed them into a soft ball in my hand. I held beauty within my hand. I held the blood of the sassafras. I crumbled these leaves in my hand and threw the contents upon this yellow earth. There wasn't a topsoil here. But the sassafras roots went down and held firmly in the yellow dirt. They grew here, thrived, and multiplied.

My father's plow, pulled by a skinny mule, had once turned over this slope. My father's skinny hands with the big blue veins guided the handles of the plow he had made of yellow locust, strong and durable to break the roots in this rugged land. My mother's hoe cut the weeds on this slope and raked loose dirt around the fragile stalks of corn. And I followed my mother, imitating her with a long gooseneck hoe in the hot summer sun.

Before we cleared this hill, almost forty years ago, the blackberry briers and red sumacs grew here. But after we farmed this steep slope a number of years and the eroding elements had knifed into its flank, the soil was too thin for the wild blackberry briers and the sumacs to take over again. So the sassafras moved in.

My father, mother, and I, and our little skinny mule, Barney, took sustenance from this soil when it should have been left in the earth. We didn't own this land. We rented it. We cleared and plowed this land, planted our own seed, furnished our own mule, plow, hoes, labor, and sweat. We learned to be patient and coax corn to grow here. And we prayed for rain. If we got plenty of rain, we grew fairly large corn and were modestly paid for our efforts.

If we had blue skies and a season so dry the rain crow croaked for more rain, then we grew "bumblebee corn." A bumblebee could sit in the tassel of this corn and search for nectar while his stinger touched the dry, dusty ground. This was our joke. My parents were young and could spend their sweat freely then, could laugh at defeat. Steep hills were no obstacles to our plow and hoes. We conquered them. We scratched the surface of this rugged earth for our bread. We planted our salty sweat upon the sun-dried land our bull-tongue plow had furrowed. We planted our sweat along with our corn, beans, and pumpkins. We couldn't lose.

Today the prints of our old furrows are under these tall sassafras trees. These old furrows are the dim receipts by which this sweat-salted earth reminds us of our labors. This land fed our skinny mule, Barney, corn and fodder, too. Our mule was an essential part of our family. He pulled us to town in an express wagon loaded with sweet potatoes we raised on creek bottoms, wild blackberries we gathered in season from the hills, and bushels of green beans, pumpkins, and melons.

Our cows that furnished us sweet milk, buttermilk, and butter were fed from the corn that grew from this steep slope. We couldn't do without a cow, and often we had two. We liked cold milk, and we liked golden butter melting on our hot cornbread. Our cows got the soft ears of corn, they got the choice bundles of fodder. Our cows meant so much to us.

The two hogs we always fattened in autumn were fed from corn that grew on this slope. Pork was our main source of meat, except for the wild game we killed. We smoked our hams and shoulders with green hickory or with sassafras. What corn was left, the loose grains on our crib floor, we shoveled up and threw out to the chickens. Not a grain of our corn was wasted.

The very best ears of corn were selected for next year's seed and put away where mice couldn't get to them. Usually we sacked this corn and tied the sack up to a rafter in the crib. Our next best

ears of corn were selected for our bread. Cornbread was the backbone of our diet. Cornbread gave us strength. And we had to have
strength to dig and plow the rugged slopes, to be active and enduring
people.

Now these old furrows are under the sassafras that nature has
sent to this hill to prevent erosion. No one farms these hills now.
I don't know a man in this county who would work the way we used
to work for our bread. Some sort of pension would be sought instead.
This rugged slope doesn't support cows, mule, swine, or people
today. It supports the sassafras.

The sassafras is the presiding tree in the United States. It pre-
sides over what has been. It comes to cover the old scars. Here on
this slope it is trying to blot out the last remaining receipts that
show where we made our bread.

X I I

My father was an earth poet who loved the land and
everything on it. He liked to watch things grow. From the time I
was big enough for him to lead me by the hand, I went with him
over the farm. If I couldn't walk all the way in those early days, he'd
carry me on his back. I learned to love many of the things he loved.

I went with my father to so many fields over the years and
listened to him talk so often about their beauty that I know now
that he had wonderful thoughts which should have been written
down. Thoughts came to him faster than a hummingbird flits from
one blossom to another.

Sometime in the dim past of my boyhood, my father unloaded
me from his back under some whiteoak trees just beginning to leaf.
"Look at this hill, son," he said, gesturing broadly with a sweep
of his hand. "Look up that steep hill toward the sky. See how pretty
that new-ground corn is."

This was the first field I can remember my father's taking me to
see. The rows of corn curved like dark-green rainbows around a high
slope with a valley and its little tributaries running down through
the center. The corn blades rustled in the wind, and my father said
he could understand what the corn blades were saying. He told me
they whispered to each other, and this was hard for me to believe.

I reasoned that before anything could speak or make a sound it had to have a mouth. When my father said the corn could talk, I got down on my knees and looked a stalk over.

"This corn hasn't got a mouth," I told my father. "How can anything talk when it doesn't have a mouth?"

He laughed like the wind in the corn and hugged me to his knees, and we went on.

On a Sunday, when my mother and sisters were at a country church, my father took me by the hand and led me across two valleys to a cove where once giant beech timber had stood. He was always restless on Sundays, eager to get back to the fields in which he worked all week. He had cleared a piece of this land to raise white corn, which he planned to have ground for meal to make our bread. He thought this cove was suited to white corn. He called it Johnson County corn. Someone had brought the seed from the Big Sandy River, in the county where my father was born and lived until he was sixteen. When he had cleared this cove, set fire to the giant beech tops, and left ash over the new ground, he thought this earth would produce cornfield beans, too. In every other hill of corn he had planted beans. Now these beans ran up the cornstalks and weighted them with hanging pods of young, tender beans. Pictures I saw later of Jack and the Beanstalk always reminded me of this tall corn with bean vines winding around the stalks up to the tassels.

But the one thing my father had brought me to see that delighted him most was the pumpkins. I'd never seen so many pumpkins with long necks and small bodies. Pumpkins as big around as the bottom of a flour barrel were sitting in the furrows beneath the tall corn, immovable as rocks. There were pumpkins, and more pumpkins, of all colors—yellow and white, green and brown.

"Look at this, won't you," my father said. "Look what corn, what beans, what pumpkins. Corn ears so big they lean the cornstalks. Beans as thick as honey-locust beans on the honey-locust tree. And pumpkins thicker than the stumps in this new ground. I could walk all over this field on pumpkins and never step on the ground."

He looked upon the beauty of this cove he had cleared and his three crops growing there. He rarely figured a field in dollars and cents. Although he never wasted a dollar, money didn't mean everything to him. He liked to see the beauty of growing things on the land. He carried this beauty in his mind.

Once, when we were walking between cornfields on a rainy Sunday afternoon, he pointed to a redbird on its nest in a locust tree, a redbird with shiny red feathers against the dark background of a nest. It was just another bird's nest to me until he whispered, "Ever see anything as pretty as what the raindrops do to that red-bird sitting on her dark nest?" From this day on, I have liked to see birds, especially redbirds, sitting on their nests in the rain. But my father was the first one to make me see the beauty.

He used to talk about the beauty of a rooster redbird, pheasant, chicken hawk, hoot owl, and turkey gobbler. He pointed out the color of the neck, tail, and wing feathers. Then he taught me how to tell a stud terrapin from a female, a male turtle from the female, a bull blacksnake from a female. My father knew all these things. He learned them in his own way. He observed so closely that he could tell the male from the female in any species, even the gray lizard, which is most difficult.

"A blacksnake is a pretty thing," he once said to me, "so shiny and black in the spring sun after he sheds his winter skin."

He was the first man I ever heard say a snake was pretty. I never forgot his saying it. I can even remember the sumac thicket where we saw the blacksnake.

He saw more beauty in trees than any man I have ever known. He would walk through a strange forest laying his hand upon the trees, saying this oak or that pine, that beech or poplar, was a beautiful tree. Then he would single out other trees and say they should be cut. He would always give his reasons for cutting a tree: too many trees on a root stool, too thick, one damaged by fire at the butt, one leaning against another, too many on the ground, or the soil not deep enough above a ledge of rocks to support them.

Then there were the hundreds of times my father took me to the hills to see wild flowers. I thought it was silly at first. He would sit on a dead log, maybe one covered with wild moss, somewhere under the tall beech trees, listening to the wind in the canopy of leaves above, looking at a clump of violets or percoon growing beside a rotted log. He could sit there enjoying himself indefinitely. Only when the sun went down would we get up and start for home.

My father wouldn't break the Sabbath by working, except in an emergency. He would follow a cow that was overdue to calve. He would watch over ewes in the same manner. He followed them to the high cliffs and helped them deliver their lambs, saving their lives. He would do such things on Sundays, and he would fight forest fires. But he always said he could make a living working six days in the week. Yet he was restless on Sundays. He just had to walk around and look over his fields and enjoy them.

Sometimes when I went with my father to a field, we'd cross a stream, and he'd stop the horse, sit down on the bank in the shade, and watch the flow of water. He'd watch minnows in a deep hole. He wouldn't say a word, and I wouldn't either. I'd look all around, wondering what he'd seen to make him stop, but I never would ask him. When he got through looking, he'd tell me why he'd stopped. Sometimes he wouldn't. Then we'd go on to the field together, and he'd work furiously to make up for the time he had lost while he sat beside the stream and watched the clean water flowing over the sand and gravel to some far-off place beyond his little hill world.

My father didn't have to travel over the country searching for something beautiful to see. He didn't have to go away to find beauty, for he found it everywhere around him. He had eyes to find it. He had a mind to know it. He had a heart to appreciate it. He was an uneducated poet of this earth. And if anybody had told him that he was, he wouldn't have understood. He would have turned and walked away without saying anything.

In the winter, when snow was over the ground and the stars glistened, he'd go to the barn to feed the livestock at four in the morning. I have seen him put corn in the feedboxes for the horses and mules, then go out and stand and look at the morning moon. He once told me he always kept a horse with a flaxen mane and tail because he liked to see one run in the moonlight with his mane arched high and his tail floating on the wind.

I've gone out early in the morning with him, and he's shown me Jack Frost's beautiful architecture, which lasted only until the sun came up. This used to be one of the games my father played with me on a cold frosty morning. He showed me all the designs that I would never have found without him. Today, I cannot look at white fields of frost on early winter mornings and not think of him.

When spring returned, he was always taking me someplace to show me a new tree he had found, or a pretty red mushroom growing on a rotting stump in some deep hollow. He found so many strange and beautiful things that I tried to rival him by making discoveries, too. I looked into the out-of-way and unexpected places to find the beautiful and the unusual.

Once, in autumn, we went to the pasture field to hunt pawpaws. "Look at the golden meat and the big brown seeds like the seeds of melon or a pumpkin," he said. "Did you ever taste a banana in your life that was as good as a pawpaw? Did you ever see anything prettier than the clean sweet golden fruit of a pawpaw?" I never forgot how he described a pawpaw, and I've always liked their taste.

He took me to the first persimmon grove I ever saw. This was after frost, and the persimmons had ripened and had fallen from the trees. "The persimmon is a candy tree," he said. "It really should have been called the gumdrop tree." I was a small boy then, but ever since I've seen ripe persimmons after frost as brown gumdrops.

I didn't get the idea of dead leaves being golden ships on the sea from a storybook. And neither did my father, for he had never read a book in his life—he couldn't read. He'd never had a book read to him either. It was in October, and we were sitting on the bank of W-Branch. We were watching the blue autumn water slide swiftly over the slate rocks. My father picked up leaves that were shaped like little ships and dropped them into the water.

"These are ships on swift water," he told me, "going to far-off lands where strangers will see them." He had a special love for autumn leaves, and he'd pick them up when we were out walking and ask me to identify them. He'd talk about how pretty each leaf was and how a leaf was prettier after it was dead than it was alive and growing.

Many people thought my father was just a one-horse farmer who never got much out of life. They saw only a little man, dressed in clean, patched overalls, with calloused and brier-scratched hands.

They often saw the beard long on his face. And they saw him go off and just stand in a field and look at something. They thought he was moody. Well, he was that all right, but when he was standing there and people thought he was looking into space, he was looking at a flower or a mushroom or a new bug he'd discovered for the first time. And when he looked up into a tree, he wasn't searching for a hornet's nest to burn or a bird's nest to rob. He wasn't trying to find a bee tree. He was just looking closely at the beauty in one of a million trees. And among the millions, he always found one different enough to excite him.

No one who really knew him ever felt sorry for my father. Any feeling of pity turned to envy. For my father had a world of his own, larger and richer than the vast earth that world travelers know. He found more beauty in his acres and square miles than poets who have written a half-dozen books. Only my father couldn't write down the words to express his thoughts. He had no common symbols by which to share his wealth. He was a poet who lived his life upon this earth and never left a line of poetry—except to those of us who lived with him.

A U G U S T

The singing of the cicada has always meant August to me. Its energetic, monotonous song filled so many hot, still days of my youth. Walking along the narrow paths through these hills, I'd hear the cicadas in the tall trees, I'd race a few steps under them when they were in flight, I'd wonder at their loud, rhythmic voices that on a quiet August morning could be heard a quarter of a mile away.

The cicada is also called the harvest fly, though wheat, rye, barley, and oats are harvested before he arrives and he is gone before corn-cutting time. Some call him the jarfly (the name I like best) because the nearer you get to him the more his song seems to be vibrating in a jar. This broad-backed fly is of the locust family and lays its eggs in the ground, where they are hatched and larva comes up from the earth.

The cicada has a rough underbelly and six rough legs. It has a long proboscis, used for extracting liquids from flowers and leaves and water from the old stumps and the warm wet sands along streams. Near its proboscis are two feelers that extend outward and curve back like a pair of horns. Beneath the feelers and above the proboscis are lines like those in the front grillwork on modern automobiles. The large, bulging eyes, set far apart in the corners of the square, strong face, resemble headlights.

The design of the cicada's transparent wings, however, is one that man has not imitated. The powerful front wings, attached to the cicada's shoulders, have a spread wider than twice the length of its body. A second pair of wings, about half the length of the first, is set just behind them. These two sets of wings can drive the cicada through the air with terrific speed. Never have I seen a cicada's transparent wings come apart, no matter how long and fast his flight, for these fibers of interlacing strength are beautifully engineered.

But it is the cicada's August singing that, over the years, has been absorbed by my brain and heart, just as the ink juices from the oak balls I gathered as a child were absorbed by the soft paper I spread them over.

I I

The day before yesterday, in the morning, I went back to visit Anthill. Beside the lilac bush and under the shade of the big poplar, I found the city of ants very much alive. Here they had lived for a number of years, expanding from a few small hills into a large city of ants. They had carried up dirt from below until they had made a soft little hill. Now they were running in all directions in the morning sun.

I looked at their legion of guards. They were big strong black fellows, perhaps chosen especially for their size to protect their city. I watched them walking over their military roads. Other ants left the city and roamed over our back yard in search of food. Through the grass stubble, they dragged home worms, butterflies, moths, grasshoppers, katydids, cutworms, and bread crumbs our birds hadn't eaten. They dragged loads many times their own size long distances to Anthill.

Somewhere down in the underground chambers of Anthill were

storage rooms for foods, depositories for ant eggs, nurseries for young ants. Somewhere down there sat the mayor, perhaps, directing the life of the city. I wondered what these inhabitants of Anthill would do in case of attack. What would happen if the guards found another race of ants on their premises ready to give them battle? It would be interesting to see if these industrious ants would fight for their city.

In the house I got three small white envelopes. Then I went back to the walk in front of the smokehouse, where dozens of large red ants were constantly running up and down and across the cement. I caught over one hundred large red ants and put them inside the three envelopes, which I had perforated with a pin. I sealed them and stuck them down in my shirt pocket. Then I took my red-ant troops to attack the city of Anthill.

When I opened the first envelope and dumped the red ants down on Anthill, as if they were paratroopers descending from the skies, the big black ant guards met them head-on to defend their city. Two black ants would grab a red ant, and they wouldn't stop pulling at him until he was finished. If they happened to be pulling in different ways, they would often pull the red ant in two. Then each made off with a portion of the body to a cemetery or a storehouse below. In a very few minutes these big guards had polished off the first company of red ants I had dumped down on Anthill.

Now the word had spread through all Anthill, and troubled citizens came running to the surface from all directions, obviously excited over what had happened. Since they were running wildly over Anthill seemingly in search of more red ants to conquer, I obliged them by dumping two more companies of paratroopers from the low skies over Anthill. At first the black ants went after them one for one. The red ants didn't know exactly who their attackers were or how they got there, but they knew they were in a position where they were compelled to fight. And being a brave species—as are all ants, large or small, that I have watched—many waged a brilliant battle. But most of them wanted to get away. They weren't in their home territory. This strange land was more than fifty feet away, over the close-cut back-yard grass, from their native area of our yard. Many tried to escape on the military roads but were met by strong 'detachments of black ants which immediately gave battle. Ants died on both sides, but more red than black. I watched red ants being carried downstairs in Anthill while they were still alive and kicking.

Now the red ants were outnumbered two to one, for dozens of black ants had swarmed up on the hill from their underground city. More quickly than I thought possible, they subdued the three companies of red ants. Not one escaped that I could see to carry the sad news back to the packs of wild red ants that roamed over our back yard. The excited black ants ran all over Anthill until sundown. They seemed to be hunting for more red ants to pull apart and take downstairs. They ran out into the stubbled grass, and they climbed the soft ridges that old mole had made with his long snoot and his strong forepaws. They ran in widening circles around Anthill looking for these enemies until the shades of the lilac and the poplar lengthened over the yard. They had tasted victory and found it sweet.

Yesterday morning I thought I would balance the scales. The black ants were still strong. They hadn't lost nearly so heavily as the red ants. If I was going to promote an insect war, at least I should give each side an equal chance. Before breakfast I put bread crumbs on the walk in front of my writing room. I don't know where all the red ants came from. They must have smelled the bread crumbs, or maybe the first ants to the crumbs hurried back to tell others. I put thirty to forty ants in each envelope. I spent most of the morning gathering hundreds of red ants for the afternoon assault on Anthill. These were big strong country ants that didn't like to be confined in these small envelopes. I let them grow restless and heard them scratching on the stiff paper. I didn't care if they got a little mad and overanxious for their moment of battle to come.

At noon the first company of red ants fell from the skies upon Anthill. They were immediately met by the guards. Big black ants swarmed up from underground to overwhelm the already outnumbered red ants. But the battle wasn't going to be so onesided today. Hastily I reached for my envelopes and emptied one after the other onto Anthill. The red and the black mingled in combat. It was hard to see the ground under them. There were dead ants every-where, and living ants heaving their carcasses along the military roads. When the black ants, perhaps because they were fighting for their home, again seemed about to get the upper hand, I emptied my last two envelopes of reserve troops. Red ants went tumbling down through the skies.

More black ants came up to meet them, not the big, strong guardian blacks any more, but smaller artisan ants. But the reds, in equal battle at last, were no longer seeking routes of escape. They stuck it out, killing and being killed. Not a single black ant that I saw deserted his home. Now both red and black ants were being carried downstairs. I suddenly wondered what would happen if the red ants were victorious. Would they migrate from their distant part of the yard and take over Anthill? As the minutes passed into an hour, there were fewer and fewer able-bodied ants of either color left on Anthill. It was hard to tell which side had won.

I waited until this afternoon, the third day of battle, to find out. I thought that probably the black ants would have had time to recuperate and to finish off the last invader. I waited until I thought Anthill would be a place of activity again, as it had always been in spring, summer, and early autumn throughout the years.

Crossing the domain of the red ants near the kitchen, I was surprised to see only a very few scattered here and there. When I reached Anthill, I didn't see a guard on top of this city of ants. There was not a single ant crawling on the roads, the small and big turnpikes, which led to Anthill.

Anthill was quiet for the first time in three years. The big heap of soft dirt looked strangely empty. It was hard for me to believe there weren't any ants on Anthill under the lilac bush. So I picked up a stick under the big poplar and went back to Anthill and carefully removed some of the dirt. The ground beneath was honeycombed by small entrances.

In one place I found small ant's eggs. In another I found dead worms, bugs, a cricket, two grasshoppers, and crumbs of corn-bread. After a little more prodding with the poplar branch, I knew the reason why there wasn't any activity. I came upon dead black ants, dozens of them. Whether these had been buried or had crept below to die, I don't know. Then I found dozens of red ants, too, killed in the battle for Anthill and dragged below.

As far as I could tell they had fought to the last ant. Not a single black ant had deserted his city. At least I couldn't find a trace of one in the grass nearby. And there was not a living ant, red or black, in all of Anthill.

Now I had a depressed feeling about my black ants. I knew that I would miss them. I had carried them crumbs. I had made old mole crawl under their city once, something he would never do a second time. I had fed these ants grain that the birds hadn't eaten. My original question, Would the black ants defend their city? was answered. Now I wished that I had let it go unanswered, for I was lonely for them.

I I I

This morning, before the heat set in, I walked down the valley toward Dead Man's Curve and the Old Peddler's Well. The well had been filled up in recent years. But when Bill (Daddy) Myers, who owned this land for nearly half a century, was alive, he kept this well cleaned, and he, his wife, and two daughters drank water from it when they fetched their scythes and mowed their bottoms. They never used a mowing machine. They did it the hard way. All four of them could swing a scythe and work up a thirst. In those days the Peddler's Well was a famous spot. None of the children in the neighborhood would pass it after dark, and very few adults walked this way alone at night. They were usually in pairs or groups.

Back in 1850, everybody was afraid to pass this well, but with good reason. This was after a peddler was murdered here, his horse and goods stolen, and his blood-soaked buggy broken up and thrown into the well along with his body. He was fished from the water, the buggy and all the debris cleaned out, and the well's rock wall scalded and washed down so the water could be used again. But even a century later most people in W-Hollow wouldn't touch this water. They'd drink from W-Branch and risk getting typhoid

germs before they'd drink this haunted water from Peddler's Well.
Old Daddy Myers, his wife, and two daughters were not afraid to
drink this water. But they were about the only ones.

Old Mr. Daughtery claimed he saw lights around this well back
around 1850. He wasn't a cowardly or superstitious man, but he saw
so many lights in this area he wouldn't drink this water or pass
this way at night. His only son, W. W. Daughtery, often told me,
when, as a boy, I set strawberries for him at Buzzard Roost, about
the lights his father had seen. He claimed that he himself had an
awful scare there by the well. Walking by it one night, he heard a
flapping noise and looked up in time to see great white wings fan-
ning the air over his head. Other times he saw lights that stood about
waist-high in the middle of the road. When he got near, they disappeared. He told me he gritted his teeth and held his breath and
walked toward these lights. And when he got within a few feet
of one, it always went out.

Yes, W. W. Daughtery was always seeing lights at Peddler's
Well. He came into W-Hollow at all times of the night in his little
hugmetight, driving his old mare, Moll, who lived to be thirty-
one years old. For over forty years he courted a woman who lived
on his farm and never married her. Usually, after he left Sarah's
home, he tipped the bottle. He drank enough whisky, so I have
heard my father say, to float the biggest saw log in W-Hollow from
the source to the mouth of the W-Branch. So perhaps he did see
lights at Peddler's Well.

But when his sister, Mrs. Lydia Collins, told me *she* had seen
lights here, then I believed. I never knew a more truthful and fear-
less woman than Mrs. Lydia Collins. She said she had seen lights
rise up from the creek bottom near the well and trail off across
the sky, like flaming torches. And there is a possible explanation of
these lights—gas that bubbles up from the creek near the well. We
used to hold a lard can over the gas, and strike a match after re-
moving the can. I often wondered if lightning could have ignited
this escaped gas and caused these lights. For my own father and
mother and my cousin Ben Stuart had all seen these lights.

My uncle Martin Hilton, who moved to W-Hollow about 1908
and got a job mining coal in the E. K. Country, used to walk out

of W-Hollow before daylight and return after dark. He laughed
about people's seeing lights. He didn't believe in strange lights
and wouldn't let anybody talk to him about such nonsense. Uncle
Martin was a 220-pound, broad-shouldered man with big hands,
thick arms, and a neck that measured eighteen inches around.
He would have tackled a ghost and fought one. He wasn't afraid
of anything or anybody—until one morning at about four o'clock
when he passed Peddler's Well and heard a whirring sound overhead and looked up in time to see a pair of white wings pass over,
felt his bank cap, which fitted tightly over his head, being lifted off,
and saw it carried away. This scared my Uncle Martin. He never
made any more comments about the cowards who had seen strange
lights.

During the year of 1912 I was a little boy, five years old, living
in W-Hollow not two-tenths of a mile from Peddler's Well. My
sister and I played up and down W-Hollow. We went as far as
Peddler's Well and Dead Man's Curve in the daytime, but we never
dared go near there at night. We were afraid of Peddler's Well. We
had heard too many people tell what they had seen there. I wish
I'd been a little bolder. Then maybe today I could say I'd seen the
lights and heard the whirring of the wings myself.

Now cars breeze past this place. There are a few light head-ons
at Dead Man's Curve. The road is still as narrow as in the horse-
and-buggy days. But the great tall tales about this place have flown
with the winds of yesterday. Either ghosts are getting scarce or our
imaginations aren't what they used to be.

I V

The boy who mows around our place—his name is Hubert
and he stutters—was chased out of the bottoms yesterday by yellow
jackets. He was whooping and clawing the air and running to split
his trousers. I calmed him down and promised him the yellow
jackets would be gone in the morning.

I know about fighting yellow jackets. I've fought yellow jackets
since I was a small boy. I used to rush in with a small mattock
and dig up a nest while they stung me. I did, that is, if I didn't
get too many stings. Once we found a nest of yellow jackets in a

hollow beech log beside the road. The log was half rotten and wouldn't burn. We couldn't dig them out. I tried to chop them out with an ax. I plugged the hole up so they couldn't swarm from the log. I chopped in daylight when many of the yellow jackets were out working along the streams. But they came flying back and found me and set about trying to remove me. They landed on me and started stinging. There were so many I didn't know where to slap first. I dropped my ax and got away. They ate their way into the log. They made another entrance.

Later, we fought these yellow jackets long and hard by throwing rocks at them. Then we clubbed them. We beat them with leafy branches broken from trees. But we couldn't get them out of that log.

In August, these yellow jackets, made angry by our fighting them, stung the teacher when she walked past on her way to the Plum Grove School. Usually someone went early and stoned or clubbed them into submission before our teacher and the girls passed. But these yellow jackets were becoming mighty mean. There was a young girl at Plum Grove, Marcella Jones, who was very pretty. She always said I would be the first to conquer these yellow jackets, and I meant to prove her right. But I didn't know how I was going to do it.

I went back on the ridge to see Old Op Acres, who had lived in the woods with nature and knew about everything. He told me what to do. I followed his instructions and removed the yellow jackets from this beech log. I found a way, but I wouldn't tell another boy or even my teacher the secret. Op told me not to tell.

Yesterday Hubert quit work at five and hung his mowing scythe up over the limb of a tree that grew on the bank above W-Branch. He stuck his rock and file back in a hollow beech, where they would be kept dry if it rained during the night. Then he walked down the valley for home. I went to work.

In our utility room, which joins our garage and house, water seeps out from under the hill between the concrete blocks and over the floor. This makes a nice cool place for Mr. and Mrs. Toadie, who live in a damp corner behind a white oil tank. In the evenings they go out and catch themselves a mess of fireflies in our front yard, then hop back inside the utility room, where they are safe from snakes. We seldom close the garage or utility room door until very late.

I took the broom we keep in the utility room and used the handle to urge Mr. and Mrs. Toadie from under the oil tank. Then I took these two big hungry toads (one would have been sufficient if he were real hungry) to the ditch between the bottoms where the yellow jackets lived. At this time of day they were busier than ever. The heat had let up, and there was a line of golden jets streaming down in the afternoon air, landing and crawling into a dark hole in the earth. They were going to their secret underground hangar. And there was another golden line taking off every second into the still, sunless air.

I crawled over on my stomach and reached my hands over near this entrance and deposited Mr. Toadie very gently. One of the yellow jackets' guards not only stung my hand but bit me at the same time. My hand burned like fire in a couple of places. But Mr. Toadie had been placed gently and well. Mrs. Toadie was squirming in my hand, trying to get down onto the ground beside old Mr. Toadie. I sat her down a foot away, and in one hop she sat beside him.

Old Mr. Toadie opened his big mouth, and he got a yellow jacket. He got another. He got them as they came from the hangar underground. Mrs. Toadie turned her back to him and took them from the air as they came in for a landing. They went inside Mr. and Mrs. Toadie stinging, but this didn't hurt a pair of hungry frogs. I watched awhile and wondered how they could hold so much. I knew that by the time the sun had set all the yellow jackets would be gone.

This morning I went back to the ditch to get my frogs. They were there all right. They hadn't moved. But the sun was rising, and they would soon have moved away from the morning heat. They were squatting there side by side, so inflated that they looked like soft-shelled terrapins hugging the skin of earth. This was the time of morning that the yellow jackets would have been busy had they not been in captivity. They would have zoomed from their

home in a hurry and up into the bright morning air. There would
not have been a bit of dew on their wings.

This time the whole colony of beautiful yellow jackets hadn't
been brushed and clubbed to death. They hadn't been destroyed by
the heat and flames from gas or kerosene. They had been taken
in nature's way, as a tasty delicacy for frogs. There is another animal who loves them, too, but not any man I know likes to handle
him. He is the polecat. When he finds a nest of yellow jackets in
an old field or in the woods or by a stream, he digs them up. He
eats the old and young and all the food, similar to the bee bread
made by honeybees, that they have stored in the cells in their nests.
But the toads are the ones who really like the yellow jackets. A
frog may even gorge on them until he dies. This was the reason I
had brought two frogs instead of one.

I looked my toads over very carefully before I picked them up.
I supposed that all the yellow jackets were dead and partly digested
now and that there was no danger of their stinging me through
the thin skin that covered these sagging stomachs. So I picked up
old Mr. Toadie. He was content for me to pick him up or leave
him alone. He didn't want to hop. He felt like a soft ball of lead,
actually heavier than a terrapin, which is almost all bone and shell.
And Mrs. Toadie, who pretended she was going to hop but didn't,
was about as heavy. They looked at me and blinked their sleepy
eyes. They had overloaded their big stretchy stomachs and were
none too comfortable. I handled them carefully.

Old Op Acres knew the way to do it, and he had told me. I
thought about this true man of nature as I walked back home in the
rising morning sun with a loaded frog in each hand. They wouldn't
be leaving the utility room for a week. They were so heavy I worried about them.

V

One Saturday morning in August three years ago, my
father came and asked if he could take Jane to the far pasture with
him to see about water for the cattle. Jane was delighted to go, so
Naomi fixed sandwiches and filled a thermos jug with lemonade.

The pasture was more than a mile away. The day was beginning to get hot. Jane and her grandfather walked away talking and laughing. He had a hoe across his shoulder and the thermos jug in his hand. She carried a notebook and pencil and a sack filled with sandwiches.

The sun had set when Jane came home, very tired. Her grandfather didn't stop to tell us what they had done. He hurried on toward his home, for he always had work to do feeding his livestock and horses.

"Daddy, come here," Jane said. "I want to ask you something."

She was sitting with an open notebook in front of her. She had filled twenty or twenty-five pages in her close handwriting, and between the pages she had pressed a collection of leaves and barks. I knew my father hadn't cleaned many water holes for the cattle that day. I knew what he had been doing. He had been teaching Jane from the only book he knew.

"Daddy, what kind of a leaf is this?" Jane asked.

Without my seeing the tree, I couldn't identify this leaf.

"Grandpa said I'd catch you on this one," she said. "Grandpa said you spent too much time with other things and not enough with the things he had taught you."

"I can't identify it," I said.

Yes, my father's caught me, I thought. He's right. I've not spent the long hours in the woods alone reidentifying old trees and flowers and learning new ones. I was slipping.

"It's a red-oak leaf, Daddy," Jane said. Then she chuckled because I'd missed. "Grandpa showed me more red oaks than any other trees. And he told me you used to help him cut red-oak saw logs and make red-oak saplings into crossties. He said you used to help him clear ground and cut the small red-oak bushes. He laughed when he told me you wouldn't know a red-oak leaf any more."

Neither my father nor my mother ever looked into a scientific book on wild flowers, plants, and trees. My father had never gone to school, and my mother had finished only the second grade. But the whole face of this upheaved earth, the only section of America my father and mother ever knew, was their book. They read the earth's surface as children today read their textbooks. Before any of us entered school, we could identify from ninety to ninety-five per cent of the trees by leaf and bark and the flowers by petal and leaf and stem. We would have been mighty poor students if we had not been able to identify them after the games we had played.

Occasionally my mother would find a flower she couldn't identify. She would dig it up carefully and set it in our yard. Then she would ask everybody who came by what kind of a flower it was. Since the flower was put before us as a strange one without a name, we worked hard to find the answer. We couldn't rest until we had identified it. Finally, one of us would get the answer.

Very seldom was my father unable to name a tree. Once, I remember, he failed to identify a silver maple he found growing wild among other trees. This was the only one of its kind in the forest. He wasn't long learning its identity, for he went to a doctor in Ohio and found the same kind of tree growing in his yard. This was worth far more to him than the medicine he got from the doctor.

But the tree that gave him the most trouble he found growing in a deep valley among some beeches on a new farm we had bought. I would like to know how many men my father took to see this tree. There was a path worn to it from our home uphill and down valley and through the woods for more than a mile. He had James and me searching hill slope and valley for another of this strange species. Finally, after three years, we gave up. Then a member of the University of Michigan faculty visited me, and my father collared him and dragged him out, and he identified the tree. It was a coffee tree. And it is the only one I've ever heard of in this county. How it got on our place we will never know. But my father took great pride in this strange tree. He visited it often.

Once when my youngest sister was sick and we had the doctor, my father complained to him that he felt all right during the day but was short of breath at night. The doctor followed my father into the room where he slept. In this small room, the two windows and the door leading outside were shut tight. My father had built a deep shelf and a table which occupied over a third of the room, and both were full of potted flowers, tame and wild. Flowers in pots and shrubs in lard cans filled with rich loam from the woods were growing in this small room as if in a greenhouse. My father and mother's bed was crowded into one corner, for the vegetation didn't leave them much room.

"You mean to tell me you sleep in this room?" Doctor Morris said, looking at my father.

"Yes. What's wrong with sleeping in here?"

"Don't you know flowers use oxygen, too?" Doctor Morris said. "No wonder you're short of breath sleeping in a greenhouse! Looks like your wife would be, too."

"Well, she is," my father admitted. "But we never dreamed it was the flowers causing it."

We moved about two-thirds of these flowers to the cellar. But my father and mother wouldn't let all of them go. They disagreed on just about everything else—politics, religion, and each other's friends. But there were two things they were always agreed on: education for their children and love of the earth and everything that grows on it.

They were the least book-educated but the best earth-educated people I have ever known. No wonder my father was alarmed at our daughter. He had tested her, and although she was eleven, living in the country, she didn't know a persimmon from a black gum. He set about doing something about it that August Saturday three years ago.

V I

If there is a greater flycatcher in all America than the lizard, I would like to know what it is. The pewee, the toad frog, and the hornet are all clever, but the lizard is the slickest of them all. To observe this apparently sleepy fellow at his work is the only way to learn about him. When you see one lying on an old log or a rock in the sun, or scurrying over the scaly bark of a tree, sit down and watch him a few minutes.

Today, walking up our hill behind the house, I found five lizards. The first one caught ten flies in twelve minutes. The second one caught four flies in ten minutes. The third one didn't catch any.

The fourth one, lying on a lichened rock, caught eight flies, a firefly, and a bug. The fifth lizard, an active and aggressive fellow, caught sixteen flies in twenty minutes. And when I left them, each of these lizards was still hungry, still on the alert for the next mouthful.

Nature has prepared them well for the task. Their skin is almost the same color as the black- and gray-barked oaks and beeches they crawl over. All a lizard has to do is lie in wait with his mouth closed. When the right moment comes for him, he simply opens his mouth and catches the fly.

He is more agile than a frog. He catches more greenflies than a spider, and I have even seen him catch bean beetles. Find the farmer a better friend if you can.

V I I

There is an old superstition in this hill country that if one intentionally kills a toad frog his cow will give bloody milk. This is because of the kindly feeling farmers have toward the toad frog. I have never known country people in my lifetime who deliberately killed them. They know too well that a toad frog is another one of the farmer's valuable friends.

The toad frog is loved by children because of the many stories in which he is personified and dressed up in little boy's clothes. The toad is always a good character in stories, often the good-humored butt of jokes and pranks. Old Toad in *Wind in the Willows,* for instance, is a most colorful fellow. The toad is loved for his clumsy way of hopping around, for his gentleness and good nature. The gentle old hoptoad likes to live in your cellar, under your doorstep, your rosebush, or in some other cool, protected place. And in the winter this cold-blooded fellow goes to sleep in some hole under the ground to await spring.

Most farmers never heard of Old Toad in *Wind in the Willows,* but they know that his mouth is big, and they have seen him catch and swallow a June bug, a jarfly, and a horsefly. They have seen him catch mosquitoes, gnats, fireflies, and moths. Being practical folk, farmers value the toad for his usefulness rather than for his personality.

V I I I

A hornet, if let alone, never bothers a man. But once a man gets too near a hornet's nest, he is likely to be hit hard enough between the eyes to get knocked down. An angry hornet, stinging and biting at the same time, is harder to handle than a polecat under the bed or a bear in the kitchen. Yet this hornet, though mean when angry, is a friend to man not many people know about. The hornet is another great flycatcher.

A hornet's nest is usually as large as a three-gallon water bucket and shaped like a pear, with the little end hanging downward. The nest is made of wood that the hornets chew into a pulp, a substance very much like paper. Hornets build their nests up in the eaves of old buildings and in trees. When frosts come and the wind sweeps the leaves to the ground, the large gray hornet's nests swinging on barren branches of trees are easy to find. A man wonders why he didn't see them before. But the wise hornets choose a place where the green leaves will camouflage their nests. They usually build close to a house or barn where food—flies—will be more plentiful.

The hornets hover about our porch in summer and take every fly that comes by. I entice the flies with sugar and watch the hornets at work. Every few seconds a hornet leaves with a fly. Though I don't know where their nest is, when autumn strips the trees of leaves, I'll probably find it less than a hundred yards from the house.

I have watched these bees fly down and take a bloodthirsty horsefly from a horse's back. I've seen cow flies drink blood from an unsprayed cow until they were saturated and red. And I've seen hornets from a nearby nest wipe out an entire swarm in a matter of minutes. I've seen them catch knit flies trying to fly under a team in harness. Knit flies sting horses and mules on their legs and bellies and lay eggs at the same time. But the hornets get the knit flies before they can either sting or lay. The hornet, first cousin to a red wasp, is the only bee whose staple diet is flies. That alone is reason enough for our appreciating him. We just have to remember not to get him angry.

I X

In late February or early March if you are awakened some morning by the call of "pewee," you'll know a pair of Virginia flycatchers is looking your place over to build. These birds won't eat anything but insects. They will rid your yard and garden of insects and clean your air in late evenings of gnats and mosquitoes. Over your door or under the eaves of an outbuilding, these two will go to work carrying mud and straw to build a nest that will withstand rainstorms and winds and bear up under the weight of young birds. And you needn't feel obliged to feed them, for they don't eat grain.

These birds are equipped by nature with long, sharp bills and a wide wingspread, which makes them like lightning in the air. The greenfly, moth, butterfly, horsefly, housefly, bean beetle, cabbage worm, and aphids don't have a chance. Virginia flycatchers clean the aphids from the rose vine and spirea bush. They pick the cutworms from the cabbage plants. But their first choice is a fly or a moth, and most of their shopping for food is done in flight.

X

To many people the death of a butterfly doesn't mean anything. But it upsets me more than the death of most other living things on this earth. The butterfly is a thing of such beauty, and there isn't any harm in one. The butterfly doesn't prey upon any other creature for its food but gathers nectar from the flowers. I saw a butterfly, whose black wings and body were decorated with red dots, lying dead in the middle of our lane road a few minutes ago. I had to stop and examine this fragile thing for signs of the life and beauty it held an hour ago.

When I was just past three years old, my sister Sophia explained death to me. We lived in the Middlefork of W-Hollow and had just walked down the path to the W-Hollow Road in time to see a hearse behind a span of big horses come from the Collins' house with Mr. Collins in it. This was in 1910. Behind this hearse was a long line of buggies, surreys, people on horseback, and many on foot.

"Mr. Collins is dead," Sophia told me. She was seven years old then and understood about death. "They are hauling him in the front wagon. He's taking his last ride."

"What is 'dead'?" I asked my sister. "What do you mean 'dead'?"

"He can't breathe, and he can't move," she said. "He's dead. He is buried in the ground and goes back to the earth."

But I still didn't understand.

Then, as the last slow walkers in the long funeral procession went around the bend and out of sight, my sister tried to explain about death. She fetched two stones, laid one stone in the road, and held one in her hand. Then she ran after a butterfly. Though I didn't understand, I hoped she wouldn't catch it. She didn't, but she did find an ant. She laid it on the rock in the road, and with the other rock in her hand she crushed the ant. The ant didn't move any longer. Life was over for this ant. It was crushed and would soon return to dirt. This was when I was first told about death. I didn't like it.

So, when I see a butterfly crushed and lifeless on the ground or watch the hundreds of other multicolored butterflies winging through the bright warm August wind, flying to the rows of flowers on either side of our front walk, flying to the little stream whose warm waters flow slowly and gently across the hot sands of the miniature sand bars—when I see these butterflies, alive or dead, I think of the butterfly my sister didn't catch to show me what death was.

X I

From the ridge road I had seen the blue-slate dumps where my father used to dig coal. When I saw them, I knew not many days would pass until I would return. Now, with a stick in my hand, I walked up the path. I carried a stick, for this was copperhead country. Sweat ran down my face and dripped from my nose and chin. Sweat soaked my shirt collar until it felt wet and limp around my neck. I was happy my health permitted me to walk here. This was a desolate section of sandstones, scrawny pines, persimmons, black sumacs, sawbrier, greenbrier, pennyrile, and high lonely skies. Only the vegetation that could survive in a thin, starved soil would grow here. But fortunately for my father and my

father's father when they lived here, there was coal to be mined
under these sandstone hills.

I wanted to return to the place where I was born. I wanted to
see once more the ugly gaping mouths of the mines on the slopes of
these high desolate hills. Now I climbed up a path that wagonloads
of coal had once rolled over. Cattle, mule, and horse teams had
pulled the jolt wagons of coal, heaped high with big black lumps,
over the winding indentation that was only a faint path now. Once
it was filled with tracks where animals had dug deep with their hoofs
as they strained at their heavy loads.

I followed this old road to the top of the ridge. Then I followed
the ridge road to the sand gap. Here I took the old wagon road to
my right down the sandy point.

This old road had grown up in poison vine, bittersweet, bullgrass, and briers. The ground had never been rich enough before
to grow such heavy vegetation, but this season we had had plenty
of rain. Through the years past, the dwarfed bushy-topped oaks
growing along the banks of this ancient road had shed their leaves
season after season, and the leaves had rotted on this infertile land.
These few old trees had done their best to refertilize this barren
earth. Now the forest of worthless trees and briers was closing in,
and soon this old road would be a part of the jungle.

I broke grapevines and bittersweet with my hand and laid my
weight against the tangle of vegetation. Once I sat on the exposed
roots of one of these old trees that many times had shaded the hot
oxen, mules, and horses as they toiled up this point with a load of
coal from the mines below. Not many would think this tree had
served a purpose in its earlier years.

I walked down to the bushy-topped whiteoak that stood in the
yard of the house where I was born. But that one-room structure
was in ashes now. In the spring of 1954 a forest fire which burned
over more than two thousand acres got this little shack. This was
my first time back to the scene since it had burned. Where this
house had once stood and its ashes had helped to refertilize the
ground, weeds had grown taller. I could calculate the exact spot.
Where our old garden had been, someone had planted corn, but
it wasn't even up to my shoulder. This was not land for corn. This

was starvation land. It had always been. The Stuarts starved out when they moved here from Big Sandy. No one could have lived from the sustenance of this infertile land had he not also mined the coal from under the sandstones.

Here I could smell the pennyrile, that aromatic herb which is death on insects, especially mosquitoes. But mosquitoes would never come to this hilltop where there wasn't any water. There was a sulphur spring near the coal mine when my father and mother lived here, but this water was too full of minerals to use. So my mother used to climb this mountain with a lard can of water on one hip and a child on the other. How my parents ever were able to live here I never understood. And why had I returned now?

The rabbit returns to the hole where it nested in the ground. When dogs follow its tracks, the rabbit returns to its place of nativity. The dogs had been on my tracks since that day I fell on my face in Murray. For months I had thought of the place of my birth. This was the reason I was returning. I was born on this desolate acre of infertile earth, in a one-room shack, without a doctor. How many spots upon this American earth, now forsaken and forgotten, have given birth to America's children? How many of us have come from the inaccessible places, lost coves and hollows, beneath the rugged hills?

Not anyone passing could now tell that people had once lived here. The jungle had moved in again. But my people had pushed the jungle back and mined the coal and raised gardens. They had cut the sassafras and the sawbrier with their garden hoes. They had salted the earth with their sweat and won a meager pittance in return. And they had mined the coal. Then they had moved away, and other people had come to mine coal and work the land for a bare existence. Now all had moved away. And the sawbrier, greenbrier, wild grapevine, sassafras, persimmon, and scrubby pine were moving in. This land rightfully belonged to them in the first place.

I turned away from where the shack had once stood. I walked down the old wagon road toward the mine. The jungle had grown over this, too, but there were still faint prints of the old road my father had walked. I found the place where the scales used to be, where they had weighed the coal when it left the mines. This was the only mine in this county that had scales a few feet from its entrance to weigh the coal. Where the scales once were, there is now a slight depression in the earth.

Finally I reached a high blue cone where vegetation didn't grow. Here was a clean place surrounded by bush, brier, thorn, and vine. This was the old blue-slate dump I had seen from a distance. My father had wheeled much of this slate from the coal mine above. Now the coal mine's mouth was a dark cavity, surrounded by earth's woolly lips. The lips of this ugly mouth were sealing tight, vegetation would soon cover the mouth. I wondered how many times my father had gone back under the hill here, how many times he had lain on his side, on his back face up, and on his belly face down, and picked the coal from the narrow seam. How many times he had come from the cool bowels of this sandstone hill out into the sweltering heat of a summer day. How many times he had made a fire of coal outside the mine and sharpened his coal picks on an anvil. And what were his dreams? Did he dream that his children would do well in life? He and Mom were young then, and their days, despite the poverty, were happy ones.

Now this was a land where dreams lay buried. Under this hill, in all directions, the coal mine ran. Under this hill the old bank ties and wooden rails have turned to dust. The dreams of men are deep, deep down in this hollowed-out hill. Men who sat before their blazing fires, men who saw giant teams strain as the big wheels rocked under the heavy weight on the sandstone road. My father had seen the drivers leave the mine with loaded wagons for the scales. My mother had seen the teams pass on their way up the sandstone point to the ridge. As a small boy, I had waved to the drivers when they passed. I don't remember these drivers, but my father told me about them, and about walking over this land, the two of us. He had held my hand and led me to the scales and showed me the mine entrance.

Now only the wind sighs and the crows caw and the sulphur stream of water flows from a hole in the hill where the mine used to be.

XII

     Even before I left Murray Hospital last November, Naomi made a suggestion of one way I could spend the long days of convalescing ahead. She suggested that I get a TV set. And to encourage me along this line, she reminded me of how much I liked to attend football and baseball games.

     "Just think," she said enthusiastically, "you can sit before your TV and watch the best baseball games, Jesse. In the autumn you can watch football. It will be wonderful for you. You can see the best and never leave home."

     But I have never agreed to get a TV set. Jane would not read books if we got TV. I could either watch TV or leave it alone. And I believed Naomi could do the same thing. But I had certain fixed ideas about bringing up our only child. I wanted her to be a reader and an active observer, instead of a passive watcher and listener.

     She kept the radio on for hours at a time. She listened to all sorts of programs. There wasn't much I could do about it with four radios in the house. But she only listened. There weren't any pictures for her to watch. So, while listening to programs on the radio, she read books. She painted pictures. She did things with her hands.

     "Look how wonderful the radio has been to you here in the hospital," Naomi went on. "What would you have done without it?"

     And this was true. What could I have done without the little radio at the head of my bed? I had even listened to *Little Orphan Annie.* This was hard for me to believe. I listened to a women's program I had never heard of before, *Queen for a Day.* I was entertained and remembered the queen from week to week. I could have done well on this program if they had called me by phone and asked me about the last week's queen. I listened to Amos and Andy. I'd not heard them for years. I listened to news broadcasts, weather reports, hillbilly music, Sunday symphonies. I'm no snob, never have been. The radio was fun, and it helped.

     When Naomi suggested TV to me, I considered. But when I was brought home in the middle of the winter, the bleak and barren hills looked good to me. I heard the December winds moan around this house, and that was sweet music to my ears. I was contented

with my views through many windows of the dark hills and the
sound of cold winter winds whining around my room. Naomi reminded me a few times about the TV set, but I didn't say anything.

And while lying in bed, I had time to go back over my youth.
What had given me powers of observation? Why could I write a
winter scene in hot July and make people shudder with cold when
they read it? My powers might not be too important, but whatever
they amounted to, I wanted Jane to have the same chance to develop
hers.

When I was a child, I'd never seen or heard of a movie, a radio,
or a phonograph. All I had to read were my textbooks, poor as they
were, at our one-room rural schoolhouse. But as I walked over the
hills and down in the valleys, so many questions were thrust before
me by nature that I had to find the answers. I couldn't help but observe the world around me in all four seasons. Animals, birds, bees,
insects, and even snakes became my friends.

I wanted my child to share a little of this now, even if some of
the nature I knew had been tamed by man. I wanted her to know
something truer than the prefabricated, artificial man-made substitutes on the little silver screen. I wanted her to roam free, make
her own choices. Why people think their children have to be entertained all the time anyway is something I can't understand. And
why did I have to be entertained? Why would I sit, two or three
worlds removed, and watch baseball and football games of other
men's choosing?

When a man is near death, he will listen to suggestions of what
he should do. He'll listen to the doctors and nurses who tell him
what medicines he should take. He'll listen to anyone who paints a
rosy picture of how happy he will be when he can sit and watch
TV. But even while I was still flat on my back in bed, I started re-
belling against the idea of somebody's entertaining me all day on
TV. I would convalesce in my own way.

Slowly the winter passed. I didn't get a TV set. I wasn't listening to as many radio programs. I had learned to walk again, at first
only a few feet down the front walk. I was feeling the winter wind
now. I watched the redbirds fly over. I saw the snowbirds under
the old ragweed stems hunting something to eat. I heard the water

singing past the ice-coated rocks. I didn't need a TV set. I needed to get back to the natural things that excited me when I was growing up. These things had not only entertained me, they had educated me, made a man out of a boy. There weren't any substitutes for winter hills, bare branches against dark skies. There weren't any pictures to take the place of winter walks.

Jane was disappointed for a time, but she got over it. In the meantime she was winning prizes at school, reading and understanding major novels at the age of twelve, learning the names of the trees and birds and flowers in our hills. Jane hasn't suffered any from not staying indoors on beautiful afternoons peering at visual soap opera on the little silver screen.

I was reminded of all this the other day when I asked her how many legs a grasshopper had. She didn't know. Instead of looking it up in the dictionary, she went out and caught one. She drew a picture of a grasshopper and wrote a two-page description. She described him as a minor kangaroo, because of the powerful legs with which he did his jumping. If she had looked up *grasshopper* in the dictionary or a science book, she would have found out how many legs he had. But she knew that now anyway. And she wouldn't have seen with her own eyes how far he could jump or the pair of legs which reminded her of a kangaroo's. I know, because I compared her description to the ones given in two dictionaries. Hers was the best.

So I figure Jane hasn't lost too much by not having TV.

SEPTEMBER

This morning as the sun came over the hills, I felt a renewed strength and vigor. I walked up the W-Hollow Road to the tool shed and then to the knoll behind. This knoll was once clean of brush, and we farmed it and the high, rocky hill beyond. In my high school days I had the longest row of corn in the county here. The row of corn went around and around like a corkscrew until it reached the top. Now this hill where we once raised corn for bread was covered with broomsedge and brush.

My father had sat on his porch and looked toward this portion of his farm in his last days. Once, when I was visiting him, he said with disgust, "The bushes are closing in on me. They are pushing me back. I wish I was young again. I'd like to go after them with a bush blade and a mattock."

He was right, the bushes were closing in on him. The land I had cleared for my father in my youth was growing up. This was land we farmed for three years and then sowed in grass for pasture. We scythed the bushes each late summer. Now it was in the process of going back to the forest—proof, if such were needed, that nature whips us in the end. My father sat on his porch, a defeated old man. But he never gave up. He had hopes of getting his fields cut again, despite the Army's taking his grandson, Gene Darby, the last help he had. But before he realized his last dreams, earth accepted the dust she had loaned him to use in his stay here.

How long, when a man had to lie in bed, did it take his fields to grow up and the winds to blow the tin roofs from his cattle and tobacco barns? How long did it take his line fences to go down, his fence posts to rot, and the bluebirds to find holes in them for nests? How long would it be before the forest fires in March blew from nowhere and raced over the top dry leaves in a hurry to get to the young pine forests he had set? How long would it take all his once-cleared fields to go back to forest again and not leave a sign that work had ever been done here?

I could answer this. Not long. It had not been long since I had had a heart attack and had gone to bed. But even before this heart attack I had neglected my farm. I'd not had time to walk over this land I love to see what needed to be done.

Now I had the time. I had worlds of time. I was happy and contented to be able to walk again over this farm. I had torn roots from this ground with my plow. I had followed mules and horses over this pasture when it was new-ground earth, and I had grown tall corn. I had played and hunted over every foot of this small world, these rough acres, these folded hills and valleys.

I walked up the winding sandy-floored road to the hilltop. Here was an empty house, over there were two barns. One, my old sheep barn, was now used for hay and tobacco. The other, still older, was falling apart. For twenty years I had filled both of them with feed, with sheep and cattle. Now these sheep and cattle and the good teams of mules and horses and the dogs that followed the wagons were only dreams of what had been.

I was in the world of long ago, with my mother and father, with the Dick and Dinah mule team, and with Jerry-B and Red-Rusty, our dogs, running behind the wagon. Our pasture fields were clean, and our haylofts were filled. Our corn cribs were bulging with white and golden ears, and I was writing my first novel and was in love with Naomi Norris and walking over the high hills to see her three times a week, carrying her armfuls of flowers picked on the way.

I would like to start my life over—borrow this same dust from the earth, have my same parents back, be born in the same little one-room log shack. I would like to write my high school themes again, use the same old fountain pen, see the same wild flowers, hear the same wordless song of the leaping stream. I would like to have my sheep back on this hill, have the hill green as it was then, with the clouds dropping down occasionally to visit and hide the woolly sheep. I would like to sell my first poem and my first story again, and write my first novel.

After one has been through the agony of a heart attack, after he has learned on what a slender thread life hangs, after he lies flat in bed five months and has time to reflect, he realizes how great it is to live life fully. No one knows how wonderful it is to be alive until he knows how it feels to die.

I had seen the past. It had spoken to me, and now I had the future to face, not such a bleak future since I was up and about. But while I had been in bed, only my oaks had maintained their imperturbable blind watch over my farm. I knew these acres belonged to me as much as my fingers belonged to my hands. I must begin measures to reclaim them.

I I

Any man who has once lived a normal life hates suddenly to be isolated as a special case. No matter how well-balanced a man is, how filled with good humor, if he has ever had a serious heart attack and becomes known as a "cardiac," he'll never make a joke about it, as he will about his "operation."

Never before have I been isolated in a minority group. First, being a white man in this country, I belonged to the majority. Second, I belong to the largest religious group, the Protestants. I do not know what it is like to be Jewish or Catholic. Finally, I have been healthy, I have belonged to the "well" majority.

After an article I wrote about my heart attack appeared in a large national magazine, I received letters from almost every state in the Union. A fat bundle of letters arrived each day. Who was interested in writing me about my heart attack? Was it the person who had never had one? No, not the man in good health. If a healthy man sees another man fall of a heart attack, he'll continue on his way positive it will be some other bystander, not he, who will be the next one to fall. No, my correspondents are cardiacs themselves. We are in a closed circle.

The isolation of a cardiac can be very depressing. When I walk in a crowd where it is known I am a cardiac, heads turn and I hear whispers. People seem to have the feeling I might just topple over any time. For the first time in my life I feel on the defensive. Before, I was respected as a strong, sturdy physical specimen. I was welcomed as a member in normal human society. Now if I am ever again to be fully accepted, it appears that it will have to be among people who don't know I have had a coronary occlusion.

Yesterday we drove to an East Kentucky state park, where my wife, daughter, and I went in swimming. We didn't know anybody there, but before the afternoon was over, everyone in swimming seemed to know I was the man who had had a heart attack. There were whispers and troubled looks and shaking of heads. One woman, a complete stranger, took my wife aside and told her the water was too cold and I shouldn't be in swimming. I didn't know what was wrong until my wife walked out of the shallows, where we had been playing, to the warm sands and motioned for me. Then she told me. It hadn't been my imagination playing tricks when I noticed people shying away from me when I was in water waist-deep. They didn't want to be pinned under and drowned when I toppled over.

Our enjoyment of that outing was ruined. I had not gone out into deep water. I swam but a few feet at a time. I watched myself. We had consulted our doctor, and he had answered that a gentle swim might actually be beneficial to my health. A little exercise in the water tightens the soft muscles after one has been forbidden activity. And Naomi, who felt more responsible for my well-being than anyone, was happy to see me in the water and was watching me carefully.

Yet my presence there deeply troubled this group of strangers, and they did what I prayed they would not do—they built a wall around me. A cardiac has no defense against such ostracism, for it is true that he has had a heart attack and is likely to have another. He might say, "Yes, but it can happen to you, too." But no healthy person ever believes that it will happen to him. I didn't.

Ninety-five per cent of my letters for the last month have come from cardiacs. They have written me wonderful letters, for it is they who understand. After they read my article, they knew I belonged to their society. They complimented me on the honesty of what I had said. Perhaps in my small way I had spoken for all of them, for they, too, had been through the fiery furnace. Although I don't know them, I feel that they are my true brothers.

In one of these letters, a cardiac in Chicago had an idea of building a "Cardiac House." His dream was to build a special apartment house for cardiacs where there wouldn't be any climbing for the patients, where special foods would be served, and where a direct communication system from one apartment to the other would make help immediately available in case of emergency. His idea had the approval of one of the great heart specialists and of the health department of that city. If his cardiac dream house is built and is successful in Chicago, there will be other cardiac houses in other large cities in America to take care of our growing minority group of approximately three million.

I thought his dream splendid, and at the same time awful. Here it was again. The wall around the cardiacs. They would be isolated, like lepers. People would pass a cardiac house and whisper and point and shake their heads sadly.

Yesterday a friend of mine in good health, a college graduate and former teacher, wrote me a letter. He had every intention of being polite. He would never have hurt me knowingly, of this I am sure. We have written each other for the past twenty-five years. But in his letter he reminded me that I "belonged to the society of cardiacs now," and he went on to say, "of course this is not of your choice but you do belong." Such expressions, well-meaning and accurate though they may be, are knives between the ribs to cardiacs. A cardiac doesn't want to hear this from a friend. He is well aware of it without constant reminding.

After I got my friend's letter, I fell into a terrible mood. He had started a chain reaction in my mind. Try as I might, I couldn't break the pattern of my thinking. The past returned, and I began to worry. I thought of my many lecture tours, when I rode trains, planes, and buses all over America. No more, for now I belong to the society of cardiacs. I remembered the time I had written a novel in three weeks. Not again. And how was I to make my living? Only yesterday, my attorney advised me my income for the year was way down compared to what I had been averaging annually. When something strikes at a man's livelihood, it strikes directly at his heart. And in this case it was also the other way around: my heart had struck at my livelihood.

Then I thought, What if I have another attack? Now I was in a dangerous area. Once I wrote a short story about a man's thinking he would be burned to death some day. The man was burned to death. His friends had tried to keep him from thinking he would. But the man thought so much about this it actually happened. There is much to the way a man thinks.

My thinking had always been positive. The day I toppled over with a heart attack, my last thought before unconsciousness was that I would live. And despite the odds against me, I had managed. But if I had thought at that moment that this was my last conscious breath, that I was going to die, I believe I would have died.

Now I lay on the bed restlessly kicking the covers. I wondered what was left for me to do. I thought of the articles I had read about employment for cardiacs. While in the hospital, I read where the Jewish people, as far back as World War II, had made special efforts to see that their cardiacs were employed. They had done war work, made gas masks. They, as a people, had understood. They had done more for their cardiacs than any other group I had heard of.

I had been happy up until I had received this letter in the afternoon mail. Now I was afraid I might have another heart attack. Restlessness, worry, fear, fatigue, and cold are the dangers for a

cardiac. Rather than wrestle with the first four, I would brave the
fifth. I got out of bed, put on my shoes and robe, and walked out
into the September night.

I walked up the center of the road, where I would be discovered
if I toppled over. I had to find something I liked to do, hear, or see,
to change my way of thinking. The way he thinks is ninety per cent
of the battle of a cardiac. I knew that I wanted to live, but now I
was wondering why. Then I heard the wind in the pines and the
water flowing over the rocks. I had been upset this way because of a
letter from a well-intentioned friend. Now I walked over well-
traveled paths through the bright moonlight, listening to the night
sounds. I grew sleepy and contented. I came home, went to bed, and
immediately to sleep.

Cardiacs, after the initial shock, don't expect any special treat-
ment. They want to enjoy life quietly, but as normal people. They
want to find something they can do to make a living. They want to
belong. They want to live, as much as is possible, the same way
they did before anything happened to them. They do not need people who are not doctors to tell them what to do and how to live.
Above all they should not be segregated. People should not write to
tell them they belong to a society not of their choice. They should
tell them a heart attack is but a temporary setback, that they are
still as much a part of everything as they ever were.

I I I

The car came up the lane pulling a long cloud of autumn-
oakleaf-colored dust. When it stopped down front, the cloud poured
over and around it like thick soup. A short, stocky man with a broad
grin got out and walked toward the house, leaning forward, with his
short, thick hands pulling against the wind as if he were climbing a
hill. This is the way a mountain man walks, the way my father
walked. The man was old John Bates, and he had come to talk to me
about renting the house which he now lived in and which I had
bought from him three months ago.

"Good morning, Mr. Bates. Sorry I forgot to see you this week."

"It's all right, Jesse. But you know a man worries about a place
to live."

Mr. Bates was grinning almost from ear to ear. He had a fat moonface and his eyes were blue and pretty for a man of his years. His hair, partly gray, fell in good lengths from under his battered brown hat.

Mr. Bates was like my father in many ways. In other ways, politics for instance, they were at opposite poles. Mr. Bates was an uncompromising Democrat and my father a stubborn Republican. Therefore, my father didn't have much to do with Mr. Bates in his lifetime. But they were very much alike about land. They both loved it. My father owned a fifty-acre farm most of his life. Mr. Bates owned a forty-five-acre farm, from which he deeded an acre each to his two sons, leaving him forty-three acres. My father died and left his land. Mr. Bates got too old to farm his.

Year by year it grew up. Finally he set his price and tried to sell to anybody who happened by. But people thought eight thousand for a six-room house and forty-three acres was too high. He'd been trying to sell his place for several years. He didn't like to give up, to release his hold upon this land, but time had forced his hand. Time and my cousin, Stanley Hilton, who had bought one of the acres Mr. Bates had deeded to a son. The son had lost his job, rather he had been replaced by machinery, and had had to move to a new job in Michigan, otherwise he wouldn't have sold.

"It's that cousin of yours, Stanley, who's pushing me to sell," Mr. Bates said on a day last summer when he had walked the two miles over here on the hot, dusty graveled road. "I don't want to sell, but he's forcing me. Stanley Hilton is a man of strange actions. He's like a mole. All he wants to do is dig. He's dug a basement under the house, and he's buried hundreds of tile in deep ditches. Now he wants to hire a bulldozer to put a road right up through my place past my front door. My old lady almost had another stroke over his doings."

"But Stanley has a road out," I said to him. "He's got a fill across the ditch in front of his house to the hardroad."

"I know that," he said, excitedly. "That's why I can't understand what he's up to. He hired Erf Bailey to do the bulldozing. I heard about it and went to Erf and told him if he put a bulldozer in there and scared my wife, I'd have to sue him. After I talked to Erf

I went to Greenup and got Judge Sparks. I had him out here. I wouldn't let Stanley tear this farm up. I've owned this place for twenty-nine years. I love my little farm. But I'm ready to sell. I want to sell it to you. That's why I've walked all the way over here."

I was lying in bed taking my afternoon rest that day three months ago when Mr. Bates came.

"I hate to disturb you after you've been sick so long, but if I don't sell my farm and get out, my old lady is going to keel over with another stroke," he told me. He sat by my bed with his hands and arms shaking until he couldn't control them. The tears streamed over the rough skin on his face partly covered with thin white beard. "That cousin of yours is worrying me to death. I didn't know there was a man in this county like him. Do you think you'll be interested in my farm? Will you be able to look my farm over? The land isn't steep. I think you can walk over every acre. I climb my sloping hill every day, my heart flutters like a bird." He clutched at his chest.

"Yes, I can look at your farm," I promised him before I thought. "When do you want me to come?"

"In the morning," he replied.

Mr. Bates had spent two hours with me. Naomi took him home in the car, for we were afraid for him to walk back. He was that wrought up. But on the way home, he gave her a sales talk on how fine a place I'd be coming over tomorrow to consider buying. She didn't know I'd made this promise. When she returned from taking him home, she said, "What do you mean? Are you crazy? We don't need more land. You're not able to look over that farm."

"Well, I don't plan to buy it," I told her. "I just couldn't deny him when he asked me to come over and see his land."

"You've got more land than you'll ever be able to take care of now," she said. "You go to the Sandy River road this way. And you almost reach the hardroad the other way."

"That's just it," I teased her. "If I had the John Bates farm I'd go from hardroad to hardroad. My land joins the John Bates place on two sides. I'll want you to go along in the morning to see what I'm talking about."

"Of course I'm going along," she said. "You and Mr. Bates out there together. You might topple over. He can't help you. And now you're getting interested. Yes, I'm going with you."

Next morning Naomi and I drove over to the Bates farm. Mr. Bates and I pulled ourselves up by the bushes as we slowly climbed the gentle slope. Below us was a rolling saddle of beautiful building land, parted by a ribbon of hard asphalt road. The Bates acres were covered with dogwoods and persimmons. Here and there were greenbrier and sawbrier clusters and patches of wild berries. Even Naomi was impressed with this land. On the way over she had asked me the price Mr. Bates had put on the place. I wouldn't tell her. I knew the price would shock her, as it had shocked others when he had approached them. Everybody had tried to pull his price down. Not one had agreed with him.

In just the way my father would have done, he told us about the land. He had raised big corn here, potatoes and turnips there, hay on this flat hilltop, and wheat on that slope. He would touch the dirt gently with his shoes and pat the few walnut trees affectionately with his fat, wrinkled hands.

"Jesse, you love land," he said. "I know you do. That's why I'm interested in selling to you. You'll be kind to this land and these trees." Then he turned his eager old moonface toward Naomi. "Don't you like this farm, Mrs. Stuart? Ain't this a purty place?"

Naomi had to admit it was. The three of us rested on the hilltop. Then we got up, for a rain cloud was approaching from the north, and walked down along a path cattle had made last summer.

"This is fine building land," Mr. Bates said, as we were leaving. "I'll give you a week to let me know. You can let me know by that time, can't you?"

"Jesse doesn't need this, Mr. Bates," Naomi said.

"It's a nice little place for somebody," Mr. Bates said.

"A young couple," she told him.

As Naomi drove through a hard shower over the W-Hollow road, I sat in silence, watching the windshield wipers trying to keep the water off.

She asked, "How much does he want?"

"Eight grand. Do you think that's too much?"

"Too much!" She gasped for more breath. "You know it's not worth that."

"I'm not so sure," I said. "That farm is on the hardroad. It's the prettiest little farm left in this area. There's only an acre too rough to be cut over with a mowing machine."

"I am more interested in your health than land."

I didn't know whether the price was too high or not. Naomi finally agreed that we should have Mr. Calvin Clarke, our friend and advisor and attorney, come to look this place over and that we would do what he said.

"I'll be up this afternoon," he said on the phone. "I know that farm."

That afternoon he and I drove over on the W-Hollow Road, where we parked at a good distance from the Bates home. We climbed the gentle slope near the Three Mile Cemetery, but we didn't go too close to old John or his property. I was afraid that, if he saw me with a stranger looking at his farm, he might know I was seriously interested and up the price.

As we drove back home for supper, Mr. Clarke didn't say anything. I thought he was against buying this place. If so, I'd stand by my bargain with Naomi. We were eating supper when I said, "Mr. Clarke, what do you think about the farm?"

"I was just waiting for you to ask me," he said. "Buy it."

Next day we bought the John Bates farm. I paid him more money than he had ever seen at one time in his life. Like my father, he couldn't write his name. When Mr. and Mrs. Bates asked to live on in the house until September, I told them they could stay rent free, but beginning with September I would like to have the house for rent.

Now September was here. And here too was Mr. Bates, asking to rent the house he sold to me.

"I just can't stand to move away," Mr. Bates said. "I love that old place. It's home to me. I would like to rent it until March. I might even want it longer. How much a month do you ask?"

"Well, Mr. Bates, you know how much money I've got in that

place," I said. "I've got eight thousand. Or rather you've got my eight thousand." He didn't laugh. "I've planned to ask thirty-five dollars a month. One man has already offered me this."

I thought Mr. Bates was going to fall over.

"Do you think that's too much?" I asked him.

"Oh, yes, it's too steep," he said. "Jesse, put your hand here over my heart. It's running away."

I put my hand over his heart. I felt it running like a mad wind. My father used to have me put my hand over his heart when he got excited, and it raced the same way.

"What do you think the rent should be?" I asked him.

"Not over twenty," he said. "Twenty would be about right."

"I said thirty-five and you said twenty, so we'll split the difference and make it twenty-five," I said.

"All right," he said. "That's a bargain."

Then the old man walked slowly back to the car. I was relieved. I knew it didn't pay to buy property from old people where so much sentiment was attached.

I V

Today, I got to thinking of the buckeyes of my boyhood years. I knew where they grew. I remembered seeing their broad leaves last spring in their race to get dressed before the other trees around them. I put my hands deep into my pockets and thought of the days when I had filled my pockets with buckeyes. I was on my way to the buckeye grove.

When I was a boy, growing up with Aaron and Eddie Howard and Glen Hilton, each autumn we'd go to the woods about the time the buckeyes ripened and fell from the trees. Many of the old people called them horse chestnuts. They were not good for a thing except for boys to play with. I don't know why we loved them so. We went around with our pockets bulging with buckeyes. We carried them to school. We played "anti-over" the schoolhouse and our homes with a big buckeye. We caught and tagged with them same as if they were twine balls. And always we carried buckeyes in our pockets. I used to like to put my hand down into my overall pocket filled with buckeyes and rub them together.

When Mom found my pocket filled with buckeyes, she made me empty it. Then she took the buckeyes to the fireplace and laid them on the fire. If it was still early in autumn and we didn't have fires in the fireplace, she lifted a cap from the woodstove and dropped them down into the firebox. Mom always wanted to be sure they were burned to a crisp and would never sprout. She wanted them burned so her cows wouldn't eat them. Anything that was a threat to a cow she got rid of in a hurry. She didn't have any use for the beautiful buckeyes. And this hurt me very much when I was a boy.

Big Aaron Howard, who could throw a buckeye like a bullet, Little Ed, Glen, and I used to get into a buckeye fight out in some open pasture field where we could see and have plenty of room to get out of the way of one that had smoke on it. "Playing buckeyes" we called it. When one of us got hit, he had to leave the fight. Usually he wanted to leave it anyway after he got hit. I've been knocked down with many a buckeye Big Aaron threw. He was a baseball pitcher in later years.

How my father hated buckeyes that poisoned his animals! And laurel, too. After Naomi and I were married, she found laurel growing in the woods and asked me to dig up bunches to set in our front yard. I warned her my father wouldn't like it.

As soon as my father found it growing in our yard, he grabbed a hoe in the tool shed and took off running toward these evergreens. He whacked them down. "What on earth is the matter with you people?" he asked Naomi and me. "Who had the idea to set that poisonous stuff in the yard?" Naomi admitted she was guilty. "Well, you grew up in town," he excused her. Then he told her about all the sheep we had lost, accusing the laurel of poisoning them. Next he accused buckeyes. He got so wrought up explaining to Naomi all the damage they could do that he took off with his ax and hoe to search the woods for both.

After he had cut the laurel in our yard, he felt a little bad about it, despite thinking that he'd probably saved the life of an animal. He went to the woods and found holly bushes, a nonpoisonous evergreen, and brought them in to set in our yard to replace the laurel. Then he felt better about what he had done.

Early in the spring, when they leafed and he could locate them easily, Dad went out to cut the young buckeyes. "The only thing I've ever heard a buckeye was any good for," he once told me, "is to carry in your pocket when you have rheumatics. I carried one, and it didn't work. I did it just to see. I never had any faith in a buckeye's being good for anything. But a body always likes to try out every remedy he hears about."

This afternoon I was content to pick up the worthless buckeyes from the ground until I filled my pockets like in the old days. I picked up buckeyes until my pockets bulged. I thought of the days when Big Aaron, Little Ed, and Cousin Glen came here with me. In this valley many a throwing game had started. Now Big Aaron was somewhere in California, far away from the hard oaks and buckeyes, but under the palms. Little Ed was still around somewhere, partly paralyzed from overexposure, the result of sleeping on the ground on winter nights while he listened to the hounds after the fox. Glen was living in W-Hollow, running a sawmill. My father and Uncle Martin were eight feet apart in their Plum Grove graves.

With bulging pockets, my hands down among the buckeyes, I started for home. It was wonderful to feel them again in my pockets, though I had no one to throw them at now.

V

You are not sure whether you're going to live from one day until the next. But you go out for a walk and take a few steps up a hill too fast. You get warm, and perspiration flows down your face as it once did. You enjoy perspiring, but the old ticker starts acting up. You begin to get a hurt feeling in your left side. Maybe it feels as if you've been stabbed there once and the place never came together very well. And now after your climbing and getting hot, this place has pulled apart. You sit down beside the road in a hurry. You are in the shade. You stretch out flat on your back on the ground. And the first thought that comes to your mind is, I'm liable to go any minute.

All right, you have these thoughts. You can't help it. You can't close your mind to them. You lie there quietly on the ground. You're just about afraid to move. You think about reaching for your pocketbook, opening the little bright box if your clumsy fingers don't do too much fumbling, getting a little glycerine tablet out, putting it under your tongue. That will help you. The doc did that for you a couple of times before you had the attack and all the heart damage.

Once you carried all the bills your billfold would close on. You've had it stiff with bills in the good years that have passed. And now, because you carry that little box around, which you never want anybody to see, you don't have the bills in your billfold as you used to.

No, you don't need that glycerine tablet. That's a better state of mind. After lying on your back on the dry ground under the oak, you'll be all right. Just take a rest. Be careful not to overdo next time. Listen to the people who have told you to "take it easy." They knew the right words to say even if they never had a coronary occlusion. Maybe a lot of them know more about it than you.

As you lie there, you think of a letter you got. Think about the hundreds of letters. That's it, stop thinking about your ticker. There was that letter from Canada. By golly, that fellow got fixed up all right. He was back working and as good as new. That's what he told you in his letter. A doctor with a new idea, well not exactly new, had converted this cardiac back to his old self again. He left our happy society of nondoers. In this letter he said he would never return to our "Cardiac Party" again, unless he had to.

What that doc did to that Canadian fellow goes through your mind as you pull your legs up to relax and hope no one comes along to ask you questions. You took an untraveled road because you didn't want anybody around asking you questions. Questions to a cardiac are unpleasant. But somebody might be out squirrel hunting, find you, take off screaming you'd had another attack. Have people running around and an ambulance driving as far as it could toward you, then men with stretchers. This goes through your mind as you think about that letter and what the doc did to that fellow who left your society. It was some operation all right.

You thought about it so much you could feel the doctor operating on you. Now the man was back in his store lifting barrels and hundred-pound sacks of feed. He was a man again. He wasn't like you. Even a brisk walk knocked you out. You who used to walk twenty-six miles to visit your sister. You who used to run cross-country. Boy, the old ticker was a good one then. But you never told it so. You never petted it like you do now after accomplishing a mile walk. Once you went over two miles, and you really talked baby talk first time in your life to your old tired ticker.

But about that doc. Maybe you could have the same thing the other fellow had. Would you like to leave the Society of Cardiac Joes? You say you wouldn't, just to be nice. You say it's not so bad. And you lie there and know in your heart, your crippled heart, that every man in your society would leave it if he could. He wouldn't say he wanted to leave, but deep down we're all like the fellow who had found that doc and had left. But you had your doubts too about the letter. You were a little cautious in your thinking.

The docs had a lot of banks nowadays. Funny about so many banks, blood banks, eye banks, artery banks. Time was you thought about banks as a place to keep money. You had to laugh about that one. But gently, don't laugh too hard.

You think about taking out the old damaged coronary artery where the clot was and having the blood find some other way. Well, a plumber removes joints and angles of pipes that had filled up until they wouldn't carry water. When he substitutes a new piece of pipe, the old line is about as good as new. And a man has to keep his pipes open, so the pump can send the fluid around the body to generate warmth and life.

That doc was a good plumber to remove that man's pipe and still keep the old machinery going. It was quite a trick, but he'd done it. Sounded wonderful. You thought these things as you lay and rested and looked up at the oak leaves trembling between you and the blue sky.

You had a good engine, you still had a serviceable body. Only thing wrong was that piece of coronary where the blood went around a little bend. There was once a clot there. The pipe was filled up. Well, your doc was a pretty good plumber, too. He got the pipe unstopped, but it took a long time and he couldn't use one of his eels to do it. He unstopped your pipe by putting some drug into the water that reached the stoppage. Dissolved it. That was the thing. That scar tissue was corrosion in the pipe. It loused up your circulation, and that was the reason you had to lie under the tree on your back and have all these thoughts.

Now you were getting a little easier. That feeling of something pulling apart had eased. That little bit of perspiration had dried on your face where the September wind blew over you. And you thought of that second letter you got, about twenty pages, from that crackpot electrician. He gave lectures and sold pamphlets on the old ticker and must have heard of you as a prospect. He wrote you something about getting hold of the spine, giving it a few shock charges, and the old ticker came sound.

He compared the spine and the ticker to the points and the engine of a car. It took twenty pages of longhand to tell you how he lectured to people about his new theory of body mechanics. You thought you'd better skip him. You got a lot of strange letters about breathing deep ten times before breakfast and drinking weed juice. A man just had to have a little horse-sense to know what to laugh off. He had to know what to skip. For when the old ticker acted up, a man might grab for almost anything.

Now you really felt relaxed. That was another thing. You were not indispensable. You knew darned well the world could go on without you. The world wouldn't any more miss you than the wind would miss a single leaf from the oak that shaded you from the September sun. There must have been thousands of leaves on that oak. And you were just a little leaf in the vast forest of green leaves where squirrel hunters might be approaching at this very minute . . . You still hoped no one would find you.

The old ticker was rested. It had just gotten a little tired of pushing life through that series of corroded pipes over your big body. Now it had rested and everything was all right. As you lay there and looked up through the trembling leaves at the September sky, you had humbled yourself. The world would go on without you. This same thing had happened to millions of others. And, anyway, you knew your life was in the hands of your Great Designer. When He wanted to take you off the road, He was sure to take you. You'd always liked travel, this would be your longest trip. So why do a

lot of worrying? Take care of yourself and do what the docs say.
Never quite trust your mind. Your heart is the better judge.

V I

This is the time of year when the old feeling returns. My
feet get to itching. I get restless. Yet I know that I cannot go
back.

Every September for the last fifteen years, except for two war
years, Naomi has always seen to it that my suits were cleaned and
pressed for autumn wear. She would have the right ties laid out
for the right suits, the right shirts and socks. She sometimes had
as many as forty shirts ready, too. For I needed clean shirts to wear
on the platform when I spoke. Shirts slightly frayed at the collars
I wore on planes, trains, and buses, but I had to wear my best on
the platform.

If my suit was wrinkled and I had only an hour before I left the
hotel for my talk, I called a bellboy and got quick service. Often
there were only minutes between the time I had my pants pressed
and the moment I was to go on the platform. I can't count the times
I've put on hot, freshly pressed pants that warmed me more than
the exercise of giving an hour's talk.

Naomi saw to it I had dozens of handkerchiefs. She knew how
I used from one to six every time I gave a talk. Talks in the deep
South on summer evenings took at least six handkerchiefs. They
were wet when I was through. After they dried, they were rough
with little grains of salt. When I spoke up in Minnesota, Iowa,
Michigan, even if the auditoriums were not overheated, I needed at
least one handkerchief, sometimes two. Naomi had traveled with
me over America. She knew just what I needed wherever I'd go.

She could pack enough in two suitcases for me to get along
on for three weeks. Once I gave twenty-five talks in three weeks.
Each was a major talk. At least it was for me. If I gave three talks
in a day, I had to change shirts and undershirts three times. I wore
a topcoat, tan and good-looking, which served as both overcoat and
raincoat and as a quilt to cover me when I couldn't get a room
and had to sleep in a hotel lobby or a railroad station. I took a few
difficult, slow-reading books, notebooks, ink, paper, fountain pen,

plenty of extra pipes and tobacco. On lecture tours I had lonely hours. When I spoke to thousands, I often didn't speak to one person I knew.

This time of year was always an exciting time, for I was getting ready to leave and I had dreams of seeing the old places again and visiting many new. I watched the weather reports for days beforehand if I went by air. Naomi took me to the airport at Greater Huntington, West Virginia, and before that airfield was constructed, I went to Charleston, West Virginia, or to the Greater Cincinnati Airport. From these airports I went to all parts of this country.

I want to get into a plane again, rise up into the blue, see the hills and rivers and towns below. I want to see the lines of street lights at night, and car lights inching along the highways. I want to feel the plane hit a white cloud and lurch. I want to have coffee at twenty thousand feet up, flying east into a morning sun. I want to land at night on an airfield outlined below in lights, like going home to a port in a distant land. So many airfields I've landed on at night. I remember these things.

I've had train rides across the flat Midwest. I've ridden on all the lines in Indiana, Illinois, Ohio, and Iowa. I've ridden them in September, October, and November, when the corn pickers in the fields of buff-colored corn reminded me of giant prehistoric animals, risen again after thousands of years locked in the earth. I've seen tractors in Iowa pulling truckloads of yellow corn to steel-wire cribs with meshes open to the weather. I've seen corn hauled on frosty mornings to hundreds of hogs in a field in Indiana. I love this fruitful land seen from a train rolling across the flat plains.

The southwest—New Mexico, Arizona, and Texas—was the best country I ever found to travel through lying in a pullman at night, looking out the window and up at the stars. They looked so bright and far apart, so clean in these Southwestern skies. And in the bright daytime, I watched the jackrabbits run over the sagebrush land. I liked to eat breakfast on a Texas train, looking out the window at the country's vastness.

I liked to be in Kansas when the wheat was green. I have ridden trains over Kansas in dust storms and through white level planes of snow. I have traveled by train, bus, and plane over Iowa. I liked autumn best in Iowa, where once I saw teachers getting their first pay, buying, laughing, talking. I liked to see the harvests coming from the fertile fields to the big barns, and the fine cattle, and the farmers making the kind of money they should make everywhere.

I've traveled in Minnesota when it was thirty-two below. I stayed weeks there once, until the temperature changed almost to a heat wave. It rose to twenty-two below. Snow was six feet deep. I liked the air, the people, the food—all healthy. The peninsula of Michigan got me, even for a small fee, when they wanted me. Then Detroit, and all the little towns of Michigan I know by heart —Cheboygan, St. Clair, Gaylord, Petoskey. I memorized Michigan and Ohio, for they were home. Illinois was becoming still another home when I had to stop. I was on my way to a private plane to take me to Illinois for my next talk when my speaking ended.

Autumns in the Poconos in Pennsylvania. Seeing apples ripen in upstate New York, the dairy herds, the farms, the fine homes. Flying over Louisiana, which is half land, half water.

On my first trip to the Carolinas and Virginia I hadn't yet learned to drive a car, and Naomi did the driving in our new Plymouth, the first car I ever owned. This was shortly after we were married. I got fifty dollars a talk then. If I was booked twice on the same day, I'd give the extra talk for twenty-five. I was told Carl Sandburg had done this, too.

But sunshine always followed me. I remember train rides across Georgia, Alabama, and Mississippi. Down on that flat land, pines were everywhere, bending with the lonely winds. So many nights on trains I looked at the stars above the pines. Nights when the stars were dim I often saw the large moon fastened in the tops of the pines. I traveled over America and learned about the American people by shaking their hands.

When I went on a tour, I always hoped that for the first talk I'd get the money instead of its going to my agency. I always needed money this time each autumn. But before autumn was over, my pocketbook would be stiff with bills, and I'd have debts and taxes paid and money for Christmas. After my agency's fee of thirty-five per cent, travel, hotel, and food expenses, I never got more than thirty per cent of the gross. After taxes I had less.

People who employ speakers for what they believe to be big fees are surprised when they hear how little the speaker gets to keep.

This life is hard to get out of my blood after two thousand talks to two million people over twenty years. I spoke in thirty-nine states. Most of my talks were booked by my agency, talks near home were not. Sometimes I talked for nothing, sometimes for expenses. I enjoyed talking most to young people of college age. Someday I'll go back to visit the colleges and universities where I stood on a platform behind a lectern while sweat dripped from my face, soaked my shirt, and faded my necktie on my collar. If I had to rush to another talk, my wet clothes dried on me, winter, spring, or autumn. I relaxed by smoking my pipe when I traveled between talks.

I was always frightened when I was introduced and stepped onto the platform. I had to tear into a talk the way I'd hit a football line in my youth. I couldn't hold anything back for the next one. Though I will never be able to do it again, my memories will stay fresh of all the auditoriums, the small clubs, the luncheons, the big colleges, where I dug one toe into the platform, stood stiffly on one leg, looked at my audience, took a deep breath, and then let the words tumble out.

When September comes, I get the urge to go again.

V I I

I met a minnow today who loved life.

This was the time to walk down the channel of the stream. Everywhere the land was dry and parched. There had not been rain for weeks. And across the long bottom where the yellow soybean leaves were dropping to the ground, gray soup-bean-colored clouds of dust arose. They swirled over and over trying to catch each automobile.

Gray dust had settled over the strips of late-summer green an acre in from either side of the lane road. Dust had settled in the tops of trees sixty feet tall. Dust had sifted down among the soap-bellied leaves that made a preening sound when the dry cotton-mouth winds blew. This was the time for me to be hunting water down this dry creek channel in the midafternoon of this hot

September day. This stream had stopped flowing for the first time in many years.

My shoes clicked against the bottom of the stream's channel on the rough rock floor. Dust rose up in tiny clouds where I stepped. This was very strange, to see dust coming from the bottom of the creek's channel. My eyes were just even with the soybean bottom, where I watched the yellow leaves dropping like rain and smelled the dust that had blown from the lane road. Dust had settled on soybean gold, poplar green, sourwood purple, and sumac red like a thin, gray snow.

Farther along, the stream had dropped over a strata of dark hard rock the color of pig iron. This rock had withstood centuries of flowing water. Below, there was a deep bowl where water had once poured over. Now this bowl was filled with water like some ancient iron vessel entrenched in solid earth.

This stagnant pool of water had an unpleasant smell in this sultry afternoon world under the high channel banks. Streams of perspiration were running from my face. But I had found water. Had the animals found this spot? Did they fight over this last water hole?

As I sat down on the hard dry bank, I saw one minnow in the water hole. He seemed greatly disturbed. He swam the length and breadth of this six-by-four-foot hole a half-dozen times. When a little ground squirrel came to the hole to drink, the minnow saw its shadow. He swam faster than ever in his decreasing world. He couldn't go upstream or down. He was the only occupant of this small pool. The butterflies sat back a few inches from the water's edge to drink from the soft sand. How much longer would this water last?

While the ground squirrel was drinking, he looked upstream and saw me sitting under the locusts. He gave a shrill bark, leaped across the sand bar, and scurried away. The butterflies, frightened, rose up like a bright cloud, their fragile wings bouncing on the waves of heat. They fluttered in the air scarcely a minute before descending again to their fountain of sand.

When the shadows from their wings fell onto the little pool, the lone minnow swam for his life. He raced forward, around, across, a single streak of living silver, three and a half inches long. Once this minnow and his family swam lazily in a clear pool of fresh water, waiting for a fly or bug to drop from the willow leaves. They could swim upstream or race down through their world without limitation.

I heard a rustle on the dry stems under the wilted bullgrass. I sat so still I stopped breathing when I saw the long water moccasin emerge from under this wilted canopy of grass. What had he been doing under there? Waiting for a ground squirrel, perhaps, or getting the last frogs sitting by the pool catching the greenflies as they came to drink. The snake didn't see me. I sat like a statue of stone under the locust with the pods of wilted leaves. I sat thirsty in a land of thirst where the minnow ran wild in his limited world and the big snake crawled toward him.

When the butterflies saw the snake, his skin the color of gray dust, coming across the sand, they rose up in a cloud, though he didn't intend to disturb them. He knew where he was going all right. There was purpose in his movement toward the water hole. He put his head down into the water, sliding down like a long submarine. But he didn't stop, he went all the way in. He'd not come to get a drink. He had another purpose.

The long snake started chasing the minnow. He chased him around the pool, but the minnow was too fast. Then I knew the snake hadn't caught a frog or a ground squirrel. He was hungry. He had come for the last minnow. He had caught the other minnows in this family when they had come down the dwindling stream to be trapped in their last little world. He had feasted here at ease, for his prey couldn't go beyond these rock walls.

This water snake chased the minnow until I was sure he had caught him. It didn't matter a great deal to me. Among these wild creatures, it was life preying upon life. Then the flapping and flopping of the big snake ceased. Already the pool was stirred until the brown sand rose up discoloring the water. The water snake had caught the minnow all right. Since this was the last one, perhaps I should have stopped him. But I was lazy, sitting under the locust shade in the hot dry-mouthed wind.

I kept my eyes glued on the pool. The snake was still under water, but I knew he would have to rise. He couldn't stand the muddy water too long. Maybe the sand in the water hurt his lidless eyes. He could stay under a long time without air, but still he had to come up to breathe. Watching for him, I thought about the times when I used to wait for a water snake to stick his head above the muddy water when I was a boy. I'd stand over the muddy pool with a stick. When he stuck his head up, I'd batter him over the head.

There was a lull, then a ripple in the pool where the hard lips broke the muddy surface. Slowly, the bulletlike head came up, the two eyes shining in the sweltering heat of the white sun. You feel satisfied now, I thought. You've eaten the minnow. He didn't have a chance. I ought to have got up, found me a stick, and finished you when you crawled over the sand. A stick?

I started looking around for one. It was too late now to save the minnow, but when a snake is near, it isn't a bad idea to have a stick anyway. I located one the length of a cane and as big around as the small end of a baseball bat. It was just across the channel on the bank where a swollen stream had once deposited it.

I looked back at the clearing water. To my surprise, I saw what appeared to be a quick movement across the pool again. I watched closely. Again the quick movement through the water. The sediment dropped more, and I saw the minnow still alive, a silver streak of life in the brown water. The minnow had been too fast for the snake, and too much in love with life, even in this stagnant remnant of a stream.

The snake saw, too. He gave a great lunge. Low sprays of sluggish water went up and fell back into the pool. This second lunge was filled with desperate effort. A ground squirrel came, saw the commotion in the sand-stirred water, and turned tail, running fast toward the wilted bullgrass.

How would I react to being in a cage with a tiger the size of an elephant? How would I like to be shut in a closet with something fifty times my size trying to swallow me? Just the two of us, my pursuer and I, locked in my small dark world? Would I lie still and wait to be devoured, or would I fight back? I began to feel active sympathy for the little minnow.

He was fighting for his survival while I sat under the locust and wondered if I would fight for mine. I had wondered a few times in the recent past if life was worth the fight. A few months back, under an oxygen tent that reminded me of my own grave, I had idly sought some handy exit. But the little minnow, by instinct, found life worth fighting for. He had thrown off one attack. If he could only survive this second . . . but the minnow didn't have a chance without me. I sat by watching.

The sun dipped under a black cloud that blew up from nowhere. A soft wind pressed against my flushed face. In the far distance I heard a sound like a road crew dynamiting a cliff. A distant sound. The sound that disturbed me now was the swishing water. I jumped up without thinking further and grabbed the stick. I stood over this pool of muddy water. Suddenly the snake gave up his chase. This time he'd surely caught the minnow, so frightened and bewildered. I watched for his head to come up. I waited and watched for a water snake, club in hand, like in the days of my youth.

Then I saw the hard lips rise up like a periscope. I held my club over my shoulder. When his head was two inches above the surface, I came down in an arc like striking at a golf ball. There was another flapping in the water, but it was brief this time. A creamlike substance like oily milk spread slowly over the water hole. With the end of my club, I raked the writhing snake out onto the bank. I beat him twice again with the stick, for I had suddenly become involved in this animal world of survival of the fittest. I was the minnow in the pool. This was my life. This was my enemy trying to take my only true possession.

Standing above the pool, I watched the water as sediment dropped for the third time. I watched for a flash of silver as the whole heavens above me darkened. I hadn't deliberately wanted to kill this snake. I hadn't wanted to take sides, to get excited.

I saw a silver flash in the murky water. The minnow who loved life had thrown off his enemy's third attack. And now rain had

begun to fall. A storm was coming that might fill this channel.
The dust would be washed from the leaves. The time of the cotton-
mouth winds had ended.

V I I I

Unfortunately, everybody in the United States doesn't
know Old Op. Twenty-five years ago I found him squatting on a
piece of ridge land I had bought. I liked him so well after he told
me he owned the ridge in his heart even more than I who had a
deed that I let him stay on my farm. He has been with me ever
since.

Old Op, two years older than my father, has outlasted most
men in this hill country. This morning I sat in a chair at my card
table on the hill, with my typewriter before me, while I watched
him work. I had to be out with Op again. I had to be close to
him. I had to be close enough to see the sprouts fall before his
mattock and bush blade and a tree or two go down before his ax.
Old Op, at seventy-seven, could still use these tools. I watched him
stand on the steep bluffs gracefully swinging a bush blade. I saw
him walk up to a sycamore two feet thick and make the chips fly
like leaves from an autumn sourwood in a stiff morning wind. I
watched the tree break from its mooring to fall with a crash. Old
Op could do more work at seventy-seven than any teen-ager who
ever worked on this farm.

For the past twenty-five years, instead of sitting at a card table
with a typewriter, I had worked beside Old Op. He was one of the
two men who could do more work than I, even if he was older than
my father. Old Op didn't weigh over 160 pounds, but no tough-
butted whiteoak ever grew as tough as this man. After the keel was
laid for Old Op, someone must have torn up the plans. We don't
have any more coming in like Old Op.

He married once, had a family, loved his wife and children. After
her death he raised them the best he could. The two younger ones
were adopted because his oldest daughters were not old enough to
care for them when their mother died. Old Op cut timber, fished,
worked for the WPA, or for anybody who needed a hired hand.
His children left home as they grew up until only one son was

staying with him part time in a cabin on my ridge. Later, when he was going blind, his daughter came back. She and I got him to an eye specialist and had a cataract removed from his eye. Then she married and left Old Op alone on the ridge.

Old Op has worked over every foot of this farm. He has fished and hunted when he wanted to, lived the kind of life he likes to live. And most of the time that has been alone. Whenever one of his children has returned to spend a few days in the cabin, the result has been a quarrel. Op doesn't want anybody living with him. He has gone out with many women whose character might be considered questionable, but as close as any one of them ever got was to his cabin door. Old Op's cabin has always been his private castle.

He has washed his own clothes and cooked his own food. He has done his own sweeping and dusting, despite his being almost blind for the last twenty years. He can't tell his neighbors apart when they are a few feet away. Yet he can still course bees to their den trees. He knows where there are more bee trees than any other man in Greenup County, and he has them marked. When he takes a notion for wild honey, he goes at night alone, chops the tree down, robs the bees, and brings his wild sweetening home. He sweetens his sassafras tea with wild honey. He has never bought any sugar.

He has never bought meat at the store. Instead he has fished in the Sandy River, spring, summer, autumn, and winter. And he has walked along the streams and caught turtles with his hands. He has killed wild game in season. He kept my dog, Jerry-B-Boneyard, for three years once. Jerry-B had been shot three times. He was terribly gun-shy. But this didn't bother Old Op. He didn't hunt with a gun anyway. He and Jerry-B went into the dark woods at night. Jerry-B would tree a possum, and Op would climb up and put him in his sack. If Jerry-B holed a possum or mink, Op would work all night digging it out.

Once Jerry-B holed a possum in a tile under the highway. Old Op started digging, for there wasn't any traffic on the road at three in the morning. Before five o'clock he'd dug up the asphalt, removed the tiles, and stacked them up like corded wood. He caught the little possum all right. He spent a lot of labor and sweat for a possum whose hide would have been worth no more than a quarter. But Op didn't kill this little possum. This one was a female. He turned her loose near his cabin to produce possums for his future meals.

That morning cars had to detour until the State Department of Highways was called. Men in trucks were dispatched to the scene, and the road was fixed before noon. Old Op was in his cabin asleep with Jerry-B in bed beside him. On that night they caught a half-dozen possums. His digging up the highway was one of the secrets he kept. He told me ten years later that he was the one a reward was once offered for by the State Department of Highways.

When Op was sixty-five, he could climb trees, bend their tops over, and swing into larger trees. Op laid himself in great supplies of nuts. He'd climb up to shake persimmons, walnuts, and hickory nuts from the trees. He laid in supplies of roots for winter medicine. Up until he was seventy-five, he had never had a tooth pulled and had never taken a dose of medicine given him by a doctor. He had his own medicines. He had some natural remedy for every disease he knew about. He boiled roots, barks, and leaves to make himself spring and autumn tonics, and sweetened them with wild honey.

Old Op never had much money. He would sell a few extra roots, animal pelts, and wild berries, but only to the people who got their orders in first, for he'd make just so many dollars and then quit. He often told me he could live a whole year without making a dollar. All he had to do was lay himself in a few extra fishing lines and hooks, an extra ax and mattock, some clothes and shoes. Op never cared for money. Until I insisted on his getting a tiny old-age pension, he never had over ten dollars at one time in his pocket.

He had a well-to-do brother living in another state who returned to see about him after Op reached seventy. They were no more alike than two strangers. His brother had the manners, dignity, and dress of a governor of a Southern state while Old Op walked slowly along in pants he never pressed, in shirts he had washed and never ironed, with a rabbit's foot in his pocket for good luck and the dozen other charms he always had with him concealed somewhere in his slouchy, wrinkled clothing. Before his brother left, he gave Op money. Op never wanted the money, but the brother insisted on his taking it for use in case of sickness. His brother, much younger than Op, died of a heart attack at sixty-five while Op, living on his ridge, was helping me cut timber at seventy.

It used to be my ambition to beat him with an ax when we cut saw timber, cleared land, or hung tobacco on tier poles in the top of the high barns. Now Old Op was cutting sprouts this morning while I sat at my typewriter near him. I wanted to work with him, but I wasn't physically able. Yet, Op was twenty-nine years my senior. This made me wonder what kind of clay Old Op was made of. He was made of a different clay than most men.

He had lain down on his belly, put his beardy face into the streams, and drunk the water. I had seen him do it. He never had typhoid fever in his life. He never had diphtheria. I got typhoid twice from drinking out of streams. My friend Adder Heck got typhoid from drinking out of the Little Sandy River and almost died. He got so thin they had to turn his six-foot-seven frame in a sheet. Lin Gore got diphtheria from drinking in a stream. But Old Op drank at these places and got nothing. Once he did tell me a story about almost getting hurt while drinking from a stream. He was lying across a big log to get himself a drink and the log started moving away. It was a snake—according to Old Op.

If I ate green apples, they cramped me. Old Op could eat every bite he could hold of green anything. He would never have the slightest stomach-ache. He didn't need to take all that herb medicine he made by the gallons and drank like water. He could wade through fields of poison vine, and it would never bother him. Wasps, honeybees, and bumblebees might just as well not waste their stingers on him. Their little stings didn't faze him. Old Op was immune to about everything.

I know a copperhead bit him once. He told me about the cure his father used on him—the black-powder cure. You take the bullets from the cartridges and shoot the bite with black powder. I had never heard of such a cure. Old Op said it was worse than the snake bite. I never saw Old Op sick but once. I got Doc Raike, aged eighty-one, and he drove out to see Old Op. Doc Raike diagnosed Op's trouble as lobar pneumonia.

Old Op didn't tell Doc Raike what had caused it. But late that autumn, about October two years ago, Op was out hunting one night with an old stray hound and a gallon of wine. I found him passed out on Seaton Ridge with his face turned up toward the skies. It had rained that night, and mists were rising from his wet clothes in little clouds. Old Op's eye sockets were little lakes of water which shone like silver in the morning sun. He was lying there dead to the world with pools of water over his crippled eyes. But he pulled through lobar pneumonia in three days and was out hunting again with a jug of wine he had made from locust blossoms.

I watched Old Op work this morning. I knew he wouldn't be working many more days. Before long, autumn and the hunting season would be here. Then Old Op wouldn't have time to work no matter how much I needed him. He'd soon take a basket to gather pawpaws, a sack to gather nuts. He knew where they grew. He didn't like to waste his time working when leaves changed color and beauty came to the autumn hills again.

I X

This afternoon the doorbell rang. I went to the door where a man and his wife were waiting.

"Don't want to disturb you," said the man, smiling. "But I've come to see how you are getting along. Remember me?"

I looked him over. I'd seen him someplace, but I couldn't remember where. But I'd met this man, probably years ago. Before I could search my memory for his identification, he said, "I'm Joe Smith's boy. You remember old Joe Smith out at Hopewell, don't you?"

Joe Smith, I thought. It could be anybody's name. But I knew Joe Smith at Hopewell. I didn't know him well, but I'd seen him. I'd heard a lot about him.

"Sure I know him," I said. "Workingest man in Greenup County. Never wanted to stop work when night came. Best tobacco grower in the state."

"Right," the young man said proudly. "Now, I'm his son, Joe. People call him Old Joe. They call me Young Joe."

"Will you folks come in?" I invited them.

Young Joe would weigh about 180 pounds. He was a square-shouldered man of about thirty. He had large hands, but they were soft now. And when he sat down his pants legs pulled up until I could see his boots. Why was he wearing boots?

"These boots make me feel a lot better," Young Joe said when he saw me looking. "See, I had an accident last winter. And these are my climbing boots. I've been wearing boots like these for eleven years. And after I got out of the hospital, the doctor told me to wear my boots."

"What kind of work did you do, Young Joe?"

"I started working for thirty-three cents an hour climbing trees for a tree-expert company," he told me. "I worked up with my company until I had a good job. Then I had an accident. Haven't you heard?"

"I heard something about it," I told him.

But I hadn't heard anything. I was flat on my back in bed myself last January when he had his accident. But his life was his most important possession, and his job was of great importance to him, too. I didn't want to make Young Joe feel bad. The same sort of thing had happened to him that had to me.

"Well, a limb came crashing down out of a tree, struck me on the head one Friday," he said. "When I woke up, I thought it was after a night's sleep. I was getting ready to go to work again. My wife told me it was Sunday afternoon."

"How bad were you hurt?" I asked him.

"Broke four of my teeth and fractured my skull in nine places," he said. "It burst my right eardrum. I can't hear anything with my right ear."

"That was some jolt."

"But the thing that hurt me most is the thing I need in my work," he explained. "That lick destroyed my balance. I can't walk straight, but I'm improving."

Yes, a tree climber needed his equilibrium. How would Young Joe ever climb again without it?

"I hope you improve until you can get back to your work," I said. "You want back, don't you?"

"Want back?" he repeated with a smile. "I'll say I do."

When Young Joe's wife was a little girl in second grade, Naomi had been her teacher. They left us in the old living room while they walked over the house. I wanted to know more about Young Joe.

"So when I was in the hospital, I asked for my climbing boots," he said. "After wearing boots eleven years, I got lonesome for them. My doctor had my wife bring them to the hospital. A lot of people laugh when I tell them about this. They don't understand why I wanted my boots."

"I can see why you did," I said.

Young Joe Smith looked straight at me with his inquiring blue eyes.

"A man hates to lose everything, doesn't he?" I said. "You don't want to lose your profession. I didn't either when I was in the hospital. My wife brought my last book and put it on a table in my hospital room. She brought magazines with my stories and poems in them. I dreamed of the time when I would write more of them. I didn't want to be whipped. I was so near gone of a heart attack they hadn't taken my clothes off me days later. But I wanted to go back to my work."

"Now you're talking," Young Joe said. "I don't know much about books and magazines. I didn't even get to the eighth grade. Haven't read a book for years, but I understand what you're talking about. You felt good just looking at your books and magazines. And I never felt good on Sunday without my boots." He looked at me hard. "You know, I *liked* to climb trees."

He went on with a little chuckle. "My boss said I was the best climber he ever had, as big as I am, and you won't believe this when I tell you, but when we lived in Louisville, my wife forgot her keys and locked them up inside our apartment, which was in a brick building, and I climbed up the straight outside wall to the third-story window, which we had left unlocked, raised it, went inside, and got our keys. I told a man about climbing this wall. He wouldn't believe me. I climbed it again to show him."

When Young Joe spoke of his climbing, there was a new light in his eyes.

"You know, we weren't allowed to use spikes in our boots like boys who climb electric and telephone poles," he explained. "We had to protect the trees."

"Then how did you climb them?"

"Tie a johnny-ball on the end of a rope, throw it up and over a limb, take hold of the rope, and walk up the tree." He laughed with pleasure just remembering it.

I was happy Young Joe Smith had found me. I was happy to have him in my house wearing his climbing boots. I understood what he was up against.

"Yes, I could throw a rope higher into a tree than any man I worked with or any boss I ever had. I was foreman of five crews when it happened." His face cracked open in a wide smile, and his words were positive. "And I liked to climb trees. I climbed them around Hopewell when I was a boy. I'd like to climb them now. If I could only get my balance back again."

If I could only stand up before an audience without fear of tumbling over again, I thought. If I could only grip the lectern and feel the platform beneath my feet and hear the words tumbling out.

Young Joe Smith and I had a lot in common. We understood each other's situation.

"Joe, you're on some kind of compensation, aren't you?"

"Yes, I draw thirty-two fifty a week," he said with a sigh. "My wife, two children, and I can live on that all right as long as we don't have to pay house rent. But we're expecting another in our family. It will be a little tough then. But I hope to be back working. To hell with the compensation when I'm able to work. I go to see my boss real often. He thinks I'm getting better."

"Say, would you like to walk around here?" I said.

"I'd love it."

We walked slowly into the dining room. Young Joe barely missed the door facing. I knew he wouldn't climb until he had better equilibrium. He'd surely fall from a high tree if he climbed now. When he went through the kitchen door into the back yard he bumped the doorframe. He touched it lightly like a man who had hit objects before. We walked out into our back yard, where there were trees in all directions.

"You've got a lot of nice trees here," he said.

"Say, where you living now?"

"With my mother and father-in-law," he replied. "I've been practicing climbing every day, too. They've got some low apple trees for me to climb. I get my rope out, tie a johnny-ball, throw it over a limb, and up I go. People down there think I'm crazy out climbing trees with a rope. They drive by on the highway and look at me as if I were some kind of freak. Then they drive on laughing."

"I understand that, Young Joe," I said. "I lay in bed with my fountain pen and tried to write. But I couldn't read what I'd written. My hands were that stiff and sore. I had to exercise them. Yes, I understand about your climbing trees. Keep it up until you become your old self again. That's what you want, isn't it?"

"That's it," he replied quickly. "You said the right words. That's what I want. Just to be my old self again. I'll never be happy until I am."

They left a few minutes later.

"Good luck to you." We shook hands. "I hope you're soon climbing the highest trees."

"And I hope you'll soon be writing the best books," he said with a laugh. "I don't know much about books, but I hope you'll be writing them!"

Young Joe Smith went down the walk. He was very unsteady. His once-powerful body seemed to wobble off to the side as he walked. As I listened to his boots giving hollow echoes down the walk, I wondered if poor Joe would ever climb again.

OCTOBER

October is the best autumn month for me, and of all the months, second only to April. There is great beauty in the changing colors of the leaves. Those trees that were first to get dressed last spring are now racing to be the first to undress and go back to bed for a long winter of sleep. Old cold-blooded lizards that spring suns thawed and warmed into a new life now doze drowsily in the October sun. Old dogs find places where they can lie on the ground and sleep in the sun. Old people take their chairs outside the house to sit in the sun. October sun must be magical to old flesh, old blood streams, old bones. Though October can't bear to make a clean sweep of all forms of life, she is a beautiful killer. October kills so gracefully that she stirs the imaginations of poets to write about the beauty of death on the land.

Now all the flowers are dead or dying. Just a few remain, and these are autumn flowers. They will live, bloom, flaunt their beauty to a changing world until frost. Many will live on after frost, blending their many colors with the stronger tones of turning leaves. Already red leaves slither down from the sweet gums, persimmons, and sumacs, like drops of red rain.

Yellow leaves tumble gently and softly from the tall poplars. Warm-brown leaves fall from the oaks, orange-red from the short dogwoods. Everywhere there is color. Everywhere there is a grace, beauty, and gentleness in death. Everywhere the wind whispers that the time of sleep between death and resurrection will be brief. October's multicolored death is made all the more beautiful by the knowledge that green April waits to resurrect the dead.

11

This morning I walked up the valley facing a nippy wind. It smelled of frost. In other years we have had frost in late September, and a few times we have had snow before this time of year. I knew frost couldn't be far away. I could feel it in the wind.

When I went through the first gate, I heard a rustling in the leaves, which were full of autumn death and many colors. I saw an old blacksnake barely crawling in the cool morning wind. He was not sensible to the tradition of his species. He should have already hibernated. I have heard that snakes that don't hibernate soon enough go blind and regain their sight later. Old blacksnake, his blood chilled, acted as if he might be blind, creeping along, nosing the ground with his head, hunting for a mole's hole, so he could get underground.

He crawled toward me after I spoke, as if asking for help. Looking around, I found a hole where a groundhog had once burrowed in the side of the bank. Old blacksnake was frightened when I reached down and got him by the tail. I carried him dangling in the air, squirming and wiggling, to the mouth of the groundhog's ancient burrow, which was as large as my leg at the calf. When I laid him down, he went back into the cavern in a hurry.

For days I had not seen a snake. I knew they had found places in the crevices of rocks, in old coal mines, water seeps, hollow logs, under old stumps. A whole shelf of books could be written about the hibernation of snakes, or, better still, about the hibernation of the

cold-blooded animals upon this earth. Frogs, snakes, lizards, terrapins, water dogs, after hibernation and a long sleep, are awakened
to a new life in the spring. If they are not killed by their enemies
and if they find food, they may live many decades. Perhaps doctors
put it too mildly when they tell human beings to take a thirty-minute
rest after the noon meal if they want to prolong their lives. Perhaps
tired, harried humans would benefit from resting a season.

Now with old blacksnake in a place hidden from crow, chicken
hawk, owl, dog, mink, weasel, and fox, I walked on up the valley and
into the sharp wind. A yellow jacket flew in, mumbling, crying,
sighing, for he was hungry. Maybe instinctively he thought I could
feed him, for he tried to fly into my face and I had to bat at him with
my hand. I thought he might sting me, but instead he buzzed slowly
against the cool head wind toward his uncertain destiny. In a few
feet more, I came upon some yellow jackets feasting on the ripened
fruit fallen from a towering rough-barked, almost leafless persimmon
tree. Yellow jackets were as hungry this time of year as in the early
spring when sap stirred in the trees.

But now the smart yellow jackets would be getting under the
bark of trees, in the crevices of lightning-split oaks, in hollow
branches and logs, where they would sleep like the bumblebee,
hornet, wasp, and mud dauber. Weeks ago wasps were already crawling into our attics.

On every side, ground squirrels ran toward the little rock cliffs
with their mouths loaded with nuts. These little warm-blooded animals couldn't lie down and sleep half their lives away. They had to
work hard at storing food for the winter. Even then, they didn't live
as long as the cold-blooded things on this earth. I stood watching
them strip the bushes of hazelnuts and the trees of beechnuts. I
watched one carry a walnut until he got tired. He laid the walnut
down, stood on his little hind feet with his front paws folded, and
barked to his mate. She answered him but kept her distance. Then
he rolled the walnut a few feet, finally picked it up again in his
mouth, and went on.

At the foot of the hill below the Kilgore house, which is about
the center of my farm, where there is more food and more protection

for wildlife, I saw a fox. His long bushy-red and white-tipped tail rode on the wind as he trotted across the pasture. This warm-blooded fellow had no intention of hibernating for the winter. He didn't look my way to see me, and as I was standing downwind from him, he couldn't smell me. I couldn't smell him because I didn't have the faculty. I had to see him with my eye. Men were never intended to be killers, or they would have been given the nose along with the instinct.

After the fox had moved on, jumping, alert for a quail or a rabbit, I caught sight of an old gray lizard clinging to the rough bark of a persimmon tree with his four little crocodile feet. Through the centuries of evolution between the lizard and the crocodile, how many species had died out leaving only hieroglyphics in stone as their recorded history. Just to think that this tiny lizard was a relative of the crocodile made me smile. I wouldn't pet a crocodile. But the lizard made a wonderful friend.

The sun was moderating the nippy air while old lizard, pinched from hunger, climbed up high to snare himself a greenfly. Now was the time he should nose into the crevice of a tree or a hollow stump to sleep through late autumn, winter, and early spring. Old lizard didn't look to be very active. He blinked his sleepy eyes. His blood was getting colder.

What if an icy wind blew in from the north and chilled his blood in a hurry instead of by degrees the way autumn usually slips up gently? What would happen to him high up on that tree? Would he fall asleep, then drop from the tree? Would his little crocodile feet release their grip on the rough persimmon bark?

Half-asleep, he clung there waiting for a fly that didn't come. It was too cold for flies. The lizard should not be so greedy. There would be flies for him next spring. Trying to catch the last fly, he might lose his life. But nature's creatures make fewer mistakes of this type than men do.

I walked on, watching the warm-blooded jaybirds carrying acorns to the tops of oaks, where they filled up the hollow places in the trees with food for bad weather. They were beautiful, fussy, arrogant, noisy. But they had the instinct, unlike human beings, who can be lulled into a false sense of security, to lay up something for a winter day. The frosts and snows could not be far away. Not when the ground squirrels and bluejays were this busy laying in stores.

Everywhere over the multicolored pasture fields, flocks of birds, like small dark clouds, rose up toward the blue morning sky, circled between me and the sun, gathering other little clouds, until a dark patch of sky took off toward the south. This was a time of instinctive movement, of natural change. It was a time for man to walk and watch.

I looked down when I heard a rustle at my feet. I saw an old toad puffed up so full of wind he could hardly breathe. He went down into the leaves like a man trying to pull his coat collar higher on a cold day. He was very late in finding his winter place to sleep.

Then I stepped on something hard as a rock. I lifted my foot quickly and looked down where old terrapin was hibernating for winter. He was covering himself over with the good warm dirt. Spring thunder would awaken him to a new green world. If this terrapin and his mate were not killed by drought or burned by forest fire or smashed on the highway, they might live to be a hundred.

I I I

This is my formula for surviving a heart attack:

Never feel sorry for yourself. After you have had a heart attack, the most important thing in the world for you is a positive mental attitude. Wake up in the morning and think of something pleasant. Think of something funny. This will be hard to do in your first week, for you will feel depressed. You will wonder whether you are going to live, even whether you want to live. There is a saying, A man never had a heart attack while he was laughing. I like to believe this. Just never feel sorry for yourself. You won't have to. Your wife, children, neighbors, and friends will feel so sorry for you. They may even overdo it and hurt you. Everybody will pity you until you'll get so tired of it you'll want to seek out people who don't know about your condition.

Stay on your diet. Just about every heart patient is put on a diet. The greater percentage of people who have heart attacks are overweight. After you have a heart attack, you have to take off weight, if you want to live.

I am not allowed any stimulants. Why does one have to have stimulants? For his body? No, the body will do the work if left alone. High blood pressure, which is aggravated by stimulants, often brings on a heart attack. Doctors will tell you that over half their heart patients stray from their diets. Though they know they may face death if they don't hold to a rigid diet, they break the rules, and some die. Do not be one of these who value life so lightly. If the doctor wants you to take off pounds, take them off.

I have taken off thirty pounds. I am down from 222 to 192, and I feel better. I used to have terrible headaches before my heart attack. But since I have been on a rigid, low-salt, nonfat, nonstimulant diet, I haven't had a single one. Just getting rid of the headaches alone is worth all the deprivations involved in staying on my diet. And, maybe, it will prevent my having another heart attack. We are the food we eat, just as we are the air we breathe.

Actually, it was harder for me to give up smoking than to diet. Three heart men and one surgeon advised me against smoking. I had smoked excessively for nineteen years of my life but had never inhaled. I smoked cigars and a pipe. I liked to smoke. I still would like to smoke, but I'm not going to. One of my doctors said simply, "If you smoke, you will die." I think of this every time I am tempted. Why shouldn't doctors put it up to their patients like this instead of adopting a compromise attitude? A year has passed, and I have not smoked.

Avoid anger. The word *anger* should not be in a heart patient's vocabulary. Once a famous English physician said, after having a heart attack, that his life was in the hands of those who wanted to kill him. And in the end he died getting angry at those who disputed his theories about the heart. Go out of your way to avoid irritation. You, the patient, must walk away from a nasty, disagreeable person who tries to offend you. The offender of a heart patient does not deserve to be noticed. Anger can throw you back into another heart attack. Anger can kill you.

Avoid fear. Before your heart attack, you probably were a strong man. You never stopped working. You had more energy and strength than you knew what to do with. You didn't know fear.

After the attack, you find yourself on the side of the weak, quiet, and submissive. You even stop being an aggressive spectator, you no longer scream for your football team "to take 'em out" or for your favorite fighter to hit the other guy under the heart. You will never scream that way again. You won't even watch a fighter hitting another one under the heart, for you would think of your own heart. You have fears for the man taking punishment. You're not the same. Your world has changed. You are kinder to everybody. You feel others have the right to live, too. You know that fear brings on sudden excitement and tension, you know you can lapse back into another attack. You cannot afford to fear.

Avoid cold. There was a time when you could have slept on the snow on a winter night with a blanket under you and one over you. You might have even done this to show your friends how much cold you could stand. Or you might have had poetry in you and wanted to look up at the cold winter skies filled with millions of stars. But you were younger then, stronger. You ate anything you wanted to eat, bragged to your friends that you could digest nails, razor blades, and triple-decker sandwiches. You felt that way then. Blood raced easily through your circulatory system. Your heart, the life pump, was a powerful instrument.

All that is changed now. You sleep in a room at sixty-five degrees temperature. You sleep with wool socks on your feet and a hot-water bottle in your bed. You don't know whether your feet are cold or not. You can't feel much down there. The tips of your ears and the end of your nose stay cold, though, inside or out.

Now when it rains, you stay indoors. If it snows, you stay indoors. When outside, you bundle up like a mummy, and then come in to change your socks and stand by the fire. The more cold you try to endure, the harder your heart must work to pump blood to warm the extremities. This is a matter of common sense. Keep warm.

Avoid worry. Worry, anxiety—these are words that pop up in newspapers every day. The medical journals warn you about worry, too, and about strife and tension. These are birds of a feather.

Worry certainly helps to bring on a heart attack. Everybody has heard it said a thousand times: *Worry will kill you.* But how can you keep from worrying?

To find the answer, start from scratch. If you continue to worry, you may kill yourself, and certainly all your worries are as nothing when you are faced with losing your life. Relatively, then, the problem you have found is not a problem at all. It will right itself. You are not as important to the world as you think. Let other people you worry about take care of themselves. This will be better for them, for your worrying won't help them. To get your mind off whatever worries you, switch to something you like. Play your favorite kind of music. Play chess, checkers, read a good book. Don't go on worrying about something your worrying won't help.

Bear in mind that each day you live is the best day of your life. Yesterdays are gone, and tomorrows never come.

Do not overexercise. If you are a mental giant, slow down to give others a chance to think. Maybe your mind was what you over-exercised. Thinking is exercise which might be harder on a man than too much physical labor. A heart specialist made this statement to me. "The tension in hurrying to catch a plane, riding through the skies, thinking, working on a speech, landing, getting a taxi, rushing to a platform, and giving a talk was harder on your heart than pitching hay into the barn loft or cutting saw timber for ten solid hours."

Now if you are the man who had the strength of ten, with energy to burn, if you were going to climb the highest hill to a cloud and stick your hand up through it, if you wished the day had more than twenty-four hours and begrudged the four or five you lost in sleeping, then you undoubtedly abused your body.

You knew then that your body was made of stainless steel, your engine had countless cylinders, and you would go on forever without tarnish or rust and never fall apart. Well, now you know that your body is made of flesh and bone and your heart is your engine and that the best makes of human bodies, like the best makes of machines, don't last forever.

But even with a damaged heart you can go on living. Just don't overreach yourself physically.

Listen to your wife. My doctor told me this. He permitted my wife to stay in my hospital room when my condition was critical. Later, when I was allowed to dictate one letter each day, I wrote to three friends who had suffered the same fate I was suffering now. I had never understood before what was the matter with them. Each was large and strong. One was both a mental and physical giant. Two were college presidents, while the third was vice-president of a large business concern. It was strange when I got the same reply from each of them: *Listen to your wife. Do as she tells you. You'll be all right.*

Why should one listen to his wife after he has had a heart attack any more than he had listened before? How could three of my friends who didn't know each other and who lived hundreds of miles apart write me the same thing? Then it all began to add up as I thought about it. Women are kinder than men. They give us birth, love, food, and tender care. They would never have us killed in wars if it were left to them. Women are affectionate and gentle, more so than men.

My wife put my books on the table beside my bed. She told me I wasn't through. She told me that all the money we'd saved and all we could borrow and all we'd get from selling our land would see us through. All the resources we had would be used for my benefit to see me well again. All of this was sweet talk to me. She saw that I took my medicine. She watched to see that I didn't get off my diet. My wife, more than anyone else, wanted me to live. No wonder my doctor had said this to me.

Neither of these three men had been given much chance, but each had lived. Maybe their wives were responsible for their being alive. Once a man is helpless, somebody has to take charge. It had better be his wife. She will do it best because she loves him most. She'll fight even harder than doctor, nurse, children, or friends for his life. My wife was the only person who ever tried to get me to slow down *before* my attack. It wasn't her fault that I didn't listen.

Ask the Divine Physician's help daily. There is every evidence of the "Divinity that shapes our ends." This is something we don't have to prove. We are on this earth for a purpose. The world itself didn't just happen without the Greater Power's laws and intent. Life didn't come into being without reason. All around us, we find evidence of a Divinity.

He can help us restore ourselves to health if we humbly ask Him. All other physicians work under His guidance. Often people give up hope for a loved one. There is only once chance in a thousand, they are told. And yet the person lives. That chance belongs to God.

I V

Since last October, my most adventurous excursions in search of man-made entertainment have been to the movies in Greenup. After many Saturday evenings of watching others, I have learned just how to behave in a small-town theater.

After you get your ticket, by all means stop and buy yourself two bags of warm, buttered popcorn. That's why they've got it at the theater. Now, as there are fewer than forty patrons to call to and wave at when there used to be a hundred and fifty, a little popcorn helps fill the gap. And while you are spending for popcorn, look under the show window at the chewing gum, candy, and peanuts. After you take a bite of popcorn, it's nice to switch to a chocolate bar and then over to peanuts. This is the regular procedure at a small theater. If you want to behave well, spend your money for these essentials so you can eat and chew while you relax and watch the show.

This theater doesn't handle the soda pops, but you'll need something to wash down the popcorn. A soft grain might lodge in your throat. So you had better buy yourself a soda pop before you come in. You need to bring something to drink if you want to live up to the standards. Now you're ready. Walk through the door and down the aisle to the seat of your choice. If someone is sitting in this row, step on his feet if he doesn't draw them back under his seat.

You must come early to the theater. You must be there firstest with the mostest. Just sit back, open your mouth wide, for no one can see you in the dark, take a handful of popcorn, and put it all in your mouth at once. After you have finished this first handful, reach down on the floor beside you and pick up the bottle of soda pop. Take a sweet swig to wash all the loose grains lodged in your gullet on down into your craw.

Now take a bite from your chocolate bar. After the popcorn and soda pop, the chocolate tastes wonderful. And after the chocolate, go after the salted peanuts. Well, this is fine. You are relaxed and happy as you watch others come down the aisles. They talk and laugh, and they have their arms full, too. They look to their right and left, choose seats, sit down with good things to eat, and get relaxed and unbuttoned and ready to watch the show.

If the seat feels a little hard or a little too straight to lean back in, put your feet up on the seat in front of you. No one will be wanting the seat in front anyway. This theater is never crowded any more. In this small-town theater they used to stand in the aisles on Saturday night to see a show! You don't like to think of the way you had to stand. Somebody would holler, "Buttin', buttin', who's doin' the buttin'," and patrons would shove and you'd all go together and smash popcorn sacks, knock soda pops from hands, spill them on pretty dresses and clean suits, and then everybody would laugh. Those who got mad would be considered bad sports.

Everything has changed now. Not so many come to the theater any more, unless you count the groups of boys and girls from the country on Saturday nights. In those days they came to see the big monster get loose on the screen and carry a pretty blonde around for some time before choking her to death. Not a sound went up from the audience until the end of the show, when they finally killed the bulletproof monster and women were safe in the town. That kind of show was breath-taking.

Now you thought about those great thrillers while you waited to see what was coming up. It was a good title for a show all right, *Deep in My Heart*. Show you something about the life of a man named Sigmund Romberg. Now who was he? You try to think as you become more relaxed eating popcorn from the palm of your hand, washing it down with soda pop. Yeah, that man, Romberg! Say, he wrote some music, didn't he? Didn't he write songs? Well, you can't be sure, but it doesn't matter a lot anyway. You've come to the theater to relax and be entertained. You'd better be enter-

tained! You feel that way. If you're not, you can get up and walk
out of the theater. You've done that many times before. Why sit
through something you don't like? You didn't come in here to think
about that man Sigmund Romberg.

Whoever he is, his life story can't draw the Saturday-night crowds
that fearful monster who tried to kill all the blondes in a big town
drew. Say, that show brought them out! When you saw the preview,
you went home and marked the date on the calendar. You had to
be there. Sigmund Romberg didn't make you mark a date on your
calendar. You just didn't have anything else to do. Well, about all
the small crowd was in. Maybe thirty-five had come. Pretty good
for a picture you didn't know too much about.

The soda pop was gone now, and you didn't want the empty
bottle down at your feet. A little kick from your toe started it rolling
down under the seats. You heard it hit another bottle. Didn't know
whether it turned the other soda pop over or not. Didn't matter
much one way or the other. You heard many bottles rolling over
the slanted floor down to the front. Easier for Old Dollie, who
cleaned the theater, to pick them up down there than to bend over
to get them under the seats. You'd finished one sack of popcorn.
You'd finished your candy. You'd kept a few of your peanuts. You
might need them along with a few grains of the unpopped corn
you'd found at the bottom of the sack.

There was a lot of pleasant talk all around you. Some of the boys
who liked the big monster from the deep were here. They didn't
bother to take their caps off. Hadn't it always been the custom for
women to sit in the theater in front of you wearing broad-brimmed
hats? Better not ask one to remove her hat either, even if you had to
move from behind her. Well, these country boys wore skull-fitting
caps with long bills. Sometimes the bills got in the way, but not
very often. Why should a man take off his cap or a woman her hat
in a theater? A fellow paid his good money to see a picture, and he
liked to see it his way. He liked to have a little personal freedom.
If the manager came in and said something, best thing to do was
tell him off, get up and walk out, and make him give your money
back at the ticket office. You were smart, you liked freedom and

independence. You liked to have a good time at the theater—your way, which was the right way.

Bottles were still making a lot of noise clinking and clanking under the seats, clattering down toward the stage in front. But only a few were broken. There wasn't too much shattered glass for Old Dollie to sweep up in her little dustpan. She ought to do something to earn her money anyway.

The popcorn fell around you like snowflakes. It was fun to see white flakes of fluffy popcorn in the semidarkness, coming down around you like snow on a dark night. Reminded you of winter. You tore into your extra sack with a smile. You sent the white snow flying four rows below you. You made them look back. Old John Graves was down there. He looked back, his eyes were shining in the dark. He didn't like to be hit with popcorn any more than he liked the movies with the monster of the deep. He even walked out of the theater on the first one. He liked movies, but he never returned for a thriller-killer-diller monster show.

One thing you've never done was put your chewing gum down in the empty seat next to you after chewing it. You always stuck it up under the seat. Some unmannerly people didn't know it should be put up under the seat instead of on top. A few people got stuck to their seats every night. When they rose up they had long white tails hanging to them. A man had to chew something while he was waiting for the picture to begin, but you'd always been careful with your gum.

People got loud if they had to wait very long. A man wanted to be entertained, didn't he? That's why he had come to see a picture. That's why you had come to this unknown picture about this Sigmund Romberg. You had to be entertained. You had to have somewhere to go, something to see, something to keep you from getting restless.

There was a burst of sound and a flash on the screen. The news came first and then some ads. You knew what they were. You had seen them so often. About the Chevrolet dealer and the Ford dealer and their new cars and trucks, about the furniture, clothing, and grocery store in your home town. You were so tired of these ads.

They didn't thrill you except the first time you saw them. Well, you could always throw things up front. Old John Graves looked back once during the cartoon of the worm and bird to see who was throwing the peanuts. You know he thought you were throwing them at him. Well, what if you did? Somebody was throwing at you from behind.

Then *Deep in My Heart* flashed on the screen with a big orchestra and a man in a swallowtail coat up front directing them how to play music. You didn't like that kind of music. That wasn't your kind. But you figured there'd be something in the show you'd like. Only thing that interested you in the first part of the show was when Mr. Sigmund Romberg took two men and went to a village where he was trying to write music. A girl and her mother came to the little cottage, and he went through an act of his show. Well, you thought that was pretty good. A lot of action and entertainment, especially when he jumped through the window and took window-pane, sash, and all with him. This brought a laugh from you. You liked the way he sailed out that window.

When this Helen sang his early songs, well, it wasn't anything terriff. You just couldn't appreciate her singing. Let's see, her name was, you believe, Helen Traubert—something like that. You'd never heard of the woman. Well, you always know right away when a picture is going to be good, like the monster pictures for instance. If it's good everybody is quiet. If it's not good, they talk. And that's where Old John Graves comes in again. The picture went right along through the life of this man Romberg, and by the time they played something he had written about Maytime, there was a lot of talking and carrying on.

Honest injun, if Old John Graves didn't rise up and stand by his seat and stare back at you. He was awful mad about something. There was a beautiful scene of flowers in bloom and two lovers who sang to each other. But you'd never heard the song. Guess it was a song Mr. Romberg wrote. Old John Graves must have known all about Sigmund Romberg and his songs the way he acted.

The talking got louder, and Old John clawed his neck and looked back with his hands shading his eyes. He was catching the peanuts.

Popcorn fell over him like the white blossoms of Maytime fell from the trees when the soft summer winds blew. Everybody was talking. This wasn't any thriller-diller show. What was Old John trying to do? Did he think he owned the theater? Were all the rest wrong while he was right. What happened to a theater or a town when one man tried to run the whole works? It went to seed, didn't it?

Then, after a few more scenes, there was one about a show called *The Student Prince.* A voice said it had once been a smash hit. You got a smash hit of peanuts on the side of your face. John Graves got up again. There was a lot of loud talking and laughing now. Many of the thirty-five customers were getting up and leaving. Forty-five cents didn't break anybody up. But you liked to get your money's worth. You stayed on just as long as you thought you could stand it.

When you got up to go, which was toward the end of the show, that orchestra was back playing "When I Get Too Old to Dream." Gee, you liked that. You didn't know this man Sigmund Romberg had written that one. You had actually started to go. But if you had gone, only Old John Graves and four others would have been left. So you decided to stay on to the end of the show with Old John and make it a half-dozen.

V

All my life important things have happened to me in October, the middle part of October particularly. Naomi Deane and I were married by a (retired) Methodist minister on October 14—actually at 12:05 in the morning, so as to avoid getting married on Friday the thirteenth. We were that superstitious. Then my first book, *Man with a Bull-tongue Plow,* was published on October 14, 1934. For one reason or another—I never asked for it—eight of my books have been published on October 14. When one of my books became the selection of a book club, my publisher gave me a big party in New York on October 14. We ended up at the Stork Club at three o'clock in the morning. That was the only time I was ever in the Stork Club.

This year a group of my friends, citizens of Riverton and Greenup, and some civic groups chose October 14 on which to pay me a great honor. Then they changed it to October 15, a Saturday, so that schoolteachers could come from around the state.

I don't know exactly how to describe this occasion. They had the Governor proclaim it Jesse Stuart Day. The president of the University of Kentucky came down to speak. Hundreds of my friends, hundreds of other people I'd never set eyes on, newspaper reporters, and radio people came here to wish me well. They unveiled a stone marker set on the green in front of the courthouse in Greenup with my name and face and a few kind words on it. It turned out that my friends around here had been planning this occasion for a long time, ever since I was so sick that they didn't know if I was going to pull through.

I gave a short speech today, the first one I've been allowed to give in a year and a week. Maybe it's the last one I'll ever give. And it wasn't much of a speech because my doctors said I had to write it all out beforehand and then read it very slowly. I'd rather speak spontaneously, and in the old days I would use hardly a note. But this is what I said today:

My friends, I've spoken to many audiences over America, but this is the greatest audience I have ever faced. This is the highest honor that has ever come to me, to stand here on this spot in the courthouse yard and speak to you. All along this has seemed like a dream, but now I know this is reality.

It is a fine tribute to anyone to be so honored in his home town. And it is most unusual for a writer. When you travel over America, you see but few markers up for writers. Those few you find were erected after their deaths. What makes this occasion unique is the fact that this tribute is being paid to me in my lifetime. I have not always been a good boy in my home town. But I never was at any time in my life without ambitions and dreams. Because this is my country that I know so well. I've written so much about this town, changed its name three times, on paper that is, to Greenwood, Blakesburg, and Honeywell.

The Tussies and Bushmans, Didway Hargis, Sparkie, Arn and Peg Sparks, Shan, Finn, and Mick Powderjay, Old Op and Lucretia Acres, Doshie, Hootbird and Ben Hammertight, Alf and Julia Pruitt, the Beatinest Boy, Scrappie Lykins III, and Red Mule—all are my children. There are a whole host of lesser known children, too.

Maybe because my friends here know these people so well is why I am honored today.

Perhaps another reason why this has happened is that I have dared to dream of lifting the education of our youth to a higher level and of doing something for the teaching profession. I have learned that sound teaching, tolerance, and love are the greatest things on earth. I know I've had teachers who have influenced my life.

You who visit Greenup, Kentucky, today, see the jackets of my books enlarged and displayed over the street intersections. When each of these was published, I always had two fears. I wondered what the repercussions would be on my people and my friends, and I used to think there would never be another book of mine published. But there have been more published. There will always be more published as long as I live. I am not boasting when I say this. I have too much to say, too many stories to tell, to quit now. This forces me to consider the time I have left.

Regardless of what has already or ever will happen to me, I have never felt sorry for myself. Now, I rejoice that I am living. Look today what I would have missed if those scales, holding life on one side and death on the other, so evenly balanced for so many days, had been tilted in death's favor. I wouldn't have been here speaking to you, standing before an audience for the first time since last October 8, when I spoke at Murray State College right before my attack. I am happy just to be alive. To be here to receive this honor in my home town from my neighbors, my near and faraway friends, makes me rejoice. I have so many things to be thankful for, of which the greatest is life.

Each day, I make myself believe this day will be the finest. Yesterdays are gone forever, and tomorrows never come. I feel just as surely as I am standing here that I have reached on this day the middle milestone of my life. I expect and hope to do as many more books as you see jackets displayed over the streets. I might even do more if I am given more time. This rests not only in the hands of my good physicians but in the hands of the Great Physician over all.

You know, my friends, people must have courage. The young, middle-aged, and old alike must be courageous. We must have the will to live forever. We must have the will to do forever. We must have the will to dream forever. We cannot turn back. We have to live now, in the present, rejoice, dream, and lay plans for those tomorrows that may never come.

If you read my earlier books, you will find they are now dated. I based those stories upon real incidents, real people. But things

changed here. The people are still very much independent indi-
viduals. But when I first started writing, I used dialect. Dialect isn't
spoken here very much any more. People's speech, dress, and way
of life here have changed, and they continue to change at such a
rapid rate it makes one's head swim. How can we remain isolated
when our youth have fought all over the world, when they are practically all finished high school, and a solid minority of them are
going to college? I am only forty-eight now, but I can remember
when there were only six automobiles in this county. I've seen every
foot of hardroad come. I worked here, doing a man's work, helping
to pave the streets in this town before I entered high school.

As times have changed and people have progressed, my stories
have changed. I seldom go back into history for a story. I have written of the present because I have found it interesting. I like to write
of life that is being lived around me. I like to write about something
I know and can see or have seen. And in the future I shall pursue
the same course. People live dramas so strange and incredible they
often have to be changed to be made plausible; then, they become
fiction. I like to think I was born in the right place at the right time.

Here today among my many friends are people who have helped
me when I needed help. Here in this group are people who have
given me food when I was hungry. They have loaned me shirts and
socks. They have given me a bed to sleep in on cold, rainy winter
nights when I was walking to and from high school. Among my
friends here today are four former teachers who helped shape my
life: my first- and second-grade teacher, who taught me to read and
write, Calvin Clarke, now a businessman in Portsmouth, Ohio; Mrs.
Nora Riggs Scott of Flatwoods, Kentucky, who taught me in the
sixth grade; Mrs. Earl Kotcamp of Greenup, who taught me in the
seventh; and Mrs. W. A. Voiers of Vanceburg, Kentucky, who gave
me extra of her time in high school to teach me algebra and who
has remained interested in my work ever since.

I wish it were possible for two others to be here today. They have
left many footprints on this spot of earth since the turn of this century, never dreaming a marker would be erected here to one of
their children. This was their home town, too. I wish I could, in
some way, turn back the clock and have them here for today. But
this is impossible. They gave all their children good training and
strong family ties. They encouraged us in our small but worthy
endeavors. Our family was all for one and one for all. We learned
to work, sweat, and live together. My home was the strong spring-
board from which I dove into the waters of life, believing firmly it
was my duty to amount to something.

It can never be truthfully said that you in my home town haven't been good to me. You and my fictional children are becoming chummier all the time. Minor reforms in education which seemed radical twenty years ago, when I advocated them, have come to pass. Because I have followed my profession diligently, whether I have pleased or displeased you, I am thus honored by you. And for this honor I am grateful from the depths of my heart.

V I

Reporters asked me yesterday how I felt about the celebration. I couldn't tell them, for the story was too long to tell. Only the people who have lived here know and remember. But I felt the way the Duke of Wellington must have felt after the Battle of Waterloo. Though he had won, his allied forces had taken a lot of punishment and there was great suffering. I felt the way General Meade must have felt after the Battle of Gettysburg. He had repelled General Lee's invasion of the North, but his losses were great and his forces were battered terribly. I felt victorious, but battered, too.

My battle lasted longer than the Duke's or the General's. I was never relieved of my command like Meade. My battle started on October 14, 1934, when I shocked this community with a big volume of verse. A few critics and reviewers called *Man with a Bull-tongue Plow* poetry. But only a few people here called it anything that was repeatable. These few were enlisted as my scouts. If they had not rallied around me, I couldn't have made it. They remained my true friends over the troubled years. They rejoiced yesterday when the marker was unveiled on the courthouse square in Greenup. Many of the older ones actually wept. But I didn't. I didn't shed a tear. I wouldn't let myself. To keep from doing so, all I had to do was to think back over the years.

My war actually started before October 14, 1934, when my first book was published. It started about 1929, when I did my first high school teaching here, though there were clashes even back in 1924, when I was barely seventeen and did my first rural school teaching. The condition of our schools, and education generally, at that time was just miserable. Kentucky youth wasn't being given the chance, in these schools, to develop into an enlightened citizenry.

It didn't take a smart man to see these obvious injustices, but it took a stubborn one to do something about them. After my first taste of teaching, I vowed to escape it forever. I hadn't planned any war, I liked to laugh a lot and have fun with my friends in town. I was not a radical. I was a hill-country Republican who voted and lost.

But in 1929, 1931, and from 1933 to 1937, I got into a series of violent school fights. I made more enemies than I'd ever believed a man could make in such a short time. I wrote article after article about schools and teachers, stupidities and abuses in education, and my beliefs—they never got published. Finally, I burned all these articles no one would accept. But I couldn't burn away my ideas.

The ideas and changes I fought so hard for in those days seem like only common sense today. Most of them have been accepted, bills passed, legislative action taken. I fought for consolidation of the schools, even though I lived and taught in a small backwoods school district, because I knew that bigger schools would bring finer facilities and better education to the outlying districts. I fought to do away with local district trustees. In my early years of teaching, each local school district (and there was only one school to a district and one teacher to a school) had three trustees, five members of the county board of education, and a superintendent. That meant that a single teacher had nine bosses to report to and, sometimes, nine hounds breathing down her neck. She didn't know which way to turn.

I fought the school board when it passed a rule that married women couldn't teach. As early as 1932, I fought for old-age and retirement pensions for teachers; I'd seen elderly teachers kicked around long enough. I fought the parents who wanted to keep their young children home from school during planting and harvesting seasons to work on the farm. I drummed it into their heads over and over again: school comes first, school comes first. I struggled to open up McKell High School to everyone, no matter what his age, and I had pupils from eleven to sixty-seven. I attacked and tried to have changed the unfair system of taxation by which schools were supported and which injured the schools in rural areas. I insisted that even in the lower grades the school term should last for nine months, that the thorough education of the very young was the most important of all.

I wrote articles, I made speeches, I pestered and plagued people. I fought hard, maybe too hard, anyway hard enough to make a lot of enemies.

When I was superintendent of Greenup County schools, two years before my first book was published, I finally had to go armed. I received threatening letters. I had fist fights. The people in certain county districts rose up against me. In those days I was dating Naomi Deane Norris, and we had to walk in the shadows and stay away from street lights at night. Many times my mother sent brother James to warn me not to walk on a certain road on my way home. We had friends who reported what they heard to my parents. My brother or one of my sisters, sometimes both, got a message through to me wherever I was and regardless of what I was doing, even if I was in a meeting with my school board. Certain people my secretary always let in to see me. They came only for one purpose. To warn me of danger.

Next I was elected principal of McKell High School in Western Greenup County. There I worked under a friendly county-school superintendent and helped to build one of the finest high schools in this state. Though I still received threatening letters, I disregarded them. I was a happy man, writing and teaching, buying discarded acres, setting trees, dating Naomi Deane Norris. But people still disliked me at home. My brother had an old car, for which he paid fifty dollars, and he used to drive to the house where I boarded to tell me when to come home and when to stay away.

After I went to England on a Guggenheim Fellowship, I thought that, when I returned, everything would be all right. I started a newspaper, since I couldn't get back my principalship of McKell High School. In fact I couldn't get a place to teach anywhere in Kentucky, near or far. So I crossed the river to Portsmouth, Ohio, where I had a most successful teaching year and continued to edit my paper. But once too often I went home.

The day before, my brother drove all the way to Portsmouth in his old car to tell me to stay out of my home town, that the feeling was still high there. I disregarded this warning. I wanted to see my parents, and I wanted to see Naomi Deane Norris. Besides, I wasn't afraid. I got the worse end of the fracas. On a side street in Greenup I was slugged from behind with a blackjack. I bled profusely, blood filling my shoes from the three scalp wounds, two of which laid open my skull.

There followed two attempts to bring my assailant to trial. People on both sides went armed. The feeling was so high for the first trial that it was postponed. It was postponed again for a similar reason. Although this man had tried to kill me, the indictment against him was for assault and battery rather than for a felony. I'm glad at least that I wasn't armed that night. When finally brought to trial, he was fined two hundred dollars. I understand he never paid the fine. If it was ever paid, his friends paid it. I don't know. I don't like to think about this. I don't even care to remember him.

This man left the county for reasons of his own. He later served in the penitentiary for selling illicit whisky, a charge that had been brought against him unsuccessfully many times before. And later, many years later, a marker was erected for me on the courthouse yard. This was how I won over him.

But I had shaped my life. Angry men with blackjacks couldn't change that. I knew what I wanted to do. I wanted to teach, write, conserve land, and work with American youth. I believed that educators, with their way-over-the-head theories, were missing the point. We must start from the practical bottom and work up, instead of starting at the theoretical top and, perhaps, tumbling down. It didn't take a deep thinker and a smart man to observe what I had. I wasn't either of these. I was a country schoolteacher with a little experience and a dream.

My parents begged me to leave the progress of schools to others and to get out while I was alive. One school-board member, my best friend, told me not to reapply for county superintendency, for if I served again, I would be killed. He said I had done more in one year with the scarce dollars than others had done in twenty-five. But he said I went too fast. I should leave it to others now to consolidate my gains.

Writing and World War II took me away from teaching, and I

never returned, at least not full time. Now all that could cause my unpopularity at home was the sensitivity of people when they read one of my books. These books were admittedly about them. People declared I had hurt my part of America, my state, home town, and friends. They claimed my books were not true pictures. The criticism that hurt me most was of *Foretaste of Glory*, which appeared early in 1946, shortly after I was released from service. This book was so unpopular I almost gave up. I wondered if my writing life was worth constantly taking these insults and angry attacks. And I knew that I could write only of home, my valley, these people.

My wife and I sat down one day and discussed if we would leave here and where we would go. And when I got to thinking about leaving my country, not fighting for this land and these schools and these people I loved, I got my fighting clothes on again. The result was an article, "I Made My Home Town Mad." And I wrote another, "An Author in His Home Town." Both articles were published. I wouldn't leave now. I determined to stay and fight. The fighting had diminished to words. There wasn't any violence. There were no more near riots. I was gaining ground. Many of the people who disliked me personally at least respected my opinions now.

Also, I had a new group coming on. These were the young people I had taught. They were my friends. Had all remained close to home, I soon would have had the majority on my side. But many left here for other parts of this country for economic reasons. But things were changing for me. I was given honorary degrees by four institutions in four different states, one of which was 1,700 miles away. My stories, poems, parts of my books were published in a hundred high school and college textbooks. If the children of my enemies went through high school, studied their English textbooks, they would probably run across my name. A succession of mayors of our little town got letters of inquiry about me. The last one got so many he couldn't answer them in his nonsalaried office. He asked me to write a pamphlet about myself answering a number of stock questions so he could send it out. Slowly the people in town, almost all of them, came around.

How did I feel to end this twenty-one-year-old war, this series of battles that had lasted from October 14, 1934 to October 15,

1955? I never had such a wonderful feeling. It ended better than any book I have ever written. I wanted to be loved by the people of my town, for I loved them. What on earth could make a man happier than to be honored by his neighbors?

V I I

There are two reasons why I never left home. One, I wanted to teach Kentucky children and lift the standards of learning of my people. Second, I wanted to write of my people, of my beautiful hill country, in my day and time. I wanted to record this country's scenes, its tempo and customs, the troubles and desires of its people, just as a man photographs his children through the different ages of their lives.

My first college English teacher, Harry Harrison Kroll, of Lincoln Memorial University, told me back in 1927, when I was a sophomore there, I should return to my own country after I finished college. He told me to write of my own people. He said, "There are things in your own back yard that need to be written." Harry Harrison Kroll hadn't written a book at that time. Since then he has written seventeen novels, one biography, and his own autobiography. He is a wise man, and he knew what he was talking about.

Four years later, when I was doing graduate work at Vanderbilt University, Donald Davidson, a great teacher, a fine poet and critic, went over certain of my poems. He particularly liked those I had done about my people and my country. He revised one for me, "Elegy for Mitch Stuart," which sold to *The American Mercury* while H. L. Mencken was still the editor. "Go back to your country and write of your own people," Donald Davidson told me. "There is where your heart is. You put feeling into what you write about the people you know in your own country. You remind me so much of the Irish writers in your love for your own soil. Go back and write about what you know the best."

I never forgot what these two writers, who were my teachers and close personal friends, told me. I came back to my Greenup County hills, where I wrote *Man with a Bull-tongue Plow* within the first eleven months after I had left Vanderbilt.

While I was teaching, writing, and farming here, I was offered a position teaching English in a high school in Oklahoma. I was also offered a teaching job in faraway Portland, Maine, another in a high school in West Virginia. But when I thought about leaving here, even for double my salary, at a time when I needed money to buy writing paper and clothes, something held me here. I couldn't leave. Yet I thought if I were offered something better, I still might go.

In 1937, when I was in England, I visited the late Edward J. O'Brien at 8 Waterloo Place, London. There I was approached for a tryout in British movies. A director liked my looks, my voice, and accent, and thought these would go over well in the British Isles. But I was not interested in this offer. I was a writer, not an actor. At least I thought and hoped I was a writer. So I refused to be photographed. I wasn't cut out to be an actor.

Before I left the British Isles in 1938, I had a brief part on a BBC program which was broadcast all through the British Commonwealth and to her territories over the world. I got letters from every place, with the result that I was offered a program on BBC just to tell stories of the people in my native Kentucky hills. But something drew me back to this side of the Atlantic. Stronger than gravity, it was W-Hollow that pulled me back.

In 1940, when I was put on a program in Hollywood with a half-dozen other speakers, we were each allowed four minutes. I spoke an hour. They applauded me. They told me to keep on going. I was offered a radio program in Hollywood after this talk. I wondered why they liked to hear me speak so much when each man on the program was better known and had accomplished more than I had. One had written thirty books. I had written four at that time.

I figured the reason they liked me was because I had remained true to my country. Maybe I had held on to what these men had lost. They were making money so big the figures staggered me. They made my head swim. I was making hardly enough to live. But I had held onto my heritage without exploiting it. So I didn't take this radio program with a big salary and a promise of something bigger. Naomi, who was with me, wondered if I had acted wisely. But something told me to return to Kentucky. I came home and became a city-school superintendent on an $1,800-a-year salary while I wrote *Taps for Private Tussie.*

During the war another offer came through which floored me. I was offered a thousand dollars a week to be a script writer in Hollywood. Instead, after dieting and resting to bring my blood pressure down from 196, I joined the Navy. I didn't belong in Hollywood anyway. I knew that.

Then, after my discharge, I was offered a position teaching creative writing at Columbia University, where I had been speaking. This offer was very interesting. Writing for me had come to a standstill after the war. Two years away from my native land had done something to me. I couldn't sell anything I wrote. I was ashamed of everything I put on paper. I wondered what Manhattan would do for me. I was tempted by this offer. I even inquired about housing and learned it was difficult to get. But then, when the decision had to be made, there was that something here in Kentucky that held me. I was a small puppet tied to a string, and my native land held the other end and pulled me back every time I tried to escape.

Since the publication of my book describing my teaching experiences, *The Thread That Runs So True,* I have been offered teaching positions at Iowa State Teachers College, Baylor University, the University of Nevada, the University of California, the University of South Carolina, and elsewhere. Each time I considered, or thought I did, but each time my high prison hills—bleak and lonely in winter, bright with butterflies and wild flowers in spring and summer, and filled with a thousand shades of brilliant leaf colors in autumn—pulled me back.

Going back over the years, I have tried to answer the question so often asked me: Why have you remained here when you could do so much better elsewhere? But could I have done better elsewhere? What if I had gone to teach in Oklahoma, West Virginia, or Maine? What would I be doing now, I wonder. What if I had become an actor in the British Isles and become a British subject? Or if I had become a radio personality or gone to Hollywood as a script writer? Why have I been offered these things? I can answer this now. My country has been my fountainhead, my source, my inspiration, my everything. These people didn't want me. They wanted my land through me.

The man I am, my country has helped to make and shape. I ate food grown from this thin soil. I breathed winds that blew over cone-shaped hills and down deep valleys. I am the seed of my father and mother, whose home was these hills. I cannot desert what has made me. I tell people there's something in the land that won't let me leave and that I am nothing without the land. This is the truest answer I know.

V I I I

Checking over the brief record that I have kept of the number of letters I have posted each day, I figure that if I continue writing letters the next two months as I have in the past ten, I will have written for this year of 1955 approximately six thousand letters. According to my expense account, if I continue buying postage at the rate I have been for the past ten months, I will have spent somewhere between seven and eight hundred dollars for stamps. At my little combined store and post office in Riverton, I am the best individual customer. The postman tells me that only the King Powder Company, a corporation employing approximately a hundred and fifty men, gets and sends more mail.

The only reason I am concerned now about so much mail is the fact that answering it takes fully one-third of my time. I do not have any form letters that I send out. I have received such letters from others, and they have left me cold. All the writer, or his secretary, has to do is insert the name, address the envelope, and send it. This is everybody's letter. Such letters are like pieces of unmelted ice come through the mail. Since I hate to receive one, I won't send one.

A business letter should be direct, friendly, and it should answer any question asked that is not too personal. Such questions as how much money do you get for a story or a book, what is your monthly income, what do you eat for breakfast, and do you love your wife should be ignored. It may be hard to believe, but I am asked them often.

I like to write a warm letter. I don't see how a writer who has any feeling can be two people, can write a warm, personal story, book, or poem and yet write a cold, impersonal letter. Many of them can do this. Not me. Once I tried to write a letter of recommendation for one of my poorest students. I kept him six years in high school and even then was reluctant to graduate him. He asked me to recommend him to study embalming. He wanted to be an undertaker. I liked this boy very much personally, for he was a warm, affectionate, colorful high school character. So I tried to write something for him, completely ignoring the issue. I tried to tell the school officials not to accept him in a polite letter that was mostly about the boy instead of his abilities.

The boy was immediately accepted. The president of the embalming school wrote me a personal letter saying that mine was the best letter of recommendation they had ever received for any student. In writing, I couldn't escape the fact that, personally, I liked this boy very much. Yet I had tried not to recommend him. He doubled the amount of time it should have taken him to learn embalming in that school. I have often wondered what the president thought of my letter later.

My letters come from people in every walk of life, from every state in this Union, from the Dominion of Canada, European countries, Great Britain, Australia, South Africa, and a few from Mexico and South America. They come from Alaska and Iceland and Madagascar. Wherever American magazines and books have gone, I've had letters from their readers. I write to editors, I enter literary debates by correspondence, I write appreciative readers. I answer every letter that deserves an answer.

A large number of my letter writers are teen-age high school pupils. I can tell when a student has been instructed by his teacher to write me. And I can tell when the letter is spontaneous and undirected. I get many of both kinds. But the pupils of one high school, within seventy miles of home, have sent me more than a hundred letters in a period of three years, each asking the same stock questions. I wonder about that English teacher. Why would she allow one writer to be bombarded with so many nearly identical letters from her pupils? She can hardly expect a hundred different answers. I finally had to stop answering these letters. In a few other schools, near and far, I have had the same experience. When I see what is coming, several letters from one school, then I stop answering them.

I receive many letters from would-be writers, wanting help. I have received in one year about a hundred manuscripts, small and large, from would-be short-story writers, novelists, and poets. Many send manuscripts without writing me first. They demand help, as if this were my duty. They soon learn it isn't my duty. If they don't send return postage, I pay it. I get those manuscripts back in a hurry. I have learned if I say something uncomplimentary, even in the way of constructive criticism, the authors are forever peeved at me. They hate my name. I have made enemies by being honest in this way. If I lie and say they are good, then I am quoted wherever the authors send these manuscripts. Either way is wrong.

Then I get a fair amount of nutty, often unsigned, sometimes threatening letters. I used to get more of these than any author I know, because many of mine came from local people who disliked what I had written about my country and people. Once I answered one of these nutty letters. In a few days a young man came from about four hundred miles away to see me. He was young, pink-cheeked, and very nervous, and said he wanted to write. He brought some westerns he had written to show me. He showed me letters he had received from people whom I knew by reputation, one from a Pulitzer Prize-winning novelist whom I knew well. Then this boy told me his father beat him with a stick. I felt deeply for him because I believed what he had told me.

The day after young Mr. X left here, he sent me a nice letter thanking me for my kindness and advice, which, he said, meant so much to him. The third day I got a manuscript from him to look over, with no self-addressed, stamped envelope in which to return it. He wrote a letter asking for my comments on each story. One of them he asked me to read, report on, and then post to a magazine. The following week he came in person with another batch of stories. I gave him advice, as I would have a high school youth in one of my classes. For I thought he had been mistreated by a misunderstanding father. I thought he needed kindness.

He listened to me, agreeing with every word I told him. It pleased me to think all this was soaking in. I felt I could help him, make him happy. When he went away, I gave him a couple of my books, first editions, and inscribed them. His letters and manuscripts came to me so fast after this second visit that I couldn't answer them. I wrote him brief comments at first. Then I wrote him to slow down. Yet he kept on sending me short stories and articles about two-gun men in the wild and woolly West. I threw them into a box.

From a state university, one of my former pupils, now a teacher, wrote me a quote from one of the letters young Mr. X had sent him. Mr. X was quoting, or rather misquoting, me. Mr. X was sending quotes from my letters to editors and to his friends all over the country.

I started pulling away from him in a hurry. Then came a letter from him filled with confidential love letters from a young woman whom I knew. I wrote him a letter he didn't send to anybody. It must have burned his hands. He returned my letter. Then I told him not to write again. I sent all his manuscripts to him. Later every time a story, poem, or article of mine appeared in a magazine, I got a nasty, unsigned letter. These letters were posted in cities and towns not too far apart. The two books I had given him were posted back to me, with the flyleaves, where I had inscribed them, torn out, ripped in four or five pieces, and left inside the book for me to see.

Among all aspirant writers I have ever known, I have never found another as obnoxious and dangerous as Mr. X. The only reason he isn't a real menace is that he does not have enough writing talent. In the last letter I ever received from him, he spoke of Adolph Hitler and his book, *My Struggle* (which was Mr. X's struggle, too), with glowing praise. Since my experience with Mr. X, who taught me a most valuable lesson, I have been more cautious about the people to whom I write.

Though I like people very much and enjoy corresponding with them, it has come to the point, since my correspondence has reached six thousand letters annually, that somewhere, someplace, I must cut down. To continue would be unfair to myself and the remaining years I have in which to write for publication. I often wonder whether

I could have used all this time spent writing letters to make books of mine already published much better. I wonder about the new things I could have created with this extra time. Yet I like to write these letters, to reach out and touch all these people. And that is the problem.

I X

What is it about the wind in the sear whiteoak leaves in the late autumn woods that is so appealing? When the winter wind blows through the leaves still clinging to these trees, I like to be there. This afternoon, I went up the valley to the grove of whiteoaks that grow on my farm. These trees never shed their leaves until spring, when new buds force the old leaves from the boughs. And there is a legend that these tough-butted whiteoaks wanted to be evergreens. Since nature would not let them be evergreens, the fairies intervened to effect a compromise that would allow these stubborn trees to hold onto their leaves through the winter.

I walked under these trees as I had done many autumns. I had come to this hillside where the land was too poor to grow anything but whiteoaks, huckleberries, wild roses, and violets. I had found violets here in early March. An abundance of plush woodmoss carpeted this ground now. I often wondered why woodmoss thrived on thin soil.

In early summer I had been here when the wild huckleberries ripened. I had picked them from these spindly stems that were leafless now. I stooped over and felt the iron hardness of a stem. In a few months these vines would perform a miracle, bringing forth sweet, delicious berries from this poor sand rock soil.

And the wild rose with its single layer of petals bloomed here late each spring. Now I stood by the naked rose vines directly under the grove of whiteoaks while I listened to the winds moan and cry among their dry clouds of leaves. Then I sat on the giant brace-root of an oak and watched the wind in these treetops that looked like brown, wrinkled tents spread over stocky, durable poles. Though the wind might blow and blow, not one of these leaves would depart, because the fairies had interceded for this stubborn little tree.

X

Naomi keeps a record of all we make and what we spend. This morning we went over our accounts for October. There was a big difference between what we had taken in and what we had spent. Our outgo had exceeded our income. For this month, I sold one poem, *October's Voice,* to *Southwest Review,* for which I received five dollars. This was every cent I made in this exciting month when a marker was erected to me in my home town and so many complimentary things were said and written about me in the press. But this was one story we didn't tell to anybody.

It would be hard for anybody who works in the steel mills, or a blacksmith, railroad section laborer, farmer, clerk, or teacher, to realize a writer often makes so little. September was a lean month, too, with only a hundred sixty dollars coming in. Nevertheless both September and October have been rich months for us, rich in colors on the hills and wind to breathe and freedom to roam.

If I get depressed in spirits about my financial situation, all I have to do is to think back a few years. I know what it is to borrow money to the full extent of my credit. I know what it is to cut down on all spending. My wife knows what it is to do without a new hat and summer dresses and a winter coat when her friends all have them.

Before the publication of *Taps for Private Tussie* in 1943, I had never been out of debt. I was always borrowing money. Even in those early years people thought that, because I was a writer, I made a lot of money. From my first book, *Man with a Bull-tongue Plow,* later listed as one of a thousand great books, I made less than a thousand dollars. From my first collection of short stories, *Head O' W-Hollow,* I made approximately two hundred and fifty dollars. From my third book, *Beyond Dark Hills,* I made eight or nine hundred dollars. I owned at that time about four hundred acres of hill land, much of which I bought for twelve dollars an acre. People thought I was worth a lot of money at the very time when we had to borrow money very often to pay bills.

I had about two hundred hens then. I used to take a basket of eggs to Greenup, and on top of the eggs I would have from ten to twenty sheafs of poems going to this or that magazine, and maybe a few stories. I was sure of the sales of my eggs, for my healthy well-fed hens produced big, clean eggs, which are required daily sustenance for people in our part of the country. But my poems and short stories were not required mental sustenance; editors didn't have to buy them. I felt very fortunate when I sold something, even for five dollars.

I have had as many as a hundred poems and twenty-five stories out to magazine editors at one time. It was not that I wanted to send so many out. I had to do it. I had to live. I made talks to supplement my writing income. I didn't get many talks or big fees before 1943. Yet everybody in my neighborhood thought we had banks full of money.

After the book club selected *Taps for Private Tussie,* other things sold I had been trying to sell for a long time. Now with the local papers saying I had hit the jackpot, people around here began to think in terms no smaller than a million. This was in the early days of the government's "big spending." People were getting used to big figures. They thought I had made a million overnight. I knew what I had made. And I knew how hard money came for a free-lance writer. I wanted to save all I could.

But I thoroughly liked the idea that people thought I was worth a million. It was funny. How we laughed about it. Like in Mark Twain's short story "The Million-pound Note," people began to take a different attitude toward me. I was really somebody now I had never been before. I learned then why people like to be rich. It was a lot of fun being rich. Everybody wanted donations for this and that. People came for advice. Men looked me over carefully, as if, with their X-ray eyes, they could see hundred-dollar bills crumpled carelessly in my pockets.

Before my novel's success, I was trying to save a thousand dollars as a little nest egg for my wife and baby daughter, so they would have something to fall back on when I went into service in World War II. I had planned to take out a big insurance policy for them, too. But just before my going into the Navy, this unexpected thing happened which erased all my debts and put me on the black side of the ledger for the first time in my life.

Since that time, I have kept out of debt, expanded our house, built a bathroom, and added more acres. If it had not been for this one big success, which my friend, Calvin Clarke, has helped me to manage frugally, I don't know what I would have done. There have been times when eight months have passed and I haven't sold anything. I don't like to be bothered with the financial side. I like to write. I like to keep on writing. If something sells, that's wonderful. If it doesn't sell, I don't despair as long as we have food, clothes, and a fireplace to be happy in front of.

Six years later, while writing another book, I went almost a year before anything sold. I had to draw from my reserve. Then a portion of the new book sold to a big magazine. But this long drought hadn't bothered me too much. I knew a free-lance writer in America had more lean months than fat ones. I knew writers of international renown who were so far in debt they never expected to get out in their lifetime. Everything else was subsidized in America. But not the free-lance creator. And he shouldn't be.

The man with the hammer, hoe, ax, plane, and saw gets along fine in America. Big wages are paid skilled and unskilled laborers in this country. Even the shoeshine boys in the barbershops, where little physical skill and no thinking are required, make almost as much as the average writer whose name is fairly well known in America. A laboring man on the railway section, where the requirement is a strong back, makes more than the average writer. Certainly barbers, at a dollar or a dollar and a half a haircut, make more money than the average writer. There is a saying in my home town: Why send your son to the state university for four years to become a journalist when you can send him to the barber college in Cincinnati for six months and he can make more money?

One of the advantages I have had over many writers is having a farm where I have grown vegetables and kept cattle. I am sure that my family and I will not go hungry.

And going hungry is something I know about. When I was at Vanderbilt University I lived on a meal a day, and it was at this time that I wrote *Beyond Dark Hills*, published six years later as my third book. Many times I could afford only a nickel bar of candy. My going hungry so often in the past has put a stricture in me against wasting food. I know somebody somewhere is hungry.

I wrote many stories on the paper my friends gave me. Katherine Atherton Grimes, poet and writer on the old *Southern Agriculturist* in Nashville, Tennessee, used to give me paper when I was a student at Vanderbilt University. I wrote *Beyond Dark Hills* on the paper she gave me. I used to get paper out of wastebaskets at Vanderbilt and write on it. After I came home from Vanderbilt, I picked up chewing-tobacco sacks along the road to use for scribbling poems.

Neither poverty nor lack of food could ever stop me from writing. If I never sold another story and had to give my work away, I would continue to write. Sometimes I am afraid of wearing my name threadbare by attaching it to too many poems, stories, and articles in magazines and to too many books. But I am not afraid about making only five dollars in the month that a marker was erected to me by my friends in my home town of Greenup, Kentucky.

X I

I wonder if medical science would profit if heart specialists would make a thorough study of the terrapin. Dictionaries refer to the terrapin as a reptile. For me he has always been the finest species of his class. He is a friendly fellow and never bothers anybody. And if anybody bothers him, he goes into his shell and closes it. His shell fits him neatly. Nature has done a precise job with his protective covering. I often have wondered how a terrapin gets enough air after he goes inside and closes the heavy curtain.

After all I have read in medical journals and all doctors have told me about the human heart, I believe the terrapin follows more of the practices that contribute toward a long life than any human being I know. The terrapin by nature and by habit carries out the doctor's medical advice to heart patients. Perhaps heart patients would do well to follow the terrapin's way of life.

In the first place, the terrapin is a lazy fellow. He never gets in a hurry. Children love to hear about this old, slow, friendly terrapin winning a race over a fast rabbit. The terrapin's slow pace is the object of many jokes and stories, and the climax of each is that the terrapin will get there. But in the matter of health and longevity, the terrapin really does win the race. He can outdistance any machine of flesh, blood, and bone that exists on this continent today.

There are records in American zoos that show that terrapins have lived as long as a hundred and forty years. They are still mating at this ripe old age, and the females are still laying eggs. Who has ever heard of a human centenarian who is able to propagate his species? (I'll probably get a letter from one who reads this.)

We have found terrapins in this area with initials carved on their shells over a hundred years ago. Carving initials on a terrapin's back used to be a popular pastime. A century ago, when men didn't have many ways of entertaining themselves, they would come across a terrapin while they were out hunting, decorate his shell with their names or initials, and then turn him loose. Long after these hunters had gone to dust, the terrapin was still plodding over the earth. Why is he able to outlive man? The terrapin has a heart and a bloodstream that nourish his life, just as a human being does. Yet a man dies, and a terrapin who was old when this man was born crawls over his grave and past his tombstone with its faded lettering. We should know more about what is under the terrapin's shell that enables him to live a century or longer. We should know more about his everlasting heart.

The terrapin doesn't get angry. Men do. A terrapin doesn't get excited, he doesn't move quickly. Men get excited, they run for trains. The terrapin has a shell to retreat into. Men have none. The terrapin lives from day to day, a man worries about the past, the future. A terrapin hibernates five months of the year, a man prides himself on how little sleep he can get by on.

I've taken to watching the terrapin. I was a teacher once and know the value of the living example. Particularly a long-living example.

NOVEMBER

How exciting it felt today to be a man with a hoe again. At three in the afternoon, I walked across the footlog into my garden with a hoe over my shoulder. This little spot of earth at the foot of a steep bluff, where towering young poplars bud about the time percoon blooms beneath them in the spring, is my garden. My hoe in the different seasons, from early spring until late fall, has sliced through this dark dirt time after time, cutting the weeds and piling dirt around the roots of my vegetables. I have raised fine vegetables on this small piece of earth.

It was cultivated perhaps a century before I was born. I helped my father and mother hoe potatoes here when I was a little boy on sunny spring days in 1915, 1916, 1917, and 1918. I dropped potatoes here while my mother's hoe covered them. My father, with his horse, Sam, plowed this ground and laid it off in straight rows. Later, he plowed the young potatoes here. My mother and I hoed them. There was something magic about this dark earth back in the days when commercial fertilizers were unheard of here.

In the autumn, leaves fall from the tall poplars. They are soaked by autumn rains until they form a wet leaf carpet on the earth. Then the snow falls, weights the leaves, soaks and rots them. They go back to the earth as a rich dust which spring rains wash down over my garden. This leaf-rot loam is the wonderful fertilizer nature uses in all our forests.

This afternoon I was happy again to have a hoe on my shoulder. But this was the gathering and not the growing season. I had missed the spring and summer in my garden. Last spring I watched the weeds grow tall here, and it hurt me to see it, but I couldn't do anything about what was happening. I asked the doctor if I could plant this little patch. He said that I couldn't.

I persuaded Glen Hilton, my cousin who runs a sawmill, to plant my garden and take what he raised. He plowed this ground and planted it in corn and beans, but he didn't get a good stand of either. Twice this garden of corn and beans was cultivated hurriedly and poorly. Then a drought came. The result was thirty bushels of green beans, which Cousin Glen gave away to his neighbors. The way my father and I used to farm, either of us would have raised from fifty to a hundred bushels of beans here.

Part of the green corn was pulled for roasting ears while it was soft. Much of it was left on the stalks, and when the big frost came, this corn and fodder ripened. Each stalk turned buff-colored. I wanted to get to it with a corn-cutting knife and cut and shock it. But I wasn't quite up to this yet. I had to wait an extra month, and a little more, from September to November.

This was the reason I carried a hoe today. I liked to grip the handle of my hoe again. Eventually a little work with it would toughen my tender hands and make me feel more like the man I used to be a year ago.

I planned to cut, stack, and haul this corn and fodder to the livestock in the pasture and at the same time get this ground ready to disk and sow. I wanted my garden prepared in the right way. This was a spot of earth to which I felt a deep sentimental attachment. My hands had fondled every shovelful of topsoil in this garden, just as my mother's and father's hands had fondled it forty years ago.

As soon as I reached the first row of corn, I lifted my heavy sprouting hoe and let it fall. Two cornstalks snapped off just as I had expected they would. I walked up this row cutting, then came down the next. I can work again, I said to myself. I repeated these words to myself over and over. I can work again with a hoe!

There is no other feeling for a man like having power in his body and exerting it in some creative way and seeing what he accomplishes as he moves along. No wonder a man brags about what he can do in the fields. I say let him brag while he can. For there comes a time when he can't work. And when he has to stand by and watch others, when he can't work himself, it is a disconsolate feeling. I had watched too many others using hoes in early and middle summer.

While I cut this fodder down, I thought about the wonderful mysteries never photographed or written up in farm magazines. The power of new machines and magic fertilizers was described by word and picture every week. But dirt alone, the greatest mystery, always escaped attention. I have never seen a write-up about a ball of mud in a farm magazine. I've never read much about the dependence of the human race on a little thing called "dirt," wonderful dirt, so soothing to touch, so comfortable to sink bare feet into, to dig with a hoe. The thousands of young men who leave the farms every year never to return must fail to see the poetry in growing things, the beauty of dirt.

People in this country believe in advertising. When a way of life isn't highly advertised, it is soon rejected and forgotten. People have to be told what to like, what to buy, even what way of life to choose. People have to be sold on their jobs. Perhaps if the farm lobby were to glamorize the soil, run ads about the beauty of growing plants ... but I doubted if this would work. And perhaps it was best to keep the two worlds apart.

I stopped and put one hand to my forehead while holding onto my hoe handle with the other. There was moisture breaking out over my warm face. I looked up toward the blue sky where a pair of crows winged over. Though I felt warmth in my face all right, my feet were still cold. My hands were cold, too, when I picked up the fodder stalks. Despite these reminders, I was glad to be getting a little genuine exercise after so many months. I heard the honking cries of hundreds of wild geese going over in a big V. My father used to say, as we stood on this very same spot and listened to their lonely cries, that the rough weather would soon be following the wild geese toward the South.

High overhead in the bright wind, the wild geese seemed so certain of their destiny. I felt certain of mine too, standing in this garden. I knew what I was doing. I knew where I was going. I wouldn't work too hard and bring on another attack. I would be careful. But this land I had sifted with my hands, fondled and loved, that had produced vegetables over the years to provide my people with food, was wonderful medicine for me.

Agriculture can be taught, I know it can. More than that, the beauty of growing things can be taught. When I went to school, of my three instructors in agriculture, two were practical men. They taught the boys what to raise on their farms to make money. They taught them methods of soil conservation, crop rotation, the better breeds of poultry, livestock, and swine. All their teaching ended with the value in dollars. This was all well and good. But the third teacher—a young, pink-cheeked man, Fred Hatcher—gave them this and something far beyond. He mentioned dollars and cents only by implication.

Once I went on a field trip in the early spring with him and his agriculture class. We went to a field where the long drilled rows of corn had just broken through the soil in an Ohio River bottom. Fred Hatcher took from his pocket a handful of shelled corn and called his class around him. He showed them how perfect were these grains that had produced the young corn in the rows. Then he had his students get down on their hands and knees and observe how beautiful the slender stalks of young corn were. He discussed the beauty of a stalk of corn until it became a flower. I had raised corn all my life, but this teacher gave me a new awareness of the beauty of the grain, the seed germinating in the good earth, and the young

graceful flower that would help to sustain man and animal. He was
the kind of man who showed his boys where farming and poetry
overlapped.

1 1

Every time we have an election in Kentucky, this entire
state takes on a holiday air. People don't work unless they are
compelled to, so the majority take part in an election if they possibly
can. Today hundreds of thousands went to the polls to decide who
would be our next governor—colorful and controversial Happy
Chandler, the Democratic candidate, former baseball commissioner,
state senator, and governor: or helpless Edwin Denny, the Republican candidate, a good attorney and judge, solid, substantial, but
entirely lacking Happy's charm and color and facing a Democratic
majority of more than 150,000 voters. There wasn't much doubt in
people's minds, even among the Republicans, of the outcome. Yet,
Republicans thought there just might be one chance in a hundred.
They flocked to the polls, too.

Everywhere people were out hauling in voters. At least six people
had been promised every political appointment, and each was sure
he was going to get it. But if he didn't get it, he would still remain
a loyal supporter of his party. All anybody wanted was a promise.
This is so typical of our people. They are satisfied with promises.
They will work furiously. They will drive cars all day hauling voters
over crowded highways just for a promise, sure to be broken, or
a handshake from the hero who heads their ticket. The political hero
is worshiped in this state. Yet no one believes what he says. The
majority don't care whether he tells the truth or not, just so they
have a part in a colorful election day and get to shake their leader's
hand and hear a few promises.

We let the election day pass quietly while cars buzzed up and
down our lane road all day long hunting for more voters. There are
only three voters living near us, my sister, brother-in-law, and uncle.
They were not at home. There is an empty house above us, and a
dozen or more drivers of election cars stopped at this house, ran over,
knocked, and looked inside. They found it empty and drove away
in a hurry.

After voting earlier in the day for Judge Denny, who would surely lose, Naomi and I drove to Greenup in the evening. Cars were parked every place, yet streets were deserted. People were indoors watching ballots counted or crowding around radio and TV sets getting state-wide results. Greenup had always been a colorful town when votes were counted. Often in a contested county election, vote counting lasted two weeks. People from all over the county drove in, ate at restaurants, saw movies, bought from the stores. Business is always good in Greenup around election time. The merchants are happy no matter what the result.

Naomi and I went to Leslie's Drugstore in the center of town directly across from the courthouse. It was in this store a few months back that I had sat on a stool at the counter, unable to get up the jammed steps into the packed courthouse. This was during the hot Democratic primary last summer between Chandler and Combs, who was backed by retiring Governor Weatherby. Here I had sat and listened to Happy tell about the rug, a famous Kentucky story now that will go on and on, be told and retold to successive generations as long as Kentucky is a state. It is a typical Chandler story, a typical Kentucky election tale. According to Happy, Governor Weatherby (called Weatherbine by Happy) paid twenty-seven thousand dollars for a rug for the Governor's Mansion. Chandler promised that when he won this primary from Combs and later defeated his Republican candidate in the fall, he would invite all his friends from all over the state to come to Frankfort, visit him in the Governor's Mansion, and wipe their feet on this rug. That was Happy's campaign promise.

People loved this story. They screamed with laughter. And after Happy won his primary from Combs, the truth came out that the rug had cost just a little over two thousand. When Chandler was asked why he exaggerated the price, he replied, "It makes a good story, doesn't it? And the people like it, don't they? Don't my followers eat it up?" Happy was right. They did.

Then at the close of this same primary speech, which lasted almost an hour, Happy had sung into the loud speaker "Goldmine in the Sky" and "My Old Kentucky Home." Another favorite he usually sang was "Sonny Boy." The people rejoiced so they almost

rioted. The whole town was in a frenzy. This man spoke to them on
their level. He was an artist and an entertainer. I have never heard
in my lifetime one who could equal Happy. I never voted for him,
but I don't mind saying I enjoyed him.

But this was a peaceful election evening as compared to others.
In years past I had seen fights on the streets. We had had elections
when men of both parties had gone armed as long as two weeks
before, night and day. Women were afraid to walk down the streets.
Political parties had gone so far as to set up machine guns, bring
army rifles, entrench, dig in before their headquarters, while men
stood watching each vote counted with their hands menacingly in
their pockets. But the vote counting today was different. The old
fire had gone from this election, and I didn't really miss it.

How do you become a Republican in Kentucky? You get born
one. One man I missed around this courthouse, one who always
worked all day for his Republican party and remained that evening
to hear the first reports of the defeat, was my father. This was the
first time he had missed a county, state, or national election in
Greenup since 1896, five years before he was eligible to vote.

"Vote a straight ticket," he used to tell James and me. "We know
what the other side has done. They have controlled this state since
the Civil War. Even when we have a Republican governor, they
control the Legislature and Senate. This state was never Republican
controlled. And with one party in power all of my lifetime, the
net results are that we stand on the bottom of everything." In his
Plum Grove grave, he wouldn't know the results of this election,
that Happy had won by an overwhelming majority. But he would
have taken this defeat as I had seen him take so many others. He
would have turned and walked silently away.

My father's father, for whom he was named, Mitchell Stuart,
was a Virginian. He violently disliked slavery and thought Abraham
Lincoln would free the slaves and return them to Africa. He didn't
think the two races would ever mix. He thought the Negro would
be happier in his homeland. He became a Republican, voted for
Abraham Lincoln, and supported this ticket until his death. My
father and his brothers followed in their father's footsteps. And
James and I followed our father, a continuous line of Republican

voters for three generations, charter members of Kentucky's Republican Party.

It's not all amusement being a Republican in Kentucky. I missed an appointment to West Point because of it. (Now I'm thankful because I didn't belong there.) Also a Democratic state senate opposed my selection as state poet laureate, and then allowed me to share the post with a banker who'd written a handful of poems.

But I'm not complaining. Kentucky is my land. Kentucky, no matter what its politics, has treated me fine.

III

We have had the greatest heritage in the world here. I am speaking of those born of my generation and before. Never pity one of us. If you pity anyone at all, let it be the youth of today, those born among these hills after life had changed here. Our generation inherited a world that gave us time to think. A world that gave us leisure in which to grow in mind as well as body. We inherited a world of nature, a world that God made.

In our heritage of a few years ago we could hear the tinkling of a cowbell on a summer evening. We knew where to find the cow and we knew that all the other cows would be with her. We always put the bell on the leader of our cows. And to hear a cowbell ring over the green land, through the soft air, is summer music and a dream that stays with a man a lifetime.

Our going after the cows when we came from school was a social affair. The boys and girls of our neighborhood walked slowly to the pasture together to get our cows. We followed the little cow paths. We found doodlebugs' holes around old logs. There was never a boy in this area who went after the cows who didn't get down and try to call a doodlebug from his hole.

We drove the cows to the milk gaps to be milked. *Milk gap* will someday be an obsolete expression in our language, for the dairy business has become a big industry. Year by year fewer people have cows of their own. For with good roads and door-to-door delivery, they say they can buy milk more cheaply than they can keep cows, which is probably true. Everything in America is turning from the small to the large, from the individual to the collective.

But families who do not own cows, whose children do not have the pleasure of going to the pasture to get them night and morning from early spring until frost, have missed something.

In years past we have been late finding the cows and have seen the stars come into the sky. We have stood half-afraid on some path under the leafing trees when we heard a hoot owl, a nighthawk, or a barking fox. And on summer nights we have almost gone to sleep leaning against a cow's warm flank and listening to the drowsy chirruping of the katydids and the lonesome songs of the cicadas in the dewy grass. These are things a boy doesn't forget.

And who among us has not heard a fox horn blow at night? When we heard the horn, we knew by its message—two shorts and a long, two longs and a short, two shorts, or two longs—just whose horn it was and what message was sent. There are true tales told that neighbors, who didn't live too far apart, asked by horn to borrow coffee, sugar, meal, or flour from one another. Sets of signals were established between neighbors. There were no telephones, then, so we used horns. And we used them in case of fire, sickness, or death. We were tied together by the sound of horns in the night.

Every family had its hounds. A hunting dog was essential to keep our families in wild game. We also kept hounds to chase the fox, a sport so much enjoyed that it was a sin to kill a fox even if one carried off your chickens, pigs, or lambs. This was understandable. The foxes had to be fed, after all, if they were to be chased several nights in each week by dogs. And the man who had the fastest hound in the neighborhood was looked up to, often with a touch of jealousy, by all the others, the way a successful business executive is admired today.

Families used to go to the high ridges, fry chicken over an open fire, and have supper while they listened to the chase. Nights when the barking hounds drove the fox fast and furious, when the stars were out and the moon was up and the winds sighed through the needles of the pines on the high ridges—such nights are impossible for a man, who was a boy then, to forget. Often we spent the greater part of a night, following our hounds by ear, listening to an exciting chase. There was poetry in those nights.

And I can remember women in our neighborhood a generation

ago, women like my mother, who used a washtub and washboard and lye soap, which they made themselves, to wash our clothes. And they would talk about taking their clothes through many waters and had great pride in getting their children's clothes spotlessly clean.

Here is a poem I wrote about our heritage. I took this poem through several waters, yet I know that it is not as perfect as my mother's wash was clean.

Our Heritage

We are part of this rough land
   Deep-rooted like the tree;
We've plowed this dirt with calloused hand
   More than a century.
We know each cowbell's ringing here
   Which tells the time of day;
We know the slopes to plant each year,
   What neighbors do and say.
We know the signals of each horn
   And messages they send
At set of sun or early morn
   Upon a blowing wind.
Though we may be in bed at night
   And hear a foxhorn blow,
We often rise, take lantern light,
   Untie our hounds and go.
We like to follow hounds that chase
   The fox until the morn
Then go back home with sleepy face
   And on to plow the corn.
There is not one who does not love
   A field and farming ground,
With sky and stars a roof above
   And a companion hound.
We love this land we've always known
   That holds us and our dead,
The thin-soiled slopes with scattered stone
   That grow our daily bread.
We love the lyric barking hound
   And a piping horn that trills;
We love our high upheavaled ground,
   Our heritage of hills.

I V

There is something stirring about a flight of wild geese. Their cries are the sign that winter has come to the North and they must travel long miles south for food and warm sun. When they cross over our land, we know that our summer has passed. Their cries are as lonely as the sighs of the dead leaves on the wind.

This time of falling leaves reminds us that our own allotted time is slowly dwindling. A few more body aches each year. A pound or two more, a few hairs less. A shortness of breath, a dimming of eyesight. In each cemetery fresh earth upturned, a few more gray, white, and brown stones, deeply felt if added to our own family plots, mildly melancholy if in others.

But somewhere a violet is blooming out of season. Somewhere, protected from Jack Frost by the grass, a mountain daisy clings to life. Somewhere old people sit out in the sun, old men rake leaves while they smoke their pipes. And the smoke thins on the chill wind as it disappears up into nothingness. All of this in the time of falling leaves.

V

This is what came in the mail today:

ELECTROCARDIOGRAPHIC SERVICE
30 North Michigan Avenue
Chicago 2, Illinois

W. W. Sittler, M.D.
D. S. Raines, M.D.
Kurt Herzberg, M.D.

Patient: Jesse Stuart   Physician: Dr. Charles Vidt

EKG was taken: 11.11.55

Rate	70
Rhythm	Sinus
Electrical Axis	Left
P.R. interval	0.18
QRS duration	0.06

Conclusion: Comparing this tracing with a tracing taken 5.17.55 there is essentially no change and the present tracing is essentially within normal limits.

At the bottom of this paragraph there was a note in Dr. Charles Vidt's handwriting: "Jesse, This should make you feel good. It does me. Doc."

When Naomi brought this little letter from the post office, I thought it was a bill or statement from my doctor. I was a little slow to open it for thinking how much I owed Doctor Vidt. Then I summoned up enough courage and opened the letter to find, if I understand it correctly, the greatest message I have ever received. It concerns my life. I am no more selfish than the next person, but my life is all I really possess. And I want to live as long as I can.

When I got this notice this morning, I rejoiced to the point of getting really excited, which is something I shouldn't do. I took a quick glance backwards at the six doctors and the EKGs the doctors had done on me. The first EKG, made in Ashland, Kentucky, after I had had my initial "upset stomach" was a strange thing indeed. It showed nothing wrong with my heart. It was because of this that everything else followed: two more light attacks, diagnosed as muscular difficulties, then the almost fatal one at Murray, Kentucky, days under a tent, a small, closed room, the face of death. Dark events that now seem far away.

At Murray, two doctors showed me my EKGs just before I left the hospital. One of them pointed to what he said was one of the worst EKGs he had ever seen, made shortly after my arrival at the hospital. He said he didn't know where the extra strength had come from which had bridged the gap between death and survival for me.

This morning, as I held this brief notice in my hand, I knew again what kind of pains I had suffered in the past. I remembered thinking I might never write again. I remember thinking of the Plum Grove hill and my family dead. Wild thoughts, gloomy thoughts that I had fought back.

But now I can use a hoe gently. I can raise a little garden. I can do things around the house that months ago I would not dare to attempt. I can write stories, articles, poems that have been building up in my mind wanting to be written. With pen in hand, I can go in search once more for the people who used to populate my books.

What I have prayed for has come to pass, a repaired heart, a new lease on life, extended time. I might even take a fifteen-minute talk someplace. I am not looking for one. I wouldn't travel any distance to make one. But there might be a possibility that I could give one. Just one. Just to show that I could. And Naomi and I will travel again. Thirty minutes after I had this report in my hand, I told Naomi, "Come January, you and I will take a trip together." What a difference our never going anywhere had made in us. We have talked about it. Sometimes we thought, mistakenly, that our love and our zest for living were tapering off through no fault of our own but because of my being in bed and then housebound for so long.

With this great message from my doctor, I walked through the house. I walked out into the yard. I had been obedient a long time waiting for this report. I had obeyed every detail of my doctor's and my wife's orders. Now I, who had been so close to the grave, was almost a well man. I wanted to run like a wild colt through the wind. But I wouldn't. I wanted to shout to the world that I was well again. But I wouldn't. The best thing for me to do was to smile and keep quiet.

This fragment of paper was greater to me than a check of many figures. It was greater than an honorary degree from some outstanding university, greater than deeds for land, greater than winning a literary honor. Despite the numbers, symbols, medical terms, for me this one-page report was a literary masterpiece. More than any poem I'd ever written, it sang with life.

V I

Naomi had gone to the funeral of her Cousin Irwin Norris at Hopewell, and Jane had gone home with Jo Ann McMann for the afternoon. On this quiet Sunday afternoon I came home from church to rest and was going off to sleep when Birch started barking. When a man knows the nature of his dog, he knows his different barks. For instance, when Birch wants inside, he barks a short, gruff bark, several seconds apart, which sounds as if he is trying to say, "In." Naomi taught him this when he was a puppy. When he is disturbed, he barks as if he is ready to take hold with his mouth, though the thing that disturbs him may be several yards away. He was barking this way now.

I put my coat on to go up Shinglemill to see if I could find out what was wrong. When I walked back through the house, I saw Birch through the window in the kitchen yard, jumping stiff-legged when he barked. I opened the door and went outside. Birch ran twenty yards up the valley, barking viciously at something straight ahead.

I looked up the bank above the garden, and there stood a hunter with his gun across his shoulder. His brown hunting clothes, the color of the leaves still clinging to the whiteoak trees, camouflaged him well.

"Aye, you!" I said. "Don't you know this is Sunday?"

He didn't answer me. He stood there looking down the valley. He was a large man whom I didn't recognize. He was the most indescribable person I had ever seen. His face was clean-shaven and as smooth as a stone. He didn't have an outstanding physical feature to make me remember him. He might have been a local man or he might have been a stranger. But when I spoke, he looked up the hill as if he didn't hear me.

"This land is posted by the state," I said. "This is a game preserve. What are you doing in here? Get out!"

He didn't bother to answer me. He had invaded my land on Sunday. He stood in the heart of the little game preserve where I fed birds and animals. A black and white hound ran from a thicket sniffing over the ground. A white and tan hound followed after him.

"Do you hear me?" I said. "Get out!"

He didn't answer, he completely ignored me.

Perhaps he knows something about me, I thought. He must know I've had a long sick spell. He thinks I can't chase him off. He may even have found out that we spend many Sunday afternoons away now.

"Are you going to get out?"

He turned, pointed his gun at me, but didn't shoot. There was still plenty of distance between us. But this was an ugly gesture from an intruder. This man who had come into my yard to hunt and kill my pets was pointing a gun at me. He would defy me, the owner. Without speaking a word, he was saying to me, When a man is physically unable to defend his property, then someone else comes in to take over. In the animal world I had seen the strong devour the weak. I had seen the young devour the old among the lesser animals. I didn't want trouble, in fact I had been explicitly instructed to avoid it. But trouble had trapped me. I wouldn't stand for this.

"Are you going to get out?"

He pointed his gun again. Then, slowly, insolently, he took it down from his shoulder. He was letting me know he didn't have to go. There was nothing else to do but turn and go back to the house. But when I came out again, I had my rifle and a box of long cartridges. This little .22 was capable of carrying over a half mile.

"Are you going?" I asked him again.

He stood there like a tree, still defiant.

"Get going!" I shouted as I brought my rifle to my shoulder. My heart beat a little faster, for I expected him to put his gun to his shoulder. "I mean for you to get out!"

He didn't go. I fired about ten feet above his head. I heard the bullet hit a tree somewhere above and beyond him, then sing into space in the direction his dogs were barking on a cold trail.

"Don't bring your gun up," I warned him.

This time when I fired, I put the bullet about eight feet over his head into a pine tree. He looked up where the bullet had hit. I shot again, putting another bullet a few inches below the first one. I could tell where I was hitting for the pine bark was flying loose. Then I came down the tree by inches, putting one bullet under the other. I had the advantage of the law on my side. I had a rifle while he had a shotgun. I had asked him to leave. Now I was shooting down close enough so that he certainly must hear the whine of the bullets. One last shot and he started running like a bull across the meadow.

He had never spoken to me. Not once had I heard the sound of his voice. He didn't call his dogs as he ran. The only thing that meant anything to this man was force. It had taken whining bullets to make him move. As he ran up the hill, I fired a safe distance above his head. I fired as long as I could see him, though I didn't have any intention of putting a bullet even dangerously close to him.

Now I stood watching his dogs run under the trees, the dogs he had deserted. What kind of a man was he? What were his intentions in walking past all the signs that mark this land as a game preserve? And what of his strange defiant actions? Many a man would have apologized to me when he learned he was on posted land. But this man undoubtedly knew it all along.

I thought perhaps he might turn somewhere on the hill and circle back along the other slope where he could get above our house. I listened for footsteps among the leaves, and I watched this hill slope, too. Then I looked down at the ground. I had fired almost a box of long cartridges. I wondered about the violence of my own reactions.

This had been a most unpleasant Sunday episode. Birch was still excited, barking and running. He wanted to tell me something more, but I wouldn't listen. I walked back inside the house where I put my rifle and a few cartridges away.

There wasn't any use for me to lie down now. I would read, listen to music, do something to make me forget. I must calm down again. In a way, this stranger had shown me my helplessness, he had made me angry when I couldn't afford anger. He had made me afraid, not of him, but of myself. It was for this that I hated him.

VII

At 2:00 P.M. I walked into Chad's barbershop in Greenup, the most talked-about barbershop that has ever been in this town. No one can remember in his lifetime a barber like this one, Chad Meadowbrook. Here stood Old Chad with a big smile, alone beside his empty chair.

"Hiya, Chad," I said.

"Greetings, my friend," he said, chewing the stub of an unlit eight-inch cigar with his gold teeth. Chad was spick and span in his immaculate white coat, white shirt, black bow tie, dark trousers, and well-shined shoes. "I'm glad to see you. This afternoon has been dragging. Get up in the chair. Where have you been so long?"

"Last time I was here the shop was closed and I had to go to another barber," I said. "Hated to go, Chad. You know I've been coming to your shop since 1932. Twenty-three years is a long time."

"Yeah, it is," Chad said, as I sat down in the chair and he put a cloth around my shoulders. "I've cut your hair when it was as black as a crow's wing. Now I notice you're getting a little frost around your temples. But time changes a man's hair like frost changes the leaves."

I remembered when I first went to Chad, too. I was Principal of McKell High School. Chad's hair was as black as mine then, only his was naturally wavy. I had heard many young women say it was a shame a man had as nice-looking hair as Old Chad did when it ought to be on some woman's head. Women had told Chad this, too. Now his hair was almost as white as his coat, but it was still curly. Old Chad, now fifty-five, still had a snap in his walk.

This stocky, short-legged barber started cutting my hair when he still worked during the day at the Taylor Brickyard. He pushed loads of bricks in wheelbarrows, which was one of the toughest jobs they had. He cut hair at night. In addition to these two jobs, he sold real estate on the side to his barbershop customers or to anybody who happened by. Chad just had to do some extra work. He had seven sons, all big eaters in their growing years, and Old Chad had to order groceries by the truckload.

While I was still Principal of McKell High School, Chad's prayers, so he said, were answered when his eighth and last child, a girl, was born. Anything she wanted she got—from her colorful, talkative, friendly, five-string-banjo-playing, fiddling, fun-loving father.

Chad's wife, Tessie, was the very opposite from him. She was an introvert. The four years I was in South Shore and had their four oldest sons in McKell High School, I never saw Tessie enough to know her. She was a shy person. But in 1937, the year I left McKell High School, I got a good look at Tessie one morning. Chad had gotten drunk for the first time, and that made news in South Shore. He had never had time to get drunk before because he wheeled bricks all day at the brickyard, cut hair until midnight, sold real estate at all times, and went to church on Sunday. But when Chad jumped the traces, he was the gossip of the town. Everybody said his shy and retiring wife, a devout member of the church, was so embarrassed she would leave him. And this was the one time when I got to see Tessie real well.

One morning walking to McKell High School, I saw Old Chad and Tessie coming up U.S. 23, which was a graveled road then. They were walking hand in hand up the middle of the road. Chad was hatless, for he was proud of his curly black hair, and he had a cigar stuck in the corner of his mouth. Tessie was smiling, holding onto Chad's hand, while the morning wind lifted her red hair. She was a very attractive woman to be the mother of seven boys and a girl. Chad and Tessie had "made up" over his getting drunk. She was putting an end to the South Shore gossip that she had left Old Chad.

Then I left South Shore and went to Europe. When I came back, I taught school in Portsmouth, Ohio, across the river from South Shore, and I went back to Old Chad's barbershop. I didn't know he was getting into the drinking habit, for he quoted the Bible when he cut people's hair, sold them real estate, and carried on as usual. About this time a short story of mine was chosen by editors for a textbook, and the publisher wrote me for a picture. So I went happily to see Old Chad. I told him that what I wanted was a picture haircut.

Chad thought my getting a short story into a textbook while I was in my twenties was great. "I'll give you a real picture haircut," he said. "I'll fix you up."

So he shaped my hair by cutting and standing back and sighting with one eye, then using the clippers and comb and scissors. He'd stand off and look at me and sight at my head like he was looking down the barrel of a rifle at a target. "I'll take care of you," he said as he grabbed a lock of hair that fell down over my forehead. He whacked it off with his scissors. "I've been tired of fooling with this unruly lock of yours for a long time."

I didn't think anything about this haircut. I went on to Portsmouth to have my picture made and sent it to the textbook publishers. The editor didn't write me that he liked the picture, but he used it. After the textbook was published with my story and picture in it, students wrote in from everywhere and asked me about my haircut. They never wrote me anything about my story. Many asked me what I was trying to do to my hair. One asked me in a letter if I were sprouting a black horn on my forehead to attract attention. I never answered these letters. Later I learned Old Chad had been drunk the day he cut my hair. I stayed away from his shop for a while, until I learned he cut my hair better when he was drunk than others could sober. I told Old Chad what had happened because of his haircut and the textbook picture, and I showed him some of the letters students were writing me from all over. Chad claimed these letters showed how important a barber was. He said they proved a haircut could affect a man's destiny. He told me how proud he was when he could improve a man's appearance with a nice haircut.

"Oh, a man born of woman has only a few years here, and they are full of trouble," he said. "Yes, even a haircut will affect a man's life." I didn't know Chad was having trouble at home. Later I found out all about it.

About this time I stopped teaching at Portsmouth and married my girl, Naomi Norris. For years Chad had been giving me "courtin' haircuts" when I was going to see her. "Just a little extra free hair tonic," he used to say, laughing, with the familiar cigar stuck in the corner of his mouth. "Naomi will love this. Young fellows tell me it wows the women. I'm the only barber here who can use it. I am the sole distributor of this wonderful tonic that will wow women and grow hair on bald spots." I laughed when he told me this, but I never forgot the extra hair tonic he gave me. After I was married, I used to drive twenty miles to his shop to get a haircut.

Then, during World War II, Chad lost two of his fine-looking sons in a car wreck. The car couldn't make a curve and went out of control, turned over, and killed four of the five occupants. Old Chad was grieved over this loss, and he tried to drown his grief with drink. Things went from bad to worse for him. In the late forties he lost his barbershop and a lot of his real estate business in South Shore. But when he came to my home town, Greenup, to put up a shop, I told my father what a wonderful barber Old Chad was and Dad went to him. But he went only a few times.

One day Old Chad was shaving my father. He had lathered his face and had shaved one side. Somebody came in and asked Chad about a piece of real estate. Chad went out into the street with a razor in his hand and left Dad in the chair. He didn't return for an hour, and the lather dried on Dad's face. Dad was mighty embarrassed when he had to get out of the chair and walk down the street with half his face shaved and the other half covered with dried lather. He finally got to another barbershop, but the people had to turn their heads to keep from laughing. They thought my dad, who had always lived a sober life, was drunk.

But I knew Old Chad was slipping when I read in the paper where Tessie had sued Chad for a divorce. This was hard for me to believe, until I got my hair cut one day and asked him if it was true. "Can't understand it," he said. "I love her. Gave her anything she asked for. She never wanted for anything. Not one of our children, married or single, has ever wanted for anything if I could help him."

Then I tried to tease Chad to see if he loved Tessie the way he claimed to. I said to Chad, "Maybe Tessie has seen somebody she likes better."

Tears welled up in Old Chad's eyes. "No, it's not that," he said. "I don't think it is. I even had a nice TV set in the house. When I saw a brand of spaghetti advertised over this TV, I bought myself some. And I liked it. So I bought some more, and when I went home from the shop one night, I found my spaghetti in the yard. She'd thrown it out. Turned against everything I liked. 'Gee,' I said, 'honey, if you don't want Old Chad to have this brand of spaghetti, just name the brand you like and I'll like it too!' She didn't say anything, but the next day she went to a lawyer and filed suit against me for divorce. This almost killed me. I got uneasy about Tessie. I said, 'Honey, this will ruin us. Don't divorce me. I want to live with you the rest of my days.' "

But Tessie went ahead with the divorce, and Old Chad came to Greenup, where he got himself a room and ate his meals in restaurants six days a week. Several times, when he tried to drown his cares, we read in the papers about his being locked up in jail over the weekend. And this was the reason I'd not got my last haircut from Chad. I wanted it on a Monday, and he had been jailed on

Sunday. There were no more happy days of banjo playing, square
dancing, and joking for Old Chad.

But this afternoon, first thing, he said to me, "Well, Jesse, I am
a happy man." Then, as he put the electric clippers to my temples,
he went on, "I'm dating Tessie again. I've been trying to date her ever
since she left me. First, she let me come back once a month to see
her. Now, I get to go three times a week and all day on Sunday.
Just like it used to be when we were teen-agers."

"I was wrong that time when I asked you if there was another
man in the picture," I said. "I was always sorry I said that to you."

"Oh, that was all right," he said, gesturing with the buzzing
clippers. "I wondered about that, too, when she threw my spaghetti
in the yard. But I don't wonder now. I was down last Sunday and I
gave her money to buy a rug for the house. And believe me, I
caught that little redhead in my arms and squeezed her tight. I
kissed her like I did a long time ago. A couple of our tall sons looked
at us but didn't even smile. I guess they thought we were acting
silly, us being in our fifties."

"Think you will win her back, Chad?" I asked.

"I stand a good chance," he said seriously. He got in a big way,
cutting my hair, talking fast, and laughing. "I won her before. I
think I can do it again. I've been wanting to tell you about this. I'm
glad there's nobody else in the shop. Boy, it's really great to get
back into that old springtime love. And if I ever get Tessie again,
she'll never get loose from me. I shouldn't have ever let her had a
divorce in the first place."

Old Chad laid his clippers down. He picked up his comb and
scissors. My hair never left my head as fast as now. Chad snapped
his scissors until sparks seemed about to fly. I was afraid he would
set my hair on fire. Smoke boiled from the end of his cigar. "Love
is great, Jesse. And old love is the greatest when it is revived.
Teen-age love in a fifty-five-year-old frame is out of this world."

Here was the fastest barber in the tristate area. When he worked
late, he had often given over a hundred haircuts, not counting the
shaves, in a single Saturday, his busiest day. But now he slowed
down on me. He wanted to do some more talking. He had some-

thing else on his mind. "By the way, I've got fourteen acres and a nice little cottage at Siloam I'd like to sell you. Two fine lots at Lloyd, too, right on U.S. 23. I'll sell them to you this minute."

"Not me, Chad," I said with a laugh. "But I do believe Tessie loves you again. You're the same Old Chad."

"Well, no harm in seeing what a man might want to buy," he told me, blowing smoke from his cigar. Then Chad started pouring hair tonic on my head. I knew the kind by its aroma. This was what he had used when he gave me courting haircuts.

"Chad, this is wonderful," I said, laughing.

"I never want you to lose Naomi," he said. "I'm giving you a real courting haircut."

V I I I

Among the finest Greenup County homes is that of Jake and Margaret Lynd, where we had Thanksgiving turkey today.

As I walked along beside Jake into his house, I knew my 192-pound frame was very small in comparison to his. Mighty Jake weighs 339 pounds now. When I weighed 222, Jake weighed 369. Still in his thirties, he is as powerful physically as he is large. He could take two 100-pound sacks, one in each hand, and toss them easier than the average man could handle 25-pound sacks.

His hands are big as fire shovels and his fingers like small sticks of stovewood. His arms are big as fence posts, not soft, flabby, and white, but woolly and muscular. His legs at the calves are as large as young saplings. He has to have his suits and shirts specially made, for he is broader than a corn-crib door across the shoulders. He is Mighty Jake, a modern-day giant.

I had seen him at one meal drink ten bottles of soft drinks, eat from four to six pounds of steak, ham, or turkey, or put away two to three chickens and his share of all the other things on the table. Then, for dessert, he'd eat a pie, drink a pot of coffee, and smoke a dozen nine-inch cigars. Through the evening he would nibble on a pound box of chocolates.

After meals he has eaten as many as two dozen five-cent bars of candy. But even so, Mighty Jake eats no more in proportion to his size than the average big hungry man. Besides, he has a great capacity for work and burns a lot of energy.

Jake's father, Joe Lynd, was a large and colorful man who started his first store by hauling his groceries in a wheelbarrow. He built his little retail store into the Lynd Wholesale House, one of the largest in the tristate area. His wheelbarrow became a fleet of trucks. He was the wealthiest man in Greenup County at the time of his death. Joe Lynd was married twice. By his first wife, he had four children. At her death, he married a large woman, and by her he had four more children, among whom was Jake. One of the boys by the second marriage was even larger than Jake. He tipped the scales at 400. The daughters each weighed over 200. Tommy Lynd, who is called "the little Lynd" because he is the smallest of all, weighs a mere 210. But Mighty Jake is all muscle. Jake's face looks as if it had been chiseled out of stone. He hasn't any double chin. His features are sharp. He has a long, pointed nose, sky-blue eyes, brown hair, a big, tight mouth. His voice, when he gets excited, is like the roar of a swarm of troubled bees.

Margaret, Jake's wife, is a blue-eyed, talkative, delightful woman. She likes to prepare big meals for her friends. And who are her and Jake's friends? There is only one qualification: they must be fellow Republicans. Jake and Margaret are most unusual in that they classify people solely according to their politics. Just so a person is a Republican is all that matters to the Lynds. They like decency and honesty among people. But if there is a little less of this among certain Republican friends, they don't say anything. They think and they speak in terms of politics. They qualify their statements about people by saying whether he is a Republican or a Democrat. Politics is a game Margaret and Jake play hard. They are the most devout Republicans I have ever known.

I got acquainted with Jake and Margaret one evening at a rural schoolhouse in Greenup County, where I was speaking for Dwight D. Eisenhower when he was a candidate for President in 1952. Sitting in the back of this little schoolhouse, I saw a neatly dressed giant, so large he had to sit on two of the small seats. Later, along with my Democratic wife, who they thought was Republican, I was invited to their home for a big steak dinner with dozens of defeated Republican candidates who ran for local offices. To Jake and Margaret Lynd our defeated local candidates were martyrs to the cause. Republicanism was a brotherhood and a great crusade. Jake and Margaret loved their Republican friends.

Today the Thanksgiving table was filled with food. One big platter was full of turkey and another was stacked high with ham, the best Mighty Jake could order from his wholesale house. There was a big dish of yams, another of the leatherbritches beans that Jake liked so much. We had mashed potatoes, dressing, giblet gravy, and baked macaroni. We had hot biscuits, strawberry preserves, and garden salad. And for dessert we had pumpkin pie, with Sanka, coffee, milk, or tea. The best food Margaret and Jake could serve was not good enough for their Republican friends.

After we had eaten, we sat at the table and talked about Thanksgiving, one of the great heritages our forefathers had passed down to us. And Jake traced the history of this day, for this was his favorite subject, history. But more specifically, he was a collector of books favorable to Republican presidents. If he found an unfavorable book, he threw it out of his collection, and as far as his powerful arm could throw it. Jake went back through the years to point out the great laws and ideas our Republican presidents had left us. He was a devoted admirer of Abraham Lincoln. Each year he made a pilgrimage to one of the places where Lincoln had lived.

Jake's wife, Margaret, mentioned the lumber that was coming for his new bookshelves. Apparently he had too many books.

"I am running into plenty of favorable books about our Republican presidents," Jake said, blowing a dark cloud of smoke from his long cigar. "I don't want them stacked. This is an insult to our great men. I want them up in shelves so everybody can see them. I want to invite in a few of these rebels around here and show them something."

Mighty Jake Lynd was adding a shelf just to hold the books favorable to Dwight D. Eisenhower. He spares neither money nor time to get these books. He is the only man I ever heard of who is collecting favorable books about Republican presidents.

I X

"I have taught thirty-one happy years, nine months out of each year, and never missed a day because of sickness," Lena Wells told me yesterday. We had been visiting with this favorite teacher of mine and her husband, Gus Voiers. "I've spent forty-five years in a schoolroom, counting the time I was a student. No wonder I love it. I like the smell of chalk and oiled pine floors. Books and youngsters have been my life."

Lena Wells Lykins Voiers came from a sturdy pioneer family. Understanding this remarkable woman requires knowing her people. Her grandfather, Peter D. Lykins, was living comfortably in Morgan County, Kentucky, when the War Between the States began. He was a man of property for his day and time in a Kentucky mountain county. And he was a man who had ideas of his own. All his brothers and relatives remained loyal to the South, but he was loyal to the Union, and two of his sons joined the Union Army. With their allegiance clearly established, the Peter D. Lykins family was given the choice of clearing out from Morgan County or being killed.

Peter Lykins gathered all his transportable property, loaded it onto a wagon train, and set out with his family in one of the worst winters on record, 1861–1862. He was escorted to the border by his brothers and told never to return. He and his family, with their teams, wagons, poultry, cattle, hogs, and sheep, rolled over frozen terrain and through muddy thaws where the wagon wheels sank to the axles and two teams were needed to pull a wagon over the little-used wilderness trails. This wagon train moved in the direction of Mt. Sterling, Kentucky. Peter D. Lykins was a determined man, and so were the brothers he had left in Morgan County.

On the second night after the Lykins' wagon train had crossed the Morgan County border, the courthouse burned in West Liberty, county seat of Morgan County. One of Peter D. Lykins' family, one of his six sons on that wagon train, was accused of having ridden back and set fire to the courthouse. No one ever found out who had burned it. But a horse's pounding hoofs had been heard by many that night on West Liberty's frozen dirt streets. And afterwards the church bells rang to arouse the people to put out the fire. But the courthouse burned to the ground. "I am sure none of my uncles did it," says Lena Wells, "but they all claimed the honor."

At Mt. Sterling, Peter D. inquired of a place where he could go "where no man is held in bondage and no witch has ever hanged," and he was told by a sympathetic stranger that there was such a county in Kentucky—Lewis County—a place of high hills that bordered on the Ohio River. Peter D. Lykins was three weeks getting to Lewis County in one of the most rugged journeys ever recorded in East Kentucky. Yet not one of his family, his six sons or two daughters, got sick on the way, and he reached his destination with all his hogs, sheep, cattle, cows, and teams. The story is told that he didn't lose as much as a single chicken. He shot one timber wolf that came too close to his chicken coops one morning at daylight.

Peter D. Lykins settled in the heart of Lewis County, twenty miles from the county seat of Vanceburg. My teacher, Lena Wells, was the seventh child of Peter D. Lykins' son, Dial D. Her father ran the store and post office at Petersville and was interested in the education of his children. Each child who could pass a teacher's examination and make a first-class certificate was promised a gold watch with his name engraved on it.

"All eight of us, four boys and four girls, qualified, but Frank and Denny declined to teach," Lena Wells said. "My father died suddenly at the age of fifty-two, when I was eleven years old. But he had arranged that if something happened to him, my oldest brother, Jess, was to see that we got our watches. Jess gave me mine with 'Lena Wells' engraved on its back. I wore it twenty-three years with a gold fleur-de-lis pin until I lost it and my jewelry box in the 1937 flood."

For years this granddaughter of pioneers has been a happy schoolteacher. Though she comes of an influential family, she has not been interested in amassing wealth. Lena Wells has never taught school because she needed money. She has taught because she likes to teach.

She had it written in her will, she told me, that the marker to

be put on her grave should cost no more than fifty dollars and that
it should have this inscription only:

Teacher
Her life was full of happiness
Lena Wells Lykins Voiers
1896–19—

If you have ever been a pupil under Lena Wells and you're
stationed in Germany, France, England, Spain, or Italy with the
United States Armed Forces, or if you are working in Europe,
Mexico, Canada, or North Africa, you are likely to have a visitor
any day when school is not in session at Lewis County High School,
Vanceburg, Kentucky. That visitor will be your former teacher,
Lena Wells. She never lets you know when she is coming. She just
drops in with a big "howdy" smile that lights up her whole face, her
eyes twinkling with good humor and curiosity. Lena Wells may be
wearing a hat you have seen twenty years before in the teacher's
cloakroom. The happy sight of her when she arrives is like seeing
all the people of the United States rolled into one, and that one is
shaking your hand, greeting you, patting you on the back, and
telling you a dozen times in five minutes how proud she is of you,
her boy, serving in the Armed Forces of the United States. And right
away you will feel that she really has been thinking of you, that she
has a personal stake in your future, almost as if she were your
mother.

She may ask you every small detail about your work, remembering all that you tell her with that brilliant, inquiring mind of hers.
And if she has a chance to meet your boss or your superiors, who
will never be able to resist her, she will start pulling for your ad-
vancement and telling them what a great boy you are. In other
words, you are still her pupil. She taught you five, ten, twenty, even
thirty-five years ago, but you are her youngster. Maybe she had
something specific to do with your getting where you are today.
Maybe you don't even know about it. She will write forty letters a
day in behalf of her pupils. There has probably never been a
teacher in America like her.

There is not a state in this Union where she has not visited pupils she has taught. She spends her summers traveling, checking up on what her pupils are doing.

"I got the idea of traveling when I was in high school because I didn't like history," she said. "I don't like to read about people. I like to meet them in person, look them in the eye, and shake their hands."

She is by instinct a good mother, although she has no children of her own. There is a long unknown list of her pupils who have had trouble in some way, and the person there to help them even before their own parents was Lena Wells. She would appear on the scene with, "It's not as bad as you think, and we'll see what can be done about it," and something would be done. She never let a pupil down if she thought he was in the right, and she never let him down if she knew he was wrong but thought he had possibilities of becoming a better person.

For instance, one of Lena's "sweet little girls" was assaulted by two brothers from a family of influence and power in town. The girl's people were of humble origin but had a reputation for uprightness and wholesomeness in the community. Yet this case couldn't even get to trial until Lena Wells stepped in. She went to the aid of her schoolgirl, who had just graduated from high school. Much money was spent, the case was forced into the open, and in a trial that was long remembered the boys from the influential family were convicted.

She is loyal to her own political party, but if one of her boys is on the opposite ticket and is running for a local or state office, she will go to help him. She is a fluent speaker, and she learned political strategy early from her father and brothers. She has entered the political arena most forcefully when she thought corruption was dominant. She has been the deciding factor in local primaries in eliminating candidates whose integrity was doubtful.

"Yes, it was time to rid this county of old politicians that lived from the courthouse," she said. "I asked one of my good boys to run to eliminate corruption and waste of the taxpayers' money. He agreed, on the condition that I help him. I got out and went all over the county. He was elected, and the people like him so well he will be elected again. Now I have had to warn *him* about waste and corruption."

One of her favorites was a Jewish boy whose father was a business competitor of her husband's. But such a little thing as business didn't matter when she had a bright boy whom she thought might have a promising future. When he finished high school, she had a college selected for him and, as she did with many of her other boys and girls, she went with him to make application. But the college dean told Mrs. Voiers that they had enrolled their quota and had excessive applications on the waiting list. Mrs. Voiers then went to another college, where she heard the same story. She went to a third, the oldest college in Kentucky, and he was accepted. Mrs. Voiers learned later that the two institutions that refused this boy had accepted students with lesser qualifications who applied after he did.

"I blew my top," she said. "I knew there was prejudice. I figured the deans of both institutions were lying and looking me straight in the eyes when they did it. I kicked up an awful fuss. Then I got him in the third college, which was the best of the three anyway. I showed them his school record, told them that he was a fine boy and that I believed he'd be a great executive someday."

As I walked the ridge path with Lena Wells that January afternoon thirty-three years ago, when she was twenty-six and I was fifteen, she told me that I would write a book someday if I worked hard enough. And she told me that she would always keep in touch with me. That moment I had my first stirrings of ambition to try to amount to something in life, simply because she had so much confidence in me. But I thought when I left Greenup High School and she went back to her home town, Vanceburg, that we would not see each other again.

Yet a couple of years later, when I was working at the steel mills, there was a call at my boardinghouse.

"Stuart, a fine-looking dame to see you."

I went downstairs to the lobby, and there sat Lena Wells.

"Thought I'd drop by to see if you planned to enter college," she said.

"I plan to enter in September," I told her. "That's only a few days away. I made up my mind to go a while back and I've saved what money I could."

"I knew you would," she said.

When I came home from Lincoln Memorial, she rode over to W-Hollow to check on my activities. When I taught my first one-room high school, Miss Lykins came to visit. When she read anything about me in the paper or one of my stories in a magazine, I'd get a letter, "I'm proud of you. I always told you you could do it." When one of the algebra students I was teaching won a state-wide competition, she wrote me, "See what I told you. See how right I was! You'll make a better math teacher than an English teacher, because math was so hard for you to learn."

Then I entered Vanderbilt University to do graduate work. One day after lunch at the Wesley Hall Cafeteria, I was back in the steam and heat of the dishwashing room when someone spoke, "Well, well, look where I find you. Up among the clouds as always." It was Miss Lykins all right, only she was now Mrs. Voiers, and her husband, Gus, was with her.

When I became Greenup County School Superintendent, Mrs. Voiers wrote me letters. She visited me. When my first book was published, she was jubilant. When my name appeared in *Who's Who in America,* she even noticed that, and wrote me a long letter. When each of my books appeared, she read it and reported her opinions, good and bad, back to me. When I got a Guggenheim Fellowship, Mrs. Voiers was there to see me off, saying, "Go to Europe and travel in every country you can."

Everyone will tell you that to see Lena Wells coming puts new life, hope, and ambition in a man, that to listen to her gives him a renewed faith in his future. This is the way she has taught and still teaches, with great faith and fervor. It has proved fortunate for thousands that Lena Wells chose the great profession of teaching. More than any other teacher I know, she has left a permanent stamp on her children.

X

Breakfast tasted wonderful this morning after my walk over the snow and through the icy wind. Afterwards I went out to look again at the thermometer. To my surprise it was only ten above. When I came back inside, Naomi was calling, "Come, Jesse, look! Here he is. Back at his same old tricks."

Yes, it was old Graybar, the three-legged possum. He had come from under the house. Where the water line went through the underpinning there was a place where he could burrow. This was the hole Naomi had wanted me to close last summer. Now that cold weather had come again, old Graybar and his family had moved back to sleep beside the hot-water pipes under the floor.

"Well, he's hungry," I said. "We had a good persimmon crop and plenty of pawpaws this year, but old Graybar on three legs can't compete with the other possums. He's asking for bread."

Old Graybar was still waiting for his food when I opened the kitchen door and threw three slices of bread in his direction. Though this was fresh bread and he liked the old bread much better, I knew he would eat it. So our old friend hobbled out on three legs, picked up a slice of the bread, and went under the floor. He didn't have time to eat this one before he was back to get the second. And then he came back for the third.

"We won't see him any more today," I said.

But Graybar's plight gave me an idea. All the time I stood in the kitchen thinking about old Graybar, I imagined he was thanking me for those three slices of bread. "Thank you, thank you very much," I heard him say. "This bread is delicious this morning, since the pawpaws are gone and the persimmons are frozen hard. But when the sun shines and the persimmons thaw again, I'll take persimmons instead of bread, thank you just the same."

Old three-legs was thanking me for bread. Why didn't I, in the same spirit, go thank the birds for their spring songs?

In the utility room I filled a large white bucket with the baby-chick feed which we keep especially for the birds. I was on my way up the valley toward the pasture. I wanted to go back there again anyway. I wanted to feed the birds who had been so kind to me last summer. When I needed their kindness more than I had at any other time in my life, the birds sang for me at my window. I lay in bed listening for their singing.

And when I managed to shuffle away from this house up the valley in late February and March, they sang for me then, too, perched on the naked boughs of late winter. I had stood resting, breathing new life into lungs stale with sickroom air, while I listened to their songs. Now these birds needed food on a morning when the land was frozen and the streams were under white veins of ice beneath the low gray sky. Intermittent flakes of snow rode on the winds.

Before I reached the tool shed, I watched the chickadees trying to pull frozen ragweed seeds from the tops of the dead stems. It was slow and difficult going for these hungry little birds. So I threw two handfuls of corn upon the dark frozen land where winds had blown the light snow away. One bird descended upon the feed from its low flight, then chirruped gleefully to the others. They left the frozen ragweeds and crowded around.

When I left, there were seven birds picking up grain from the frozen ground like small chickens. At the tool shed, I stopped to spread grain on the lumber stack. Here, during the summer, I had sat by this stream under the poplar trees and listened to the water flowing over the rocks and the wind in the poplar leaves. Here I had known the rest and peace of being alone for hours at a time, and all I had heard were the songs of birds, the cawing of crows, and the wind and water. Now I could repay some of the birds that had sung for me.

DECEMBER

At 5:00 P.M. I got our paper from the box down beside the W-Hollow Road. As I started up the lane road home, I saw the smallest possum I have ever seen traveling alone. When I saw him coming up the creek bank, I stopped, for it was hard for me to believe I was seeing a possum so small that he should have been in his mother's pouch with his tail wrapped around hers so she wouldn't lose him. Lying in his mother's warm pouch beside his brothers and sisters or riding on her furry back certainly would have been safer and more comfortable for this little fellow than braving these winds Canada had sent over Ohio's flatlands to our North Kentucky hills. Though the ground was frozen harder than sandstone, not all the creek was frozen over, and this small possum may have been down to the creek for a drink.

He was so close against the earth he couldn't get much sense of direction. But as he came up the bank, sniffling among the frosted soybean stubble, he seemed to know where he was going. He didn't

look up to see me standing beside the road watching. I might have
been a tree or a stone to this lonely little possum. I rattled my newspaper in the wind to see if this animal child had any fear. But he
didn't. He came on toward me. I wondered if he was blind.

He walked over my foot, which I had planted firmly in the lane
road. I reached down, put my hand over his soft, furry neck, and
lifted him to have a look. If he was blind, I was going to take him
to the house, put him in a box, and feed him. I knew he couldn't
last long without a mother possum in a bare winter world.

"Well, little boy possum, you're not blind," I said, looking at his
black, beady eyes. "And you seem to know where you are going, so
I'll turn you loose as soon as I've looked you over."

His little silk-thin ears were buttoned back. Pink little ears they
were, covered with hair finer than that on half-grown mice. I wondered why anything of flesh and blood as leaf-thin as this possum's
ear hadn't frozen. Each spring, trees in this uncertain climate that
had leafed too early and caught a nippy frost were filled with black,
lifeless leaves. Then why wouldn't his little ears freeze in subzero
weather? As I held this little possum, not as big as my fist, in my
open hand and felt the warmth of its young body and the beating of
its little heart, I thought of the winter life ahead for it.

Possums, unlike turtles and frogs, are warm-blooded animals
that have to stir all winter long over the small wild portion of the
earth that is home to them, searching for something to eat. I have
often wondered what they eat when persimmons, pawpaws, and
old apples are gone. I have had them come to my chicken house
and eat feed with my chickens. I have had them come to my
yard, where I've given them bread. An animal with as much wild-
ness in its nature as a possum has to get mighty hungry before it
will come to a human being and almost ask for food.

Youthful whiskers grew on either side of this little possum's long,
sharp nose, fine hairs white with frost and frozen stiff. The end of
his nose was pink, his small feet as pink as a baby's hands. The bottoms of his feet were soft and tender, too. I wondered how he could
go far over the hard ground and not freeze these feet. Beyond I
saw that he had left his small stenciled tracks on the frost.

He had enough flesh on his framework for comfort, but he wasn't fat. He probably had been nursed by his mother until a few days ago. Life from now on would be difficult. This little possum would have to search under the trees for frozen persimmons, and I doubted if he knew how. If he had had parents, one or both would have been with him. They would not have allowed him to come out in broad daylight when it is dangerous for even big possums to travel.

I put him down on the other side of the road, and to my surprise here were his small tracks again where he had come down the hill. He had crossed the big open meadow, about eight acres of open space, down a gentle slope. Happy to be free from my hand, he put his nose down to the ground and took off in a hurry, his little hairless tail barely above the frost. I wondered why he didn't freeze his tail, too. His hairless tail and the tips of his ears were the extremities of his body, through which the blood, which kept his body warm, circulated last.

Now the stiff wind blowing down from the high ridge across the meadow made climbing a little hard for me. But I was just walking slowly along, keeping up with the possum that crept over the ground in the direction of his old tracks but didn't always follow them. When we reached the first ridge, he turned left toward the whiteoak grove at the edge of the meadow. This had always been great denning country. The groundhogs had burrowed here in summer months and left holes for the possums and rabbits to take over in winter.

I followed him to the edge of the grove. Here the December wind rattled among the leaves still clinging to the boughs. If the possum heard the noise above, he didn't look up. But these strange noises should have frightened him. This is the reason possums like to stir on damp nights when everything is still. The stir of a leaf makes a possum run. And fear is a built-in part of a possum.

The lonely little possum went down in a hole in the floor of a small ravine. Perhaps water flowing underground had made this hole warm inside. Maybe his father and mother were there asleep, and he had slipped away to get himself a drink. I wanted to think so, instead of believing an animal so young could be left on his own in a winter world. But knowing something about the instincts of parent animals, I couldn't make myself believe it. If one or both parents had been in that hole, he would not have been out traveling.

Now I would take the newspaper home. But I would return with some bread and shove it back in his hole as far as I could reach. I wouldn't sleep tonight if I didn't.

I I

On this day fourteen years ago, December 7, 1941, Howard Riggs brought Naomi home from the hospital in a cast that reached from below her hips to her shoulders. She had to lie in this cast three months, maybe longer, and she was pregnant. We had been in an automobile wreck in Mexico, had spent every dollar we had getting home, and we still owed the hospital.

Everything looked dark to us that day. We wondered about our child to be born. My parents and several of our neighbors were here when Howard drove up in the old ambulance, which had an extra bulldog-low gear for the muddy roads. Our W-Hollow Road was one of the worst in Greenup County in 1941. We had to learn to read the weather signs accurately for snow, sleet, rain, and thaw before we drove out and back.

My sister Glennis, who was a nurse, had come here to spend the winter with us. Naomi was laid on a hospital bed before the open fire. We didn't have electric lights then. We had oil lamps, and we burned wood in our fireplace and cookstove. I had to haul wood for fireplace and stove, write stories, work on a novel, see to the farm, and periodically walk out to a train or bus and ride a hundred miles to give a fifty-dollar talk. I knew what a hard winter was ahead for us. I would have to keep our car in the garage because our road was so terrible. I would have to carry things on my back to my family, as my father had done for us years ago in this same house.

While relatives and friends came in to see Naomi on that dark Sunday, I switched on the little battery radio in the bookshelf. Just as I did, an announcer said: *"Stand by for important news. Stand by for important news."* He said it so emphatically that everybody gathered around waiting. *"Pearl Harbor has been bombed by the Japanese. Pearl Harbor has been bombed by the Japanese. We don't know the extent of damage to our fleet, but it might be considerable."*

"That's it," somebody said. "That's war!"

Naomi didn't speak. Our friends and parents sat silently in the room. They knew this was war, too. I grew more depressed by the minute. The future looked darker than ever.

After everybody had gone that evening, Glennis, Naomi, and I, left alone in this house in this winter-dark valley, stayed up, listened to the news over the little radio, and talked. That was fourteen years ago tonight. I sat by Naomi's bedside and cheered her the best I could. I told her she would walk again, that her back would be all right, that we would have a third member in our family. But she didn't need to be cheered along by anyone. She is the most optimistic woman I have ever known. In bed with a broken back, pregnant, isolated in the country, in a suddenly war-torn and uncertain world, Naomi did not despair.

Really deep in my heart, I wondered if she would walk again. I wondered, too, after the kind of automobile wreck we had been in, if our child would be a normal one. I wondered about going away to speak to make a few dollars, leaving Glennis to carry heavy loads of wood and ashes in addition to her other duties.

The following March, after three cold winter months, Naomi was taken from her cast and fitted into a brace. She had to learn to walk again, which she did, quickly and with iron determination. And in August she gave birth to a long, normal girl, whom she named Jessica Jane. Then, with Naomi out of danger and the child born, I felt compelled to go into the service. Naomi stayed here in the valley with Jane during my first six months in the Navy. She suffered loneliness, yet she endured cheerfully. She showed wells of inner strength hard for me even to imagine. She was a woman I'd always regarded as frail.

Then, in 1954, I was struck down. Naomi had to assume all responsibility. She watched over me like a hawk, ran the house, consulted with the doctors, kept visitors away, wrote letters for me, contended with my despondent moods, and in every way breathed the desire for life, and life itself, back into me. Because of her, and because inside every man there is a powerful urge to live, I pulled through the worst physical disaster of my life. I have walked a mile, climbed the pasture hill, pitched hay to the cattle.

On this night fourteen years ago, our country was struck down by a sneak attack. Yet with the same resilience with which an individual instinctively fights physical disaster, America had begun the very next day to gather her forces to fight back. I never doubted for a moment that we would win the war, just as I never doubted in my last moments of consciousness in the Murray College Auditorium that I would live.

And maybe the reason is obvious. Man is powerful. Man will rise to an occasion. Man will endure because he can adjust himself to existing circumstances until he has his chance to change them.

I I I

    When I saw him across the street in Greenup this morning, I walked over. He had never been a robust man in all the years I had known him. He was slender, with large blue eyes in a pale face and light-brown hair. He dressed immaculately in clothes that were of the best taste and tailored neatly to fit him. I first met T. R. in 1927. He had just come to Russell's First and People's Bank as cashier. I was in college then and needed money badly. My first cousin, E. R. Hilton, took me to the First and People's Bank and introduced me to T. R. Bankers didn't need to know me. They didn't need to be too nice to me. There wasn't a single reason why one should do a favor for a poor farm boy. I was always needing money. I was always borrowing. But this was the first time I had ever left my home town, Greenup, to get money. There had been two banks in Greenup, the Citizens State Bank and the First National, and I had borrowed from both. One of these, the Citizens State Bank, failed. And the First National, for the first time, had turned me down.

Now I was desperate for fifty dollars. I was a sophomore at Lincoln Memorial University, and I had bought myself a new suit of clothes, for I had begun to have a few dates. I was working for my board and tuition, but I had to buy my clothes and books. My expenses there for one year were about three hundred dollars, and I made only twenty cents an hour. Now I needed fifty dollars to pay off the fifty I had borrowed in Tennessee to buy the suit.

I had borrowed this money from someone who I thought was a

friend. He told me I could have it for a year. But he must have become afraid for his loan, for he demanded the money immediately, after I had spent it for clothes. I was tired of wearing a pair of sailor blues with buttons across the front that I had bought in a secondhand store in Ashland. With my sailor blues, I wore a slightly frayed light-gray coat to an old suit, the pants of which were torn out. This was my Sunday best my freshman year at Lincoln Memorial.

But my sophomore year was different. I was meeting people, writing poems, editing the paper, and wanting to go more places than my old clothes would let me. I had hitchhiked three hundred miles back home to borrow fifty dollars. When I was turned down in my home town, I was stunned. I walked outside the bank a dejected young man. After trying to borrow from three others, each of whom wanted ten per cent interest, I hitchhiked to Raceland, Kentucky, to see if my first cousin, E. R. Hilton, had the money. He had a family of four to support and was paying for his home on a railroad clerk's salary.

"No, Jesse, I don't have the money," E. R. said. "But I have a good friend in the bank, T. R. Richards, and he has helped me. I'll introduce you to him and sign your note for security."

I could have hugged E. R. Hilton's neck. And that's how I first met T. R. Richards at the First and People's Bank.

"T. R., I've brought my cousin, Jesse Stuart, up to see you this morning," E. R. said. "We'd like to talk with you about a personal matter."

T. R. knew what this personal matter was. I wonder now if he didn't get such a personal matter each hour during the day. But he invited us politely into a small room, where the three of us sat down together. Then I told T. R. my story and why I wanted the fifty dollars.

"I was going to let you have it without ever hearing your story," he said quietly, "but it was so interesting I wanted to listen. I like to see a young man with ambition. Sure you can have the money."

Later, in the dark days of the depression, the other bank, the one that had turned me down, crashed. The elderly banker there, a friend of my father's and a friend of mine, apologized for not letting me have the fifty dollars. He said he didn't recognize me since I had grown up and his eyesight wasn't so good any more. He was telling me the truth, too. Each time I saw him, years afterward until his death, he always apologized for his not letting me have that fifty dollars.

But I had met young T. R. Richards, and that was more important. I paid this first loan off after two four-month renewals. I had established a good credit with him.

There was not a year from 1927 until 1955 that I did not borrow money from T. R. I borrowed from him even when I had money invested in something else. When the bank closed in Greenup, he established a branch bank here in the same building where the old bank had been. Here I deposited money and did banking business with the man who had loaned me that important fifty dollars. I have borrowed from a thousand to fifteen hundred from him many times. I borrowed fifteen hundred just on my own signature before I ever had a real book success. In later years I borrowed money from T. R. to buy land.

T. R. had sent me a card when I lay gravely ill on a hospital bed. He was positive I would live, when others, including doctors, weren't so sure. T. R. knew my predicament, for he, too, had once been under an oxygen tent. He had been kept in the hospital several days, and then was told by his doctor to take it easy at the bank. But he went back to work saving people's homes, saving their farms, lending them money for their children's educations.

When I was at home convalescing, I heard that T. R. was in an even deeper kind of physical trouble. I didn't know—never asked, but only guessed—the nature of his trouble. I didn't want to know. I felt deeply about this man. Bankers aren't usually town heroes. It has taken many people twenty-five years to wake up to the fine things this banker has done.

Many people had looked upon him only as a prosperous and well-dressed banker who they figured was worth a lot of money. And just the idea of his being a banker made many feel they couldn't get close to him. But no one thought this who had borrowed from T. R. during the depression days and knew how he loaned sympathetically, even charitably, to the fullest extent of his bank.

Now I wanted to shake his hand again. I remembered the first time I had shaken his hand in Russell, twenty-eight years ago. I had written to him while he was in his last trouble, traveling here and there, hunting, searching for someone, somebody who could do something to prolong the years of his life. I thought about how he must feel now, having weighed himself on the scales of life only to watch them tilt in death's favor.

"Hiya, T. R.," I said, shaking his hand. His large deep-sunken blue eyes seemed brightly alive in his pale face. "How are you, fellow?"

"Fine, Jesse," he said. "And you?"

"Progressing slowly but surely," I said. "Strange things can happen to one, can't they?"

"I'll say they can," he said, "when he least expects it."

T. R.'s hair was whiter now. But this slender wisp of man had changed very little otherwise. He was still the well-dressed, clean-shaven, slender banker.

"I appreciated those fine letters from you," he said. "Come to think about it, I suppose I have done something for people around here. And so many of them are appreciative. I am getting letters from them now, years later."

"Many who have not written remember, too," I said. "Has my niece, Carroll Keeney Abdon, written you?"

"I get a thrill out of loaning money to a nice young couple like that one," T. R. said, smiling. "I was happy to see them get moved into that home of their own on the hill. No, she hasn't written."

Roy and Carroll Abdon wanted a home. He had just returned from France, where he had spent two years in the Army. The banks in Ashland turned down Roy, using one excuse or another. Price too high, no collateral, no money for down payment. Then Carroll and I went to the First and People's Bank, where we talked to Leslie Moore, cashier for the branch bank in Greenup. He talked favorable. A date was set for Leslie Moore and T. R. Richards to come and evaluate the property for a loan. Carroll and Roy had to get a loan of forty-eight hundred or miss getting this property.

The day T. R. and Leslie came, Carroll was teaching in a one-room rural school. She made a little over a hundred dollars a month. Roy was working at the Chesapeake and Ohio carshops at Raceland, Kentucky, where he made twice his wife's salary using a welding torch. I took T. R. and Leslie to see this property. T. R. went through the house and looked over the hills in all directions. This house was on a flat hilltop overlooking the middle portion of W-Hollow.

"Well, Les, you let the little blond teacher and her husband have six thousand on this deal," T. R. said softly as he walked to the car. "Let them have it soon. This property won't stand long at the price."

This was twelve hundred more than they needed.

Such were my thoughts as I stood looking at the man who had loaned me fifty dollars for a suit of clothes.

"Wonderful to see you, Jesse," he said.

"Keep your chin up."

"I will, you do the same."

Then a quick shake of the hand, a smile, and we walked away in opposite directions. I wondered if I had parted forever with a man who had done much for me in this life.

I V

I have just closed the kitchen door so Jane and Naomi Deane won't hear the noise of my typewriter. I am afraid if they hear me writing into the night they will not be able to sleep. Then there is another thing I would like to do by closing this door. I can't, but I like to pretend. I'd like to close this door to preserve in this kitchen our happiness, our love, the words that we have spoken tonight. I'd like to keep it all in this kitchen fastened up forever. I wish there could be another time when all this would unfold to other ears like voices from a record. In some future day and time I'd like others to hear the words spoken, the Christmas carols sung, the laughter, friendship, and family love that lived before our little fireplace in the corner of our kitchen tonight.

I know that I cannot reproduce these sounds, this love, with cold symbols on a printed page. But I am going to sit here and write down what I can. Actually nothing extraordinary happened at all. Our family of three lived for one evening in our kitchen.

First, about our kitchen. We have a fireplace in the corner. We don't have to have a fireplace now. We could close it, for we don't need it for either cooking or heat. We have hot-water heat which comes through convectors around our kitchen wall and produces an efficient even heat all over our house. Our four fireplaces could never do this. We know this is true, for in winters here, before the heater was installed, we had all four fireplaces going, and parts of this house were still cold.

But we will never close up any of the fireplaces, even the one in the kitchen. We like to sit before an open fire to watch the flames leap up from the wood, to warm our feet on the fender. We like to pull the red-hot coals from the grate and cook cornbread in a skillet, covered with a lid to hold the steam inside to give the cornbread flavor. We like to roast sweet potatoes, which we grow in our small creek bottoms, in the ashes. We like to hold an old-fashioned popcorn popper over the flame and watch the little grains jump up in the pan to pop open like big white flakes of falling snow. We like to boil sorghum with butter and pour it over the popcorn, which makes the best molasses popcorn balls in the world. Once we used to reboil our sorghum into a thick syrup, then put butter on our hands and pull it while it was still warm into long sticks of brown sorghum candy. We shaped it into brown twists similar to those of tobacco.

Sometimes we roast apples, which come from our trees, by putting them in a pan and putting the lid down tight under hot ashes. We like to sit a comfortable distance back from the fire holding long willow wands with marshmallows on their tips over the blaze until they start turning brown. We laugh and talk as we watch them swell with heat. When they catch fire, we jerk our long wands back in a hurry and blow the flames out.

Now, how can one do this sort of thing with furnace heat, or with coal in a grate? This is the reason why we have not closed any of our four fireplaces. They will not be closed as long as Naomi and I continue to live here. If Jane lives on here after we go, since she has grown up in the tradition of the family around the open fireplace in the evening, I believe she will always have some wood to burn and a little fire, even if she is living in the year 2000 and is warmed by atomic heat.

On this very spot where I am using this typewriter, my mother and father used to sit around a table in their kitchen. Four of their seven children, for two were dead and one was born later, sat with them. Here we planned and talked and laughed. Only we didn't have an open fireplace. We had a big cookstove we called a wood range. It burned wood like a fireplace, and heat danced above its flat top like sunlight over a tin roof on a midsummer afternoon. Dad used to cut the stovewood for this range, and I carried armfuls inside the kitchen and put them inside the woodbox. In the mornings while Mom got breakfast, I used to go to the kitchen long before daylight and sit on the woodbox close to the stove while the kitchen got warm. But after the stove got really hot, we couldn't stay in this kitchen, no matter if it was twenty below outside, unless we raised a window to let the heat out.

Naomi and I rebuilt the fireplace and chimney in the old living room after we began housekeeping here. We figured that where this hearth stands is a great tradition of family life around the open fire. At least twenty families have lived here in the century and a half this house has stood. I can remember eight of these families myself. We estimated that six or seven thousand people, young and old, have sat before a blazing winter fire here and laughed, talked, joked, ate, and lived life joyously and fully in the years that have passed.

Before we tore down the old stone chimney, made by Eric Brickey, a stonemason of another century, the elements had eroded many of these large stones until they were so thin there was danger of the chimney's falling. Heat escaping from this chimney melted the snow for a radius of twenty feet around. This frightened us, so we tore it down and replaced it with one made of bricks. But this was not breaking any old tradition, for the stone chimney had replaced an even earlier one made of sticks and mud. And the bricklayer who made our chimney, Sam Brickey, was a grandson of Old Eric, who had built the stone chimney and fireplace almost a hundred years ago.

I wish the doors had been shut for each family in the century and a half past, and we could open them to look in on evenings of long ago when a man with buckskin moccasins on his feet and a coonskin cap on his head stood before the wood fire in a fireplace built of clay and sticks. I wish we could see his wife and their young children, the long rifle hanging to a joist and a powder horn on the wall. Captain George Naylor Davis (1781–1847) belonged to that time. He trained a company of men near here and took them by boat down the Ohio and Mississippi to help Andrew Jackson in the Battle of New Orleans. Later he served on Andrew Jackson's staff, for the General took a fancy to him. Now Captain George Naylor Davis lies buried in Brick Union's rural churchyard, which is six miles from here. There were no roads then, no schools, no work but hunting, fishing, clearing of land, building, and trading furs with Indians.

Then, like turning the pages of a book, I would like to see each family that shared this fireplace up until the present. I myself can remember back to 1915.

Eric Brickey made the big chimney and fireplace so large it took a mule to pull a backstick for it. It took several men to roll one over the floor to get it in behind the andirons. Sam Brickey told us that his grandfather, Eric Brickey, called his stone chimneys, so many of which he built in this area, his "living monuments." Sam, in turn, called our new brick chimney one of his "living monuments." His living monument, too, would pass away when another age developed new chimney materials. But the tradition of the open fire would not pass away if we could do anything to keep it alive.

If we could close the kitchen doors to perpetuate what took place before our fireplace tonight, here is what we would pass along to some future inhabitants of this house.

It was after dinner, and we were drying the dishes. Naomi had already brought extra wood for the fire and filled the brass kettle that stands in the corner. I stopped drying long enough to put an extra stick of wood on the grate.

Naomi joined Jane in a Christmas carol, and while we finished the dishes and the flames leaped up through the wood in our kitchen fireplace, we sang "Silent Night." Christmas was a week or two off, but its spirit always precedes it. I remembered that this same song was sung before this same fireplace in the years from 1915 to 1918. And I am sure others sang it here long before then.

We sang "God Rest Ye Merry, Gentlemen" as we sat before the fire. Naomi got up to find a nutcracker, and I went to the woodshed to fetch a peck of hickory nuts and the two bricks which we keep for this purpose. I laid them on the hearth. Naomi was going to bake a hickory-nut cake, and we had to have the kernels. Jane used one of the bricks while I used the other to crack the hickory nuts. We put them in Naomi's lap, and she took the kernels from the nuts. We then threw the nuts, clean of their kernels, into the blazing fire.

We worked slowly cracking our thin-shelled hickory nuts. Naomi, Jane, and I had gathered them in October from a tall hickory tree that grows about a hundred yards up the valley at the edge of the pine grove. We had gathered ourselves plenty for the long winter but had left enough for our squirrels. Now, by the time we had filled the crock with hickory-nut kernels, we had cracked a peck. We had sung all the Christmas carols we knew, including some we didn't know too well. Jane had recited "The Night before Christmas" without a halt. We had each recited a poem. Then Jane popped corn for herself and her mother, and we finished with an evening cup of tea and a piece of angel-food cake.

That was all, except for the talk and the gaiety and the love that I will not try to put down here.

Now Jane and Naomi are fast asleep. I have been sitting here thinking about life in front of this fireplace over the century and a half. The fire in the fireplace is now a bed of embers.

v

Although the old log kitchen that I remember so fondly is gone, when we laid our foundation for the new one we found the old stones on which it sat and I used them again in the new foundation. I have also seen to it that our table today has been placed squarely over the same space where our old table used to be. I occupy the approximate place at our table that my father did at his, and Naomi sits where my mother used to.

During my childhood, when the supper bell rang, we didn't waste any time getting to the house. This was the greatest time of day for everybody. If we were doing some little job, we dropped our tools and hurried to the house. If we were feeding the livestock, we rushed our work. This was the time when each member of the family reported to the others what he had done that day and made his plans for the next. It is hard for me to remember when our suppertime lasted only an hour. We used to sit around the table for as long as three hours after we had eaten.

Back when I had only a brother and an older sister, we lived in a three-room house and Mom cooked on a big flat-topped stove in the corner of our kitchen. After supper Dad would sit at the table and tell us how his father took leases up Big Sandy and cleared as much as twenty acres of ground the first year. He told us how his father split the chestnuts, fenced the clearing with rails, plowed the land with cattle, sowed some of it in wheat, and planted the rest in corn the first year. That was a lot of ground to clear of saw-log timber, but there were a lot of Stuarts. My father was the youngest of eleven children, and all the boys, and girls, too, worked in the fields. He told us of the great crops Grandpa had grown, how rich the soil had been for three or four years, and what handsome rail fences he had made. He told us how the neighbors would set the woods on fire in the spring to kill the copperheads, and how fire under the rail fences around the clearings had left charred embers. This part of his story would make me tense and upset. I never wanted the rail fences to burn.

Mom told us stories of her father back in Carter County, who had once cut a hundred twenty shocks of corn, twelve hills square, in a day. He tied a middle band in the shock and two on the outside. Once he lifted a rock into a wagon bed that was so large it went through the floor. In those days they had few books and no magazines and newspapers to read in this part of the country, and the winter months in a small cabin, especially when snow or thaw isolated them, could be pretty trying. They would pop corn and roast potatoes in the ashes and tell tales over and over until people got tired of hearing them. But all these stories, repeated to us at suppertime, seemed fascinating. I wanted them to go on and on. I couldn't wait to finish eating and then hear our parents talk of long ago.

After my sister and I started to school, we had something to talk about at the supper table. If I had been wild at school and got switched, Sophia couldn't wait to get to the supper table to tell it. But if I got a headmark and turned Carrie Burkhardt down in spelling, I couldn't wait to tell it. I'd report the words that the teacher gave us and who missed each one. If I won in an arithmetic match, I never stopped talking about it at supper. We told Dad and Mom about everything we had seen on our way to and from school. Our parents were good listeners as well as good talkers. At suppertime in this three-room house a family tradition of swapping the day's doings started.

One of my dad's favorite games was to take a different farm each evening and tell us what he would do to improve the place if he were only able to buy it. By the rules of this game, we owned every farm we had ever rented, and where we lived now made six, plus a lot of other farms where we hadn't lived but had rented patches on the shares. My dad would tell where he would make meadows, have pastures, build a house, set an orchard, the woods he'd leave for timber and the fields he would clear and sow for pasture. When he got through telling about these farms, not only were they beautiful and vastly improved but we owned them. We went to our supper table hungry and we came away happy, full of food and great dreams.

When we moved on to a new place, our seventh rented farm, we didn't have as much food to set on the supper table because the thin, sandy soil wouldn't produce it. A sister was born here, and my father now had a family of seven to feed. We didn't have too much to eat, but we still had fun at the supper table. This was when we started joking about the bumblebee corn we had raised, where the bee sat on the corn tassel sucking nectar while his wing tips rested on the ground. And at hog-killing time in October, we talked about how our hogs were so large and fat we'd hang four of them on the clothesline. We kidded about the washtubs being too close to the clothesline, for a hog might fall off the line into the tub and we'd lose him. Sometimes this talk at the supper table brought Dad up from his chair. He tried to turn the subject by telling us how many cattle he had broken to plow and how much money he would make breaking cattle. But we kept on talking about porkers hanging on the clothesline and about bumblebee corn because we didn't know it was hurting Dad's feelings.

It was a big thing for us when Dad got that job on a railroad section and made real money. He walked five miles to and from his work, but he had to do it to pay for the fifty acres he had his heart set on buying. His plan was to work for money on the railroad and let us farm the fifty acres when we got moved on it. And it all worked out as he planned. My Granddad Hilton and I built that house where our family lived twenty-seven years. Granddad and I began work in early July, and by that autumn we had the big house built of logs he and I had cut, scored, and hewed with broadaxes, and hauled from the woods. We had the last house-raising in the neighborhood to put logs up, and Grandpa then split a big rock, hewed stones, and built a chimney up through the center with two fireplaces. We moved into this house in the autumn, when it wasn't near ready. I could look out through the log cracks in my room upstairs and see the stars shining. I could feel the November winds blow over my bed and lift the cover. But on sunny winter days my mother, sisters, brother, and I all daubed the cracks airtight while Dad worked on the railroad section. He was proud of the way we were improving the house and farm and always told us so at suppertime.

Now was the greatest time of our lives around the supper table. Again our table was filled with food. Dad was making money, and we had begun to farm land of our own and didn't have to pay cash and grain rent. At six o'clock Mom always had our table loaded with food. That gave us time before supper to get home from school, feed the cattle, sheep, and hogs, milk the cows, and fill the woodbox beside the range. That was work enough to make us hungry.

We stopped joking about hogs on the clothesline now. We raised fat porkers for our own use and to sell. We had our mutton

and our own beef. My mother and sisters canned hundreds of
quarts of wild blackberries, strawberries, dewberries, and raspberries. We canned corn, tomatoes, and apples, and made apple
butter and pumpkin butter. Granddad and I had to build a big
cellar and put shelves all the way around for our fruit and jellies.
We raised sweet and Irish potatoes. We raised corn to feed the
livestock and fatten our hogs. We took some to a mill and had it
ground to make cornbread. We raised wheat on our hills, cradled
and shocked it, and hauled it to a thresher where it was threshed
and, later, ground into flour. We were self-sustaining, except for
salt, pepper, sugar, and coffee. And we raised cane for sorghum,
which we often substituted for sugar.

I never tasted bread baked in a bakery until I was sixteen years
old. For breakfast, we had two big pans of biscuits and a small pan
of spare "biscuit pone" so we wouldn't run out of bread. My father,
brother, and I ate ten biscuits each. We ate six fried eggs each. Then
we ate sorghum, bacon, jelly, or preserves. We had to eat big breakfasts. After walking five miles to the railroad, my father worked five
hours before noon. I got up at four in the morning and helped with
the feeding and milking, and when we had breakfast at five or five-
thirty I was ready to eat. Glennis and Mary were allowed to sleep
until six o'clock. We never got to the breakfast table at the same
time.

But at suppertime we all got there together. Sophia and I told
so much about our teachers that our parents knew them before they
had ever seen them. Dad told us about the crew he worked with.
He told us about low joints in the track, sod line, laying steel
T-rails, driving spikes, tamping ties, walking track, the section
foremen, the track supervisors, the superintendents, and all about
his new world of railroaders and railroading. At first we were
hungry and everybody ate more or less in silence. Then we talked,
sometimes everybody at once. But Dad would call for order and
appoint one at a time.

Mom told us how many eggs she'd gathered to send to Greenup
to trade for things she wanted at the store. She told us if a cow had
calved or if a brood sow had farrowed, for she kept all this information on the calendar. Sometimes in early spring she told us of

a ewe she'd found hiding in a cliff with a lamb. We talked about bulls, cows, ewes, rams, lambs, horses, mules, cornfields, wheat fields, and tobacco seedbeds. We never sat down to gossip about our neighbors. It didn't occur to us, there were too many other things. We planned to set an orchard of black walnuts which we could sell someday to make furniture or gun stocks. We talked about different grasses for hay, and my father brought home the first lespedeza seed I ever saw and the first sown in this area. "It's the real thing for these old hills," he said at the supper table. He opened a little package and let us see the tiny seed. "They tell me this grass will grow on a yellow bank."

In autumn our supper table was loaded with spareribs, sauerkraut, backbone, and highly spiced sausage. Often we had beef, mutton, and soup beans we had raised in our cornfields. We planted beans in the corn and let them vine up the stalks, and Mom cooked them in a big pot with pork jowl, and they were wonderful to eat with biscuit and onions out of our garden.

This evening meal strengthened our family and welded us into a unit that could not be broken. At our supper table, we made all our plans. We told each other of our ambitions. We discussed them, argued about them. Suppertime is a strong memory for each of us and an enduring custom to be carried into our own homes.

V I

This morning, at twelve minutes after ten o'clock, winter officially began. And I for one was happy to see it arrive. I have been fond of its long nights, the music of its winds, its sunsets, red skies, bright stars, and wagon-wheel moons, which flood the whole dark earth below with light. Although it distresses me to see many of the old traditions pass, there is an aspect of winter which characterized past years that I am happy to see go. That is winter isolation.

Here at this very house is a good place to contrast the old winter of isolation with the new. I don't mean to sound like a man of a hundred winters. But only fifteen years ago, this valley was a pocket of isolation, almost as cut off from the outside world as it was a hundred years ago; yet, only a few miles from here winter isolation had been driven into oblivion. Wherever the hardroads ran, which we called winter roads then, isolation disappeared. These hardroads became winter lifelines.

We never got a winter road here until after World War II. However, we had made strides against isolation. We had an automobile. We built a road ourselves. We put up bridges (which the heavy trucks later smashed) so that we could get over the streams when they were full. But we often had to drive through mudholes, almost swimming our car through the mud, in the early forties. Naomi and I became expert mud drivers, skilled in getting a car out of a mudhole. We read the skies and winds the best we could before we drove our car out, but often we fell short of perfection as weather prophets.

Members of my family remember further back, when the only ways we had of getting out of this landlocked valley were to walk or to ride a horse or mule. I myself remember the days when snow lay on from November until March, and we children lived in a small landlocked world with no books, victrolas, or radios to amuse us. We didn't get a paper or a magazine and had to depend on our own imaginations and what nature provided for our entertainment. I sometimes think that this taught us to be resourceful. We made up some wild and fanciful games then.

By our winter road, we are less than ten minutes from Greenup today. When I used to drive our team of horses over the almost impassable roads, through holes where the high axles dragged, it took me a half day to get to Greenup and back if I was lucky. This was a long half day and took so much freshness from the team I seldom made the return trip on the same day. If I did, I would still be traveling at nightfall on this short winter day, and I would hang a lantern on one of my horses to light our way up the dark valley.

Those were the days when my father claimed that a circle around the moon meant bad weather within three days. If the circle was unusually bright, this meant rough weather within a week. When we heard a lonesome steamboat whistle from over the high hills and down in the valley of the Ohio River or the steam-locomotive whistles on the Kentucky and the Ohio sides of the

river, distances of six and eight miles away, we knew to prepare for
a siege of rough winter. We would bring a load of necessary supplies from Greenup in a hurry, carrying them on horseback or
walking them home in a basket.

Red skies in the morning were a warning, too, as were the soft
breaths of wind that swept intermittently up the valley. When the
mules and horses ran in the pasture, kicked up their heels, and
rode each other, this was a sign. When wild rabbits ate the sassafras
bark up ten, fifteen, or twenty inches high, we looked for a snow
that deep, and when the owls hooted lonesomelike in the afternoon,
we looked for stormy weather. There were so many signs that my
father used. He would have no truck with what he called "those
hit-and-miss calendars and almanacs." We had our own set of rules,
and we were our own prophets. Accurate or not, our way was more
fun than listening to weather forecasts from a radio beside our
breakfast table.

Our isolation had its charms. Strange how so many people who
once fought against isolation in other parts of America are crying
for some of it now, so they will have a little more tranquil time on
their hands.

Much of the art of gathering nuts, picking berries, canning, and
making jellies has been lost today among our people. These were
the arts of self-sufficiency, independence, isolation. We used to
watch the blooms in spring on the wild blackberry, dewberry,
strawberry, service tree, raspberry, and wild crab apples to see
how heavy their crops might be. And we watched frosts later, and
often went to the plum, peach, and apple trees to see if a frost
or a near freeze had damaged the fruit. Not many people today
know how to judge whether the fruit is killed by looking at the
blossoms. They don't need to know, and it would probably prove
a useless piece of information if they did. Such matters are left
to the specialists. The paradox is that the specialized ingenuity of
our world may have killed our individual ingenuity. Every gadget
that has helped us has also taken away the necessity of devising
some method of doing it ourselves. We have driven away winter
isolation from our door, but we have lost something in the process.

For instance, how could a country boy get stovewood in a

hurry, when he broke his ax handle? He could find the small dead poplars which were easy to break. He could find the dead sumacs which broke easily and burned well. The dead locust and oaks had plenty of dry bark that peeled readily.

Once the larger boys ran ahead of me in the woods with rocks to knock the winter persimmons. I was younger and was forced to devise some method by which I could compete. One evening I ran up with a long slender pole and was more accurate with it than they were with their throwing. So a saying started among us that spread through the county and is still heard today: The longest pole will reach the highest persimmons.

In deliberately routing winter isolation, we have lost some of the things that made us. Will the time ever come when we will want to return to that isolation? Will man one day rebel against having everything done for him? Will he get to the point where he doesn't give a rap if Tim Spears or John Jones eats a certain kind of breakfast cereal? Won't he taste them all and then choose his own kind? Will the time ever come when it won't matter if actor Seth Lester smokes one kind and baseball pitcher Fonse Leadingham smokes another and each insists that his brand is easiest on the T-zone?

Winter isolation used to give us respite to rebuild our individual selves. I know people now who genuinely think they would like our old way of life back. I'm not sure they clearly remember the hardships and the physical labor that made up that life. But I sympathize with their yearning.

V I I

Now, while we mail Christmas greetings to friends, buy and wrap gifts, and prepare food for the Christmas holiday just ahead, I am reminded of another Christmas. This is not the Christmas of December 25 that we know, but the Old Christmas that came on January 7.

If Mom and Dad believed Christ was born on January 7, then we believed it, too. We had faith, well placed, in their wisdom and goodness. But our main concern was that people should not stop celebrating both the first and the second Christmas. It was like having two birthday celebrations every year. It wasn't until years later, in college, that I understood that the January 6–7 date was that of the Epiphany celebrated by the Eastern Church and that it had taken those twelve days between December 25 and January 6 for the Wise Men to follow the star to Bethlehem.

Our mother and father told us that on January 7 the violets bloomed again under last year's leaves and the snow. They told us that the mountain daisy and often the apple, peach, and pear would bloom. When I was a child, I searched for proof of these things. I don't remember ever finding proof. But later, whenever apple, peach, pear, and daisy bloomed early, I remembered about the legend of January 7. Often I have found violets blooming under last year's leaves and under the snow, but never as early as January 7. I wanted to believe this legend because I thought it a beautiful idea. Because of these stories, Old Christmas was the one I preferred.

My mother and father said that the fox wouldn't catch the birds and the dog wouldn't harm the rabbits on Old Christmas. They quoted the Bible where the lamb and the lion lay down together. They told us God had created all these animals and that they were kind to each other on this night of the Saviour's birth. I always wanted to see a fox and a covey of quail lie down together. I wanted to see what would happen.

Another beautiful legend of love had it that on this night all animals could speak to each other in the same language and understand each other. The owl respected the pheasant while the chicken hawk spoke to the chickadee, wren, and ground sparrow. The weak had a voice equal to that of the strong. I felt closer to this Christmas because of the special respect the animals and birds paid the birth of our Saviour. The lamb and the lion lying down together in deep discussion became a favorite idea of mine.

On each Christmas Day, the December one and the January one, my father always gave his livestock extra rations of feed. He put extra ears of corn in the feedboxes for our horses or mules, and he gave our cows more cracked corn or soft corn nubbins. He gave our cattle extra hay, and he fed our swine more warm gruel made of ground corn and food scraps mixed up in warm water. We never, at Christmas or any other time, gave our hogs swill, which we regarded as unclean.

We children used to wonder in what language the animals spoke to each other and what they said. We often wished that Christ had made it possible for them to have been friendlier with each other all year round, especially when we would find a rabbit's blood frozen on the snow on our way to Plum Grove School where a fox had made off with him in the night. My older sister, Sophia, and I used to wonder if animals went to our Heaven or if they went to a Heaven for their own kind or if they went to a Heaven for all the animals and birds. If they went to our Heaven and we had killed them on earth, what would we say to them there? I had these thoughts.

Now, if we could turn back the pages from our modern Christmas, since it is not generally kept in the spirit of our Lord, and go back into the world of legend and tradition of forty years ago, I would be happy to be that child again, searching for the violets under the snow and the lion that was lying down with the lamb. For Christmas can be better symbolized by such a fable of love than by a dozen handsome gifts.

VIII

On my solitary walk through the dark hills that were topped this afternoon with low clouds, I followed a narrow fox path. High up, in an old field where cattle had once been pastured, I stopped to watch an old man cutting sprouts with a mattock. He didn't see me. He worked on, lifting his mattock high above his shoulder and bringing it down with force against the frozen sprouts. But I didn't watch him work so much as I looked at the features of his face. Who was he? Where had he come from? He looked more like the pictures of Jesus than any man I had ever seen.

His reddish-brown hair came around his shoulders and the wind often blew it this way and that. Wind pressed the red-brown beard against his pale cheeks. He was not wearing gloves, and his hands looked blue and cold. There were a few red places where briers had scratched his hands enough to bring the blood. The shivers

that went through me as I stood on that hill were not the result of
the cold.

His pants were held loosely around him with a small rope, which
he had used for a belt. He wore an old faded jacket, which was
without buttons down the front and was torn on the sides. This
torn, frayed, and faded jacket looked like the one I'd seen on the
garbage dump near Greenup, where I had taken our garbage yesterday. His shirt was dirty, tattered, and torn. Then I looked at
his feet. He was wearing a pair of gum overshoes with thin cotton
socks. There were at least two dozen small holes in these old overshoes. Now and again I could see the white, pale skin on the tops
of his feet.

Actually, for a moment anyway, I was positive I had found
Christ. Yet I wondered if I had walked too far. I wondered if I had
climbed too many hills. Had something snapped in my mind? I
wondered if I had toppled over into another world which happened
to be very much like my own.

"Hello there, stranger," I said.

"Hello," he greeted me softly. He spoke as calmly as if he knew I
had been standing here all this time watching him. He had never
looked up from his work until now.

"You work this farm now?" I said, searching for something to say.

"Yes, I am working here for Charlie Walters," he replied.

"But you're working late, and it's Christmas Eve."

"Oh, I know, but it won't be much of a Christmas with us," he
said. "We had our house burn up and everything in it."

"I'd not heard about this," I told him. "Where did you live?"

"In the little house down on Doore's Point," he told me. "My
daughter and I lived there together. But everything we had burned
up. We are staying at Doore's now."

"Don't your feet get cold in those gum overshoes and cotton
socks?"

"I don't mind that," he said, smiling. "It's working here without
my lunch I mind the most. I've done this all week. Lydia Doore
never fixes me any lunch. And I sure need something hot to eat and
drink up here at noon. It's cold on this ridge."

"But you've never told me your name," I said, as I looked him over carefully.

"James Chester," he said. "Call me Chester. That's what everybody calls me. And I don't mean to complain. This is one of the best jobs I ever had. I never see my boss. He pays me seventy-five cents an hour. I keep my own time. Not long ago I worked ten hours for three dollars. But I quit that work."

James Chester would hardly stop working long enough to talk to me. The wind whipped both of us unmercifully. He had to work to stay warm. And I had to keep moving to stay warm. He was shivering from cold, and I was, too.

"My daughter, Frances, and I won't be having much Christmas."

"How old is your daughter?"

"Seventeen."

"Where is her mother?" I asked.

"In Heaven."

"Any others in your family?"

"Four more," he replied. "But other people have them. See, when my wife died, nobody would have Frances because she's not of sound mind. The rest of my children went out for adoption. I was a sick man then and couldn't work. So I took my little Frances—she was only six when her mother died—and fled with her. We traveled over the country."

"Then you don't have a home?"

"None now," he replied. "We had a little three-room house, a radio and beds and a dresser and stove. But now we don't have but what we have on our bodies. But I have this job cutting sprouts and I'm able to work."

"The stores will be closed now, but I think I can find you a pair of shoes at one of my friends," I told him. "I know you wear larger shoes than I wear."

"Nine and a half made on a double-E last," he said.

"If I find the shoes," I asked him, "where shall I bring them to you?"

"To Doore's," he replied. He straightened up, stopping his work for the first time. "This is very nice of you. May God bless you! These winter hills are cold to you and to me."

Then he brought his mattock down again. A brittle sprout fell to the frozen ground where the others had fallen.

"I'll be getting on," I said. "My circulation is not up to weather like this. I'm getting very cold."

"Good day," he said.

One man's Christmas Eve is so unlike another's. A man who looked like Christ was shivering on a hilltop in shoes with holes in them and a coat he snatched from a town dump, his wife dead, his house burned, his only kin a weak-minded daughter. I walked down the narrow winding path under the clouds as if in a dream. I hardly spoke to Naomi. I jumped into the car and went to town after those shoes. I got them, and a coat, too, and found Jim Chester at the Doore place. I tried not to listen to his thanks, which he spoke with dignity. They just made me the sadder. But I let Mrs. Doore know what I thought of her not fixing the old fellow lunch to take with him to the hilltop. I think that Jim Chester, the man who looks like Christ, will get a hot lunch from now on.

I X

I stood down at the end of our walk and looked for a large, light-green automobile with an Ohio license. I knew C. C. (Calvin Clarke) would be here. He was always as good as his word, and he had told us he was coming. His visiting our house for dinner was an occasion for us. Particularly now, at the end of this year that started in pain and depression and ends in health and hope. If it hadn't been for Calvin Clarke's advice over the years, I would not have been able to weather the storm.

Naomi had dinner ready and waiting. My mind went back through the years as I watched eagerly for him. I had known C. C. since 1912. He was my first teacher, and he became my friend for life. It was he who taught me to read and to write. How could I ever forget him? My father was the district school trustee at Plum Grove then. He recommended this small, slender eighteen-year-old high school graduate. Little did we children know then that we were going to school to a man who would create a legend some day.

He was born on Clear Creek on the Leftfork of Beaver in Floyd County, at that time 139 miles from a railway station. When he was six, his mother died. He can remember seeing six men lower her homemade coffin into a sandstone grave in the Newsome Cemetery, named for his mother's people. Here the graves of his ancestors were covered with little wooden houses, a few of which still stand.

Theopolis Clarke kept his three small children, Calvin and two younger sisters, together. They lived in a small shack at the foot of a mountain. Here the children attended a rural school, but it wasn't long before Calvin had learned all his teacher could teach him. Then, one day, at his great-uncle's country store on Robinson Creek, he overheard his uncle state that all lawyers went to hell.

"I decided right then I wanted to be a lawyer to see," he told me years later.

He walked a hundred and fifty miles to his grandfather's farm in Greenup County. A cousin, Jack Burke, was living with his grandfather on this large Sandy River-bottom farm, and he persuaded the old man, Jack Newsome, to let this runaway grandson stay and go to school with him. Their grandfather liked the idea of having two grandsons instead of one; so Calvin stayed, worked on his grandfather's farm in summers, and established one of the three highest scholastic records in Greenup High School's 107-year history.

After high school, he took a teacher's examination and made the highest grade in Kentucky. But because of his slight build, too many of the county trustees were afraid to recommend him. They thought he was too young and too small to discipline the large boys. But my father liked him from the first. He recommended him, and he was hired by the five members of the Greenup County Board of Education for the school at Plum Grove.

Calvin Clarke had pupils older and larger than he when he taught his first and second years at Plum Grove. The people who feared he couldn't discipline them because of his small physical stature were stunned to see him at work in a classroom. He had the best-disciplined school in Greenup County. And the people of Plum Grove, children and parents, who were here when he taught school, have never forgotten him.

He was the most alive young man I ever knew. He kept discipline at Plum Grove without ever raising his voice and didn't waste a minute teaching his fifty-six classes in a six-hour day. He brought scissors and hand clippers to the school, and at lunch and recess he cut our hair. There was a root of a big whiteoak elbowing up from the earth, and it was here we used to sit for these free haircuts. He brought needles to school and picked the honey-locust thorns from our feet. He organized us in one year's time into an efficient, disciplined, and enthusiastic school that met with other rural schools and won a consecutive string of fifty arithmetic and spelling matches. As a teacher, C. C. was that good.

From teaching he went to business college, from business college to work for the Selby Shoe Company in Portsmouth (of which he is now a director), then to Washington and a civil service job, and finally a master's degree, a law degree, and a thriving private practice in Portsmouth that has made him famous in this part of the country. He has practiced before the Supreme Court, and he is said to have the largest real estate holdings in Portsmouth. He was my first teacher in a one-room schoolhouse at Plum Grove, and he has for years handled my financial affairs. His handling of my taxes on the money from *Taps for Private Tussie* is an eight-year story in itself, which I am not at liberty to write down. I can only say that when a government attorney came one last time to try to collect more taxes from me, C. C. collected from him. That's the way it ended.

After 1944, the year I had my greatest financial success, I got a furlough from the Navy to ask C. C. if he would take care of my taxes. This was the first time I'd earned enough to employ an attorney. Heretofore, I'd made out my own income-tax returns, and I hadn't exactly overflowed Treasury Department coffers with my contributions. But getting C. C. was a most important move for me. I have learned since how lucky I have been these last twelve years to have C. C. saving a part of my earnings for me.

When my novel was selected by a book club and bought by MGM in the same year, it was announced in all the papers that I had struck it rich. In no time I had everybody coming to sell me insurance, property, automobiles, houses, and coal mines, to ask me for endowments for colleges, donations for churches, and all kinds of personal loans. Had I given ten dollars to each request, I wouldn't have had anything left. I got letters from old friends who were in "dire" circumstances and in "desperate" need of help. I got letters from people wanting me to finance their get-rich-quick schemes, profits from which we would share jointly. One friend and classmate wanted me to buy a theater for him. When C. C. asked him what security he could give, he replied, "I can't give him any security, but he can be my silent partner."

When these letters came to me, I sent them to C. C. When a man came wanting to borrow eighty grand to start a super garage, I sent him to C. C. I sent them all to C. C., for he took a special delight in handling my problems and telling these people that I didn't really have as much money as there was gold buried at Fort Knox.

They came away from C. C.'s office in Portsmouth, Ohio, a disappointed lot. They didn't believe what he told them about my financial situation. They started wild rumors that he, already a man of considerable wealth, was doing all his business with my money. I let C. C. explain my affairs to these schemers, dreamers, and that little handful of friends always in "dire circumstances" in whatever way he wanted to. After he got through with them, they never came to me again. I don't know what he told them. But I do believe he could have made straight "A's" in psychology without ever opening a book.

A few of these people who wanted to do business with my money bear mentioning. One had the idea of building a "casino" on the Sandy River, where he would have floor shows, an orchestra, expensive foods and wines, roulette wheels, crap tables, and slot machines. For his site he had chosen a farm which had a family cemetery of about twenty graves on it that would have to be removed. "But I won't let a little graveyard of twenty graves stand in my way," he told me. This fellow, as my friend of many years and a local politician, wanted to borrow a mere $450,000 from me for this project. I sent him to see C. C. in a hurry. The next time I saw this man, he smiled, spoke in a friendly way, and apologized to me because he was too late in getting this loan, which was "too big for the local bank to make."

Besides my classmate who wanted me to buy him a $30,000 theater, I had parents of several "talented" young men and women who wanted me to finance their children through colleges and universities. One of my former students wanted me to buy him a county newspaper with a circulation of 1,900 for $26,000. C. C. enjoyed lecturing this one on economics, so he told me later. A house that a man wanted to sell me for $28,000, "not a penny less," sold later for $14,000. A casual acquaintance who was building an expensive yacht to launch on the Ohio River wanted to borrow $10,000 from me to pay the mortgage on his home.

It took about four years for the word to get around that I had an attorney who wasn't willing to loan my money because he had borrowed it all himself. Nevertheless, when the American Legion Hall burned down in Greenup, they came to me to borrow money to rebuild it instead of going to the bank. Finally, the many people who had been coming to me in a steady stream seeking money slowed down to a trickle.

Had it not been for C. C.'s handling all this, I don't know what I would have done. It got to the point where I couldn't do any work because of all the people who came, like the Tussies, wanting something. We would come home in the evenings to find people sitting on our front porch waiting to borrow money or to interest me in a financial proposition. Several of these people we had to keep all night. Later I learned better and hauled them back to Greenup to let them find their own places to stay.

I had a few ideas about investing what was left after taxes in 1944, the year I was supposed to have made a million dollars. I wanted C. C. to invest it in one thing. "Leave it to me," he said, shaking his head. "I'll guarantee you won't lose anything. But I won't put all your eggs in one basket." So I left all the investments up to him. And every investment he made for me was safe and has made a reasonable amount of money.

Once, after I'd seen how much worry and trouble a little money can be, I got the idea that I would give every dollar of it to the State of Kentucky for bookmobiles. My correspondence with C. C. will show I had this idea long before this state got bookmobiles.

Said C. C., "No, I'm not for your spending all you have for bookmobiles. You might get sick and not be able to work. Then what would you do?"

"Not I," I answered, laughing at him. "I'll be able to work a full day until I'm eighty."

But leave it to my friend C. C. to be right. In less than six years I had collapsed of a heart attack. And if it hadn't been for his wise handling of my financial affairs, I don't know what we would have done when hospital and doctor bills mounted up and I had to stop working.

Once I rebelled on him and bought $3,500 worth of cattle against his advice. I fed these cattle three barn lofts of good hay and all that I had stacked in my fields, besides a lot of grain. Then I hired a man to feed and care for my cattle when I was away on lecture tours. After keeping these cattle a year, I sold them for less than I bought them for. C. C. had warned me not to buy, feed, and sell cattle at that time. He was right again. He suggested that I write short stories about cattle instead. I did—enough to pay this deficit.

Then he suggested that I stop raising wheat, chickens, and even tobacco. He suggested that I wasted too much time farming that I should use writing. After losing $309 in a year on two hundred chickens, a crop of tobacco that heated after it was bulked down in the barn, and a wheat crop that I couldn't thresh because the hills were too steep for the combine, I decided to listen to C. C. I rented my tobacco base and sold my chickens.

Why did I call on him to handle my taxes? He used to make me toe the mark when I went to school to him. He switched me for fighting three times in one week. I went back to him because I had never been away. I had never forgotten him from the first day he taught me. No one could forget him. Why did the Greenup County's Superintendent of Schools, Johnnie Prichard, give him his first school? When C. C. was a shine boy in Greenup, Kentucky, trying to make himself a few extra dimes, it was Johnnie Prichard's old rundown shoes he used to shine so well they looked like new.

C. C. has never used tobacco in any form nor drunk intoxicating liquors. He never forgets a name, a face, a property value, a telephone number. One morning C. C. came to Greenup on a tax case. He was rushing as usual, but he recognized Little Bob Griffith, one of his former Plum Grove pupils, loafing on the street.

"There's something I want to ask you, Little Bob," he said, after they had greeted each other for the first time in thirty-eight years. "I want to know if you were the one who slipped those rotten eggs in Roy Perkins' pocket and he sat down on them in school?"

"Yes, I did, Mr. Clarke," Little Bob admitted. "But I was afraid to confess it to you then."

"Did you carry the steps from the Plum Grove School to the foot of the hill on Halloween night in 1912?"

"No, Mr. Clarke, it wasn't me that time," Little Bob said proudly.

"I always wanted to clear these two things up," C. C. said.

After C. C. had gone, Little Bob turned to me and said, "He's the greatest teacher I ever had. Think about him remembering the schoolhouse steps and the eggs! And think about a man as busy and important as he is who would stop and talk to me for ten minutes on the street."

One night at our house I was kidding C. C. about the possibilities of his going to hell.

"I'll never forget," he answered, "what my uncle said when I was a little boy. He said that after a lawyer took his last breath, he went straight to hell. When I got to be a lawyer, I said to myself, 'Here will be one honest lawyer. Here will be one who wants to see his ancestors on the other side after he leaves this world.'"

X

Among the cardiacs I have met (few in person and many in correspondence) since I have become one, I've not found one bitter man or woman. I have found most of them surprisingly cheerful. They have been through a shattering experience and are happy they came out alive. They are grateful for having been spared, hopeful that many full years lie ahead. I feel this way.

One I have written to is Dr. Randall Stewart, a former college teacher of mine. In the days when I knew him, he was a handsome six-footer and weighed about 220. I never saw a better built man in a college classroom teaching English. I had heard something had happened to him, but I never bothered to write until after I had had a heart attack. When I inquired by letter if he had had a heart attack, I got an immediate reply. He closed the one-page single-spaced letter by saying, "God Bless You," and when I glanced down the page and saw this above his signature, I knew he had had a heart attack even before I read the letter itself. I knew, because cardiacs call on God. Those among us who have never called on God before call on Him now.

I have seen men physically disfigured by the loss of a limb, an eye, a hand, an arm, or even teeth become self-conscious and bitter. But I have never seen a heart patient react in this way. He feels something different. A man can't get angry at his heart. His heart is his life. When the heart goes, life goes. And when something goes wrong with a man's heart and he miraculously pulls through, he is happy instead of bitter. He can't afford to be bitter. Bitterness could kill him.

One afternoon last September I remember wishing for some of my old strength back. I was down the road with Hubert Ross and Albert Harris, two teen-agers who cut my yard and help me about this place. I wanted to show them how to mend a burning brush pile. I got a little hot standing near the fire in the September sun, and my heart gave me a warning. There was an ache, that same little weakness which I first felt the previous September, a month before I had my near-fatal attack. I turned the mending of the brush pile over to the young men and sat down in the shade. It hurt me to do it. This was the same feeling I had had as a teen-ager when we lost a high school football game. The feeling of defeat. But I was a better loser now. I smiled as I walked over and sat down in the shade. I smiled because my heart told me to smile.

Throwing brush on a burning pile is not something to worry about. But when I collapsed at Murray State College last October, I had a full schedule of talks booked for me. Counting the number of talks and the high fees, my lecturing had reached the "big time." I had worked twenty years to reach this, from my first fee of two dollars to the seven hundred and fifty I occasionally earned toward the end. Suddenly, in the passing of an instant and the beat of a heart, I lost all of this. And there isn't any use for me to say I didn't like to travel, lecture, meet people, see the country from the train windows and from the air. This was a wonderful way to earn money. If I hadn't liked it, I wouldn't have done it.

But I wasn't sad about giving up public speaking. I felt I was very fortunate that I didn't have to give up my life, too. Speakers had died on platforms a hundred years and more before I collapsed. One of these had been William Cullen Bryant. I had been spared some extra time. I was grateful for this.

When this attack knocked me low, I was writing a novel. I had the novel in my head. I had a few notes, all I needed, and I had written about seventy-five pages. Well, I had to forget about this novel. Someday I may begin it all over again. I am not sure about this. But by now I would have had it finished and in my publisher's hands.

But I can't worry about this novel. It might have been a great success, selected by a book club and made into a movie, or it might have been a flop. I think of this whenever I see the old manuscript on my shelf. But I am not bitter about it. I also think of it when I look in the secondhand bookstores and see thousands of good books by prominent authors selling for nineteen cents as "remainders." My mind is now trained to protect my heart. My mind looks at the low value the world has set on these books. And my heart doesn't feel so bad about the book I failed to finish. Then I remember the doctors' orders when they wouldn't let me write even a letter. Later I was allowed to write a letter a day, then two, and then I started cheating on them. Whenever I saw the name of a friend who had written me, sent a card, flowers, a book, I couldn't rest until I'd written him. I'd get a letter off to him soon, written by my sore, stiff hands or the thin, tired hands of my wife. And I thanked God each day that I was able to do it. I'd never thanked God in this way before. But I'd never had a heart attack before.

I never knew what a major physical disaster was. I never knew how to sympathize with others. Now I knew. But I was not bitter because I lay flat on my back, because I might never finish that novel manuscript or publish another story. I wasn't bitter because I couldn't saw down giant trees as I had once done, or sink a double-bitted ax to the eye in hardwood, or speak again to sixteen thousand people, or write poems on planes and trains, in bus stations and airports. I wasn't bitter because I couldn't show the other fellow how it was done. It was time for him to show me something. The little skinny men I used to joke with and ask if they could lift a copy of a magazine without breaking a bone could have said something to me now. But they didn't. They came in to see me, stopped to ask how I was, wished me a speedy recovery. I was learning.

Some things I wouldn't let myself think of. I had traveled in foreign countries, seen their great cities, heard the music of their languages. I had sweated on lecture platforms, eaten hastily in restaurants, laughed, talked, argued, and smoked with friends. But I wouldn't let myself think of this life now. If I had, I would have grieved. And grieving would have hurt my crippled heart.

So I shifted my entire way of living. Once my world had been the American skies, the long train trails that span the continent, the ribbons of highway across this vast and beautiful America. My world had been a thousand friends in a hundred cities, ten cups of coffee and loud talk until three in the morning. Now my world was reduced to my home, my farm, my hills. I lived more closely with my wife, my daughter, my animal friends. I thought more deeply of my God. My heart went back to these.

In a few more hours this year will be over. My journal will be finished. I will have kept a fairly accurate record of my many thoughts and few actions for the year of 1955. This is the year of my rebirth, from my death to my morning.

Tomorrow I shall put away this journal, as a child puts away an old toy when he gets a new one. Mine is an old toy that has been given me again, life.

ABOUT THE AUTHOR

Jesse Stuart—poet, short-story writer, and novelist of the Kentucky hills—is one of America's best-known and best-loved regional writers. Although still in his forties, he has written nineteen books, taught school, lectured extensively, and traveled abroad. In a nonfiction work, *The Thread That Runs So True,* he describes his experiences as a teacher and principal in various schools in Kentucky and Ohio. One of his most successful novels, *Taps for Private Tussie,* was a Book-of-the-Month Club selection in 1943. He has written literally hundreds of short stories and poems published in the country's leading magazines.

All his work, in prose or poetry, has for its setting the Kentucky hill country he knows so well. Here, until his heart attack in 1954, he lived an active life lecturing, writing, teaching, and working in the fields. Since that time he has been convalescing at his home in Riverton, Kentucky, where he lives with his wife Naomi and daughter Jane.